D1288319

Q
720.973 - W84   183097

Women in American architecture

DATE DUE			

ST. CLOUD PUBLIC LIBRARY
GREAT RIVER REGIONAL LIBRARY
St. Cloud, Minnesota 56301

Women in American Architecture: A Historic and Contemporary Perspective

Women in American Architecture: A Historic and Contemporary Perspective

Edited by Susana Torre

A publication and exhibition organized by
The Architectural League of New York through its
Archive of Women in Architecture.

This project is made possible with public funds
from The New York State Council on the Arts and
a grant from the National Endowment for the Arts
in Washington, D.C., a federal agency.

This project is also made possible with funds from CBS,
Inc., IBM Corporation, and Harry Winston, Inc.

WHITNEY LIBRARY OF DESIGN
an imprint of
Watson-Guptill Publications/New York

495556

Copyright © 1977 by Whitney Library of Design

First published 1977 in New York by Whitney Library of Design,
an imprint of Watson-Guptill Publications,
a division of Billboard Publications, Inc.,
1515 Broadway, New York, N.Y. 10036

Library of Congress Cataloging in Publication Data
Main entry under title:
Women in American architecture.
   Bibliography: p.
   Includes index.
   1. Women architects—United States—Addresses,
essays, lectures. I. Torre, Susana, 1944-
II. Architectural League of New York.
NA1997.W65   720′.973   76-54960
ISBN 0-8230-7485-4

All rights reserved. No part of this publication may be
reproduced or used in any form or by any means—graphic,
electronic, or mechanical, including photocopying, recording,
taping, or information storage and retrieval systems—without
written permission of the publisher.

Manufactured in U.S.A.

First Printing, 1977

Edited by Susan Braybrooke and Susan Davis
Designed by James Craig and Sheila deBretteville
Set in 9 point Times Roman by Gerard Associates/Graphic Arts, Inc.
Printed by Halliday Lithograph Corp.
Bound by A. Horowitz & Son

S·23·77 Baker 15.88

Contents

ST. CLOUD PUBLIC LIBRARY
183037

Foreword

This book, *Women in American Architecture: A Historic and Contemporary Perspective,* and the exhibition that it documents, outline the participation of women in architecture and the related design disciplines as they have been practiced in the United States. Inevitably, this story is tied to historical and social trends that mark the development of the nation as a whole, for, unlike the careers of their male counterparts that are somewhat predictable in terms of available opportunities and avenues for achievement within the profession of architecture, the careers of women practitioners have always been linked to the opportunities and expectations of women in the larger society. Thus, in this instance, architectural history is considered in the light of social history. For the most part, the history revealed here is not one dominated by key figures who in their work epitomize the architecture of a time and place; yet from the study of a number of individual women emerges a picture of the diversity in architectural practice and concern that characterize the energy and innovation of American architecture.

This book emerged as a part of the process of organizing an exhibition to present the achievements of women architects. The idea for the exhibition came at a time, the early 1970s, when the enrollment of women in schools of architecture increased substantially, marking a trend that saw greater numbers of women entering other professional programs, such as law and medicine. At the same time organizations were formed to examine and improve the role of women in the design professions. The conjunction of these events, no doubt a part of the dramatic shift in women's attitudes toward their lives and career choices, which has shaped the decade of the seventies, underscores the fact that women intend to participate in the design process as professionals and that many of these women feel that there are significant issues affecting their careers that can best be examined in the context of their own professional organizations. For the first time feeling the strength of numbers, and also exploring their identity in a so-called male profession, women wanted to organize an exhibition that demonstrated the range and quality of women's work as architects, planners, and designers.

The decision to sponsor an exhibition of the work of women in architecture was a natural extension of other programs for women design professionals that the Architectural League has already supported, such as the initial organization of the Alliance of Women in Architecture. However, once the idea for an exhibition was arrived at, its implementation raised a number of difficult questions, such as what purposes the exhibition should serve, what criteria should be established for evaluating work, what process of selection should be adopted for inclusion in the show, and in what manner should the material be presented.

At this juncture, the committee responsible for organizing this project decided to form an archive to collect biographical and project data about the careers of women design professionals, for it had become clear that a much broader base of knowledge was needed before any definitive conclusions could be drawn. Under the auspices of the Archive of Women in Architecture, a national survey was undertaken and extensive historical research begun. Very quickly, this need for history and context became an overriding concern.

Looking back on this process, having been a participant, I am reminded of Virginia Woolf's essay on women and fiction entitled "A Room of One's Own," which was published in 1929. One passage, in particular, comes to mind:

One could not go to the map and say Columbus discovered America and Columbus was a woman; or take an apple and remark, Newton discovered the laws of gravitation and Newton was a woman; or look into the sky and say aeroplanes were invented by women. There is no mark on the wall to measure the precise height of women.

Now nearly fifty years later, we grappled with the question of women and architecture and came to appreciate the role of the Archive. We ceased to view it as one step toward an exhibition. The Archive fostered a consciousness of historical continuity that seems essential to creative processes, whether as an enriching matrix, as a standard to be measured against, or, indeed, as a tradition to be challenged.

This book and exhibition document the participation of women in the architecture and design professions as both practitioners and commentators. The essays presented here begin to chart a territory that tells us about women as participants in the American architectural process and something about the process itself—the art and technology, the vernacular tradition as well as the monuments, the organization of space, and the needs of a changing society.

Since its founding in 1882 as an interdisciplinary membership organization, the Architectural League of New York has had a commitment to the presentation and exploration of significant issues in the fields of architecture and the related arts. This project to document the achievements of women in architecture grew out of a concern that this important area of investigation had been overlooked. It is our hope that the material presented here will enrich our understanding of the architectural process and encourage women to participate in it.

This book and the exhibition from which it developed represent the efforts of many people, but none more than Susana Torre, who in her role as coordinator and co-founder of the Archive of Women in Architecture has guided this project through its many steps. Her vision and dedication have brought this project to fruition and for this we are most grateful. For their help in the formative stages of this project, we wish to thank the other founding members of the Archive who gave generously of their time and ideas: Phyliss Birkby, Regi Goldberg, Marjorie Hoog, Naomi Leff, Dimon Liu, and Mimi Lobell. Special thanks go as well to Deborah Nevins, program director of the Architectural League, who has contributed to the success of this project in

many vital ways. Finally, it must be noted that this project has been made possible through the support and encouragement of the Executive Board of the Architectural League and in particular Robert A. M. Stern.

Marita O'Hare
Administrative Director
The Architectural League
of New York

The Architectural League of New York

Founded in 1882, The Architectural League of New York is a national, nonprofit interdisciplinary membership organization that sponsors exhibitions, research studies, and other projects which explore innovative ideas in architecture and related art and design fields.

Officers

President
Robert A. M. Stern

Vice-Presidents
Robert Slutzky
Maureen Connor
Peter Rolland
Henry Wolf
Horst Berger
Ulrich Franzen
Jaquelin Robertson
Massimo Vignelli

Secretary
Elizabeth Shaw

Treasurer
Walter Rooney

Executive Board
Jordan Gruzen
Frances Halsband
Etel Thea Kramer
Sharon Lee Ryder
Jon Michael Schwarting
Richard Weinstein
Christo
Henry N. Cobb
Wilder Green
Richard Meier
Suzanne Stephens
Steven Winter
Jonathan Barnett
Barbara Jakobson
John Margolies
Max Pine
Peter Wolf
Nina Kaden Wright

Acknowledgments

The preparation of this book and the exhibition that carries the same name have involved the minds and resources of dozens of people throughout the country: the authors who responded to our invitation to write the essays for this book and to make their research available for the exhibition; the administrative and research staff of the Architectural League of New York, who attended to the many organizational details; those institutions and foundations who generously underwrote the project; the architects who submitted their work to the Archive of Women in Architecture, without whom this enterprise would have been impossible; and scores of others who steered us toward some interesting work and gave us scholarly leads, whose time and effort were both indispensable and greatly appreciated, even though they may remain anonymous here.

On behalf of the Archive of Women in Architecture of the Architectural League of New York, I wish to express our gratitude to the National Endowment for the Arts, The New York State Council on the Arts, CBS, Inc., the I.B.M. Corporation, and Harry Winston, Inc. for supporting through grants and contributions the realization of all aspects of the project that serves to promote the worthy cause of the professional advancement of women. The Architectural League of New York initiated through a grant the Archive of Women in Architecture, which formed the basis for both the book and the exhibition.

The contributions made in both time and effort in the initial stages by the founding members of the Archive are gratefully acknowledged, as well as those made by Susan Thomases and particularly Jan Fisher, who engaged in research, contributed valuable ideas, maintained the Archive, and made presentations on behalf of the Archive at a number of conferences.

I do not know how to thank properly Marita O'Hare, administrative director of the Architectural League, and Deborah Nevins, its program director, for the able and efficient management of our resources and for making the project possible by presenting its scope to foundations, museum directors, and publishers. I am also indebted to them in a personal sense for their valuable suggestions and assistance in solving critical problems and above all for having maintained a high sense of excitement and enthusiasm throughout every phase of our common endeavor.

Judith Paine competently accomplished the initial historical research for the Archive, for which she was also an administrative associate between late 1975 and mid-1976. The information diligently gathered by her in many cities permitted us to identify the issues reflected by the book and the exhibition.

Susan Sternberg, who was an intern at the Archive during the summer of 1975, was largely responsible for gathering and organizing the information on which the Historic Chart is based. Naomi Leff is indebted to Ellen Cantarow, professor at the American Studies Program at the State University of New York at Old Westbury, for her valuable comments on the manuscript of the Historic Chart.

Meg Shore prepared with great professional care our initial documentation book, which impressively presented the case of our project to individuals and organizations. She also wrote many of the project captions in Chapter 11.

Chapter 10 is partially based on the essay, "The Education of Women Architects in the XXth Century," written by Ellen Perry Berkeley for the Archive of Women in Architecture. I am indebted to her for permitting her material to be included in this chapter, although her name does not appear as a contributor to this book; we are all in her debt for having been the first journalist in the 1970s to present the case of women in architecture to the professional public through her writings and as a senior editor at *Architectural Forum* and *Architecture Plus*.

Deborah Booher and Anne Tichich gave of their time and expertise to work with Jane McGroarty on the construction of the "American Women's Home" model illustrated on the jacket of this book.

Nancy Duplessis, a student of journalism, served as the resourceful editorial assistant during the extended process of coordinating all the parts of this book into a coherent system. She was responsible for bibliographical and picture research and for securing permissions to reproduce illustrations.

The participation of the authors of the essays in this project has been a most gratifying professional and personal experience. I am indebted to them for their support, for the opportunity to discuss with them many aspects of our project, and for their invaluable comments and suggestions.

Special thanks must go to Dolores Hayden, Sheila Levrant deBretteville, Gwendolyn Wright, and Doris Cole, who in addition to their work in the book contributed a great deal of time to enlisting support in their regions for this project. We are grateful to Marjory Supovitz, Rikki Binder, and Jan Fisher for their help in this regard as well.

We are indebted to Michael Botwitnick, director of the Brooklyn Museum in New York, as well as John Lane and Sarah Faunce, for their enthusiasm in the project and for lending their valuable time and resources to the successful realization of the exhibition and related events.

The encouragement and recommendations of Susan Davis, the thoughtful editor of this book, and of Susan Braybrooke, the acquisitions editor at the Whitney Library of Design, are deeply appreciated.

In thanking Sheila Levrant deBretteville, we wish not only to express our admiration for her contributions to women's culture but also to acknowledge her talent as a designer. We are most grateful that in the midst of her other obligations, she came to New York on our behalf to work with Jim Craig, the art director at Watson-Guptill, on the design of this book in a manner expressive of women's concerns for multiplicity and complexity in visual experience. We are thankful to Susan Davis and Jim Craig for implementing Sheila's ideas to the extent that the commercial publishing format allowed it.

In singling out Cynthia Balart, Sara Cedar, Judy Chicago, Galen Cranz, Elaine Hartnett, Ruth Iskin, Maria Karras, James Lapine, Susan Mogul, Arlene Ravin, and Laura Rosen, we wish through them to express our gratitude to tho numerous individuals who in many ways and at different times cooperated in this endeavor.

By Susana Torre

Introduction: A Parallel History

Virtually no social and political area of American life in the last decade has remained unaffected by the issues and demands posed by the Women's Movement. The questioning by recent feminist activity of the ideology of social institutions, including the professions, has occurred in two stages. The emphasis during the first phase was on immediate social and economic revindications for women; a collection of polemical manifestos is its written legacy. The current second phase stresses historical analysis of the basic intellectual issues underlying Western systems of thought and its various disciplines in order to expose those ideologies imbedded in our knowledge that have rationalized and justified the marginal role of women in the public sphere of social life. The following history of women in American architecture includes material from both phases, partly as the result of having juxtaposed the diverse viewpoints of different authors and partly because the historico-critical analysis can only develop simultaneously with a critical theory of Western architecture in general—and such a theory is still in its very inception.

This project, encompassing exhibition and book, was started in mid-1973 as a means to achieve public exposure for the work of professional women architects. During the first year of preparation it began to incorporate issues and questions of considerable complexity: Why have there been so few women architects? In which specific way is this fact related to the general situation of women in society? Is there a difference in the way men and women design and conceptualize space? If so, is it due to biological differences or to the early socialization of the environmental competence attributed to each sex? Why has the idea that women as architects are only suited to design domestic space been so prevalent in writings about women and architecture for the past 100 years? Why, although women have designed and built since the beginning of human civilization, have their achievements remained undocumented and unacknowledged in architectural histories? And why has the role of women as patrons, clients, or propagators of architectural styles been so much eulogized? Women architects have not been altogether successful in extricating themselves from the pursuit and discussion of what is perceived today as false issues in their attempt to come to grips with the roles conceived for them or with their prospective functions as social beings and professionals with public responsibilities. Perhaps some of the diversions were inevitable, but nonetheless they have become obstacles, both for the personal, existential quest and for the collective critical understanding of contextual and historical circumstances determining women's social condition and professional status. Attempts have been made in showing the work of women architects to focus on the fact that women can build imposing structures just like men, as if this were a revelation. Such attempts are certainly worthwhile as they add to our knowledge of women's accomplishments and help to change the public's banal image of all architects. However, they do not forcefully challenge the ideological assumptions underlying one persistent and reproachful question: *Why have there been no great women architects?*

Art historian Linda Nochlin has already brilliantly argued that the feminist's first reaction is "to swallow the bait, hook, line and sinker"[1] and to answer the question literally by digging up examples of modest, albeit interesting, buildings and valid, if insufficiently appreciated, careers. But this question, like so many others thrown at women with varying degrees of animosity or bewildered sympathy, "falsifies the nature of the issue," while it supplies at the same time "its own insidious answer: 'There are no great women [architects] because women are incapable of greatness.'"[2]

This book provides a discursive reply to this question, not as it is stated above but as it should be properly rephrased, i.e., by asking: What were the circumstances that supported or hindered the full technical and expressive achievement of women in American architecture? What institutional structures were made available to women to give them the necessary preparation for achieving professional proficiency—let alone greatness? What were the alleged reasons for limiting the access of women to schools of architecture? Do these reasons change in different periods of history? When have women been commissioned to design public buildings and through what channels? What efforts have women architects exerted on their own behalf for professional advancement? And finally, what are the interrelationships of woman as *consumer, producer, critic,* and *creator* of space?

One of the major obstacles to devising methods of historic inquiry and criteria for value judgments in our analysis has been the present critical debate about female *tradition* and the emerging "women's *culture.*" By tradition I mean "those influences which are so pervasive in any historical situation that the human beings who are involved in them are not aware of them at all."[3] It is through the conscious challenge of certain aspects of this tradition, especially those concerned with domestic confinement, that women are attempting to situate themselves in history. This attempt is marked both by women's increasing participation in the public domain and by the documentation of women's past contributions to culture, science, and art.

The recovery of a cultural past is crucial for any future choices made by women so that the evaluation of the conclusions drawn from this past may avoid the unconscious repetitions of traditional patterns. Until very recently tradition has been, in the case of women, a ubiquitous backdrop that has absorbed the dispersion of history. Against its seeming permanence, the few cases of outstanding achievement by women could be safely attributed to originality and genius, regardless of contextual conditions, while the broader traditional "horizon of expectations" remained limited for the majority of women.

From this perspective, this book deals with women's participation in architecture in three areas—the domestic environment, the public and professional sphere, and the esthetic

embodiment of a contemporary consciousness of space as represenation of meaning. These three aspects are treated in relatively separate fashion within the book, but we hope that those interested will be inspired to develop connections between them in order to further elucidate issues in the cultural history of women as well as in the history of architecture and building.

The dominant element in women's relationship to architecture has been, since the obscure beginnings of humankind, the relationship to the domestic, including everyday caretaking and maintenance labor. Although women were the original builders, they were only passive, marginal actors in the intellectual process that resulted in a differentiation of "building" as a function of shelter and survival from "architecture" as a function of culture.

There is sufficient anthropological evidence about the first divisions of labor evolved by the human species for its adaptation to its material surroundings: according to this first specialization, the male individuals of the species went hunting, while the females, the children, and the elders tended the harvest and built the first independent shelters. In more recent times, but in similar circumstances, as Doris Cole has noted, American Indian women of the Southwest and the Great Plains owned, designed, and produced the tepees,[4] those beautifully efficient shelters, for their migrant societies. Although at this point it is not yet possible to identify a supremacy of one sex group over another (given that each group has the control of the space and instruments of their respective activities), there is already a principle of segregation in the forced stability of building as opposed to the mobility of hunting. It is in relation to the vast, open space of nature that the first shelter can be seen as the first form of confinement, distinguishing between an outside, where man is free and mobile, and an internal, closed space, where woman is functionally and spatially fixed.

Later, when the primitive human horde developed into stable societies ruled by powerful patriarchs, the con-

tent of religion and the incipient culture shifted from the cult of the pregnant goddess (who in ensuring the continuity of human life assuaged man's fear of death) to the adoration of all-powerful male deities, no longer associated with nature and life-giving processes. As Athena is born of Zeus's head (a creation of the mind) and as social, political, economic, and judicial institutions are established, building enters a formal system of representation that monumentalizes institutions, ensuring their physical permanence. Within this scheme, woman is assigned the role of muse, the inspirer, but not of the competitor of man, the creator. By extension of this mythological function women remained the passively gratified onlookers or clients of creativity. Although the influence of women as patrons of architecture has been historically recognized, their work as creators remains widely unacknowledged.

Culture—every culture—generates and maintains systems of meaningful forms—symbols, rituals—and systems of thought and technology "by means of which humanity transcends the givens of natural existence"[5]— survival and death—raising above and asserting control over nature, however precariously. Hannah Arendt in *The Human Condition* speaks of this dichotomy opposing the concept of *labor,* the human activity that "corresponds to the biological processes of the humnn body,"[6] to that of *work,* which "corresponds to the unnaturalness of human existence" and is not "imbedded in . . . the species' ever recurring life cycle."[7] Labor is then "impermanent and synonymous with the private realm,"[8] while work is "permanent and synonymous with the public realm."[9]

The differences that do exist between men and women can only take on a connotation of superiority or inferiority within a culturally defined framework, a framework where woman is still seen as the "symbol of something that every culture devalues" or "defines as being at a lower level of existence than itself."[10] This thing is *nature,* in the most generalized sense.

This recurring opposition between culture and nature (or *labor* and *work*) is the context of a discourse developed by anthropologist Sherry Ortner to explain why women's activities, contributions, and powers are "always constrained with the assumption that women may never be officially pre-eminent in the total system."[11] Ortner argues that any focus on women's actual (though culturally unrecognized) contributions alone would be an incomplete effort, unless one also understood "the overarching ideology and deeper assumptions of the culture that render such [contributions] trivial."[12]

A parallel to the labor/work (or culture/nature) dichotomy exists in the culturally established differences between the process of *dwelling* and the products of *architecture*. These differences are made plain by the importance given to creative and esthetic pleasure, as opposed to the toil of survival or even the satisfaction of material desires. It is inevitable that certain conclusions be drawn about most women, professional architects or not, devoting the better part of their domestic and public design and planning efforts to social aspects of their environments—to a changing process rather than the formulation of absolute cultural models.

The conceptual organization of this book, reflected in the main topic for each section and in the sequence of the different chapters, represents my attempt to place the discussion of women in architecture within the larger framework of the issues outlined in this introduction, while testing the validity of this discourse against actual conditions in America. This organization reveals two parallel courses: a history of women designers and planners engaged in the process of dwelling and a history of architecture as a profession and a public art, where women have mostly stayed, to quote Gwendolyn Wright, "on the fringe."[13] Occasionally, the historic streams merge, coincidentally, at times when women organize as a social force—at the beginning of the century and at the present time.

The first section of the book, "'Woman's Place': The Design of Domestic Space," deals with the way design has manipulated the process of *dwelling* and the unconscious "caring and preserving"[14] that is the basis of all human dwelling. The chapters in this section question the assumed "naturalness" of this process, documenting the cultural ideologies that regulate how human beings dwell and how social conventions are reenacted through the material conditions of dwelling. Conversely, the fifth section, "Women's Spatial Symbolism," deals with the creation of space as a conscious creative act and with the process of dwelling as the symbolic expression of unconscious desires.

The second, third, and fourth parts—"Women in the Architectural Profession: A Historic Perspective," "Women as Critics," and "Women in the Architectural Profession: A Contemporary Perspective"—chart the accomplishments and careers of women in the architectural profession and the conditions and events under which they occur, as well as the role of women critics. *Architecture* is here considered in opposition to *dwelling,* for architecture is exercised through institutional training and technical knowledge that the process of dwelling does not necessarily require. Moreover, in the U.S. architecture was distinguished from other building and design activities as the public and civic art *par excellence*. Certainly this Beaux-Arts-derived notion was inextricably linked with the public sphere, with a political realm of action in which women as form-givers to the evolving civic and business enterprises of American democracy had not been assigned any place.

The American architect's notion of his [sic] role at the time of the profession's beginnings is neatly summarized in the following plea, quoted from an anonymous architect by Mariana Griswold van Rensselaer in her 1890 essay, "Client and Architect": "The public must first learn to trust us, as it does lawyers or doctors, before architecture can develop into a great art. Only when a public has learned to put its interest in building into the hands of trustees who are architects, can the latter do their best work. Any examples otherwise produced are accidental and not healthful developments."[15] If this view is accepted, leaving the derogatory ending aside, women architects would still have to repeat this plea nearly a century later.

Lewis Mumford has remarked that the great periods in architecture are those in which there is an essential relationship of agreement and cooperation between architect and client.[16] Historically, we find but a few instances where this "essential relationship" involved a female architect. In those cases the relationship, however, was most likely of a different nature than that implied by Mumford, namely, that the client had given free rein to the architect's esthetic expression. Generally, women, for obvious reasons, have demonstrated a great deal more esthetic tolerance in their work than most men and have accommodated more willingly the client's preferences—an attitude that is obviously at variance with the prevalent belief in the expressive integrity of artistic genius. "I agreed to design the Cortland housing for the purpose of seeing it erected as I designed it and for no other reason. . . . The integrity of a man's creative work is of greater importance than any charitable endeavor,"[17] stated Howard Roark, Ayn Rand's fictional architect-hero, after having dynamited his low-income housing in *The Fountainhead*. One can hardly imagine women architects cheering at the sight.

Current views on the proper role of architecture are divided between those who consider it an artistic act and those who construe it primarily as a social endeavor. Depending on the view taken, women's work in architecture may be considered conservative or progressive, but it must be kept in mind that it is still too early to make wholesale comparisons between the achievements of men and women in architecture from the perspective of artistic and theoretical creation, as the general conditions for this kind of production have not yet been facilitated for women in our society. Gwendolyn Wright has justly stated that the "helpmate, supportive model [of women as 'adjuncts' in the profession] is the role in which women have always been best known and most accepted."[18]

The views and ideas presented here will hopefully stir some healthy controversy, as well as contribute to change in the professional and cultural status of women in American architecture. When such a change occurs, this book will only represent a curious (albeit necessary) document of our times.

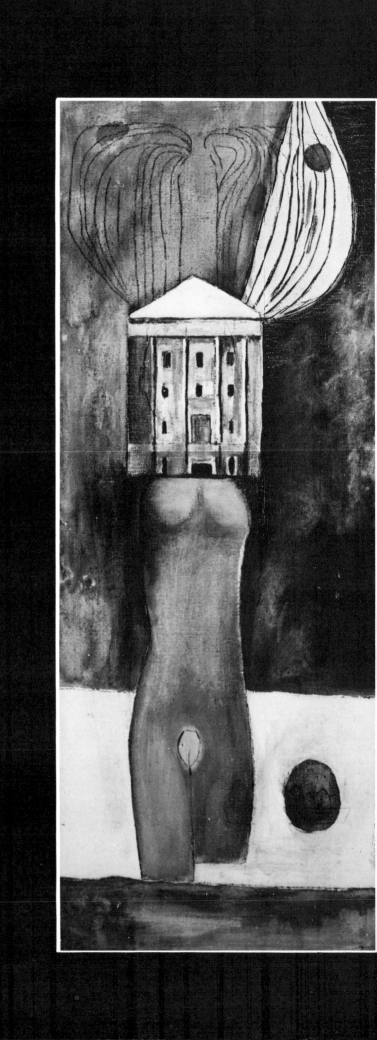

"Woman's Place":
The Design of
Domestic Space

Louise Bourgeois, Attentive Figure, *1944,*
oil painting, 91 x 35½cm/35.8 x 14 in.
Courtesy Xavier Fourcade Inc. Gallery,
New York. Photograph by Peter Moore.

In our society "the ideal happiness has taken material form in the house," Simone de Beauvoir writes in The Second Sex, *and thus the house "stands for permanence and separation from the world." Woman, the domestic keeper of that ideal happiness, has herself taken on the house's traditional attributes of enclosure and isolation. No other building type embodies such symbiotic association between occupant and object.*

Although the house has been the battleground for many avant-garde stylistic battles and the locus for many formal innovations in architecture, the basic organization and hierarchy of its internal spaces still remain unchallenged. This section provides a critical analysis of the internal organization of the house and of its transformations from the late 19th century to the Second World War.

The first chapter deals with the important role played by the women's magazines at the turn of the century in the formulation of the "ideal domestic environment," an ideal influenced by Taylorism and implemented through the principles of scientific management. These early proposals and projects by women designers and home planners were based on two prevalent views: the home as the laboratory of rational planning or as the crucible for society's improvement.

The second chapter surveys projects and actual environments by utopian communities, early feminist architects, and collective house-keeping advocates. These architectural critiques of the single family dwelling suggested provocative innovations and offered significant and inspiring social options.

The third chapter analyzes the work and philosophy of Catharine Beecher, the most influential American domestic designer of the 19th century. Her "American woman's home" project was the architectural frame for her legacy of self-sacrifice and female dominance in the domestic domain. Only the most recent generation of feminist critics has succeeded in fully breaking down Beecher's identification of the home as a female workplace, but architectural models reflecting an equality of domestic roles for both sexes have yet to replace her incredibly complete, detailed, and refined project for the ideal domestic environment.

By Gwendolyn Wright

1. The Model Domestic Environment: Icon or Option?

At least since the early 19th century women have written about homes and homelife for each other. Many women have shared their ideas with a popular female audience, while a few cultivated professional-client ties. They have played a major role in defining the market for American domestic architecture.

But did the populists who wanted to reform the domestic setting also design new sex roles? We might expect that a female who found the time to work would challenge the ways in which domestic environments constrain other women. What in fact happened is that most popular women writers seem to have reinforced the domestic status quo for their readers. Their messages about the model home have been mixtures of two recurrent themes. For some the ideal home has been the laboratory of rational planning:

Theoretically the administration of a household under conservation methods implies a perfect dwelling.[1]

Others saw the home as the crucible for society's improvement:

Better homes will give a better government, and better politics better homes.[2]

The variations on these two themes through the years do show how women have helped one another adapt to new conditions outside the home. Nonetheless, both approaches have assumed the woman's primary role to be in the home.

Women who wrote about the domestic environment have been caught in a bind.[3] The predominantly male professional structure supported those who espoused traditional domestic relations. Many women professionals still accepted sexual stereotypes in theory, even if they broke the rules in their own lives. Furthermore, their conservatism is evidence of real pressures on home life: women readers wanted improvements, yet they were cautious of radical changes that might disrupt their families.

And so the image of the model domestic environment has usually featured a traditional housewife—even when a woman designed that model.

The Progressive Home

By the end of the 19th century the traditional work of the home had undergone dramatic changes. Factories produced many of the goods women had once made themselves; schools became compulsory; professions and social services dispensed advice. Many people were optimistic about the new developments, but others cited the divorce rate, the large number of apartments, and the change in women's demeanor as evidence of social decay. Radical feminists and conservative traditionalists alike discussed the need for a new model home.[4]

Women who were home economists and architectural writers were among those who responded to the social changes of the time with enthusiasm. Most agreed that the newly rationalized, industrialized home was an improvement over the eccentricities of the preceding Victorian period. The new model would be the proper setting for the "home executive" or "home efficiency expert," as the housewife was rechristened. Yet higher standards for that housewife's performance meant that the hours she devoted to her work (if she was not employed outside the home) did not change perceptibly.[5] The new standardized dwellings, with their simple lines and functional plans, did make housework less drudgery and homelife more healthy. But few envisioned the modern home as a way of liberating women to pursue meaningful work outside the home. The progressive model modernized women's work and the setting for it, and so gave new meaning to traditions.

Cleaning can never pass from women's hands, . . . for to keep the world clean, this is the one great task for woman.[6]

Women's Magazines

Perhaps the best indicator of popular domestic ideals in the early 20th century is *The Ladies' Home Journal*, which called itself "the Bible of the American home."[7] Under the editorship of Edward Bok, it reached the unparalleled circulation of 1 million in 1900 and 2 million just before World War I. Bok had obstinately clear views about the proper place for women, but he welcomed interesting alternatives. Many of the contributions from female architects, journalists, and readers suggested how the American home could be adapted to the needs of working women.

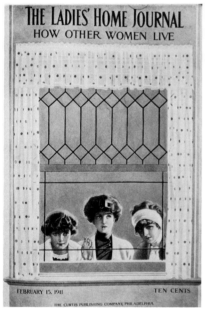

Above: *Cover,* The Ladies' Home Journal, *Feb. 15, 1911. Women began to learn about keeping house and raising children by reading magazines rather than looking to their mothers.*

Top, right: *Una Nixson Hopkins, "A Picturesque Court of 30 Bungalows,"* The Ladies' Home Journal, *Feb. 15, 1911. The communal space in this project was a "summer house" designed for leisurely sewing and visiting and not for shared housekeeping or work.*

Bottom, right: *Virginia Stern, "Two City Girls Plan Their Own Bungalow,"* The Ladies' Home Journal, *April 1912. "Easy housekeeping" was the great advantage of the one-story bungalows that the* Journal *helped popularize during the 1910s.*

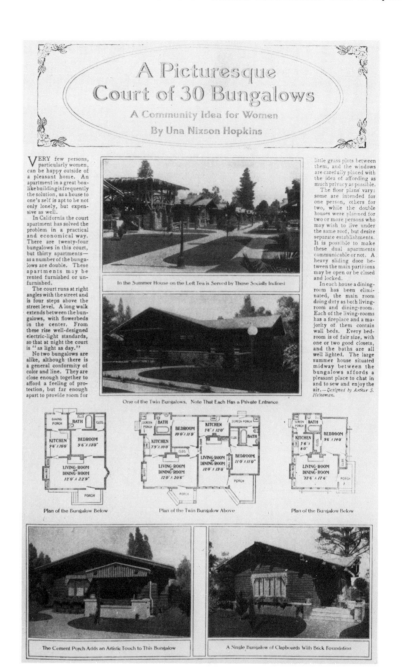

Christine Frederick

Christine McGaffey Frederick, born in Boston in 1883, was the foremost evangelist of the domestic science ideology. While a housewife in the early 1910s, she was the first to recognize the potential application of scientific management in the home. Soon she was lecturing on the Chautauqua circuit and writing a series for *The Ladies' Home Journal.* She produced a film on housekeeping in 1913 and founded a school of domestic science—Applecroft Experimental Station—in her Long Island home during the 1910s.

Frederick's work was based upon the famous experiments of Frederick Taylor, who set out to increase factory production by standardizing workers' movements and machinery. In her most popular book, *Household Engineering: Scientific Management in the Home* of 1915, she interpreted the twelve principles of Taylorism for housewives:

1. Ideals
2. Common sense
3. Competent counsel [i.e., following the advice of experts]
4. Standardized operations
5. Standardized conditions
6. Standard practice
7. Dispatching [i.e., planning chores]
8. Scheduling
9. Reliable records
10. Discipline
11. Fair deal [i.e., keeping "indexes" and "scorecards" of how various products performed]
12. Efficiency rewards

The homemaker must look at her work as it *is,* as a problem which is *interesting,* which is *stimulating,* which will call into play all her highest training, and which, no matter how difficult, *can be solved* by the twelve principles of efficiency.[8]

Frederick taught millions of women a newly defined role that combined the self-importance of the business manager with the rigid training of the assembly-line worker. She also insisted on the latest equipment, new arrangements, and modern surroundings to complement this role. Increased consumption would go hand-in-rubber glove with increased organization, for the housewife should be "training herself to become an efficient 'purchasing agent' for her particular firm and family."[9] But Frederick was something of a double agent. Her third book—*Selling Mrs. Consumer,* published in 1929—shared her ideology of domestic science with advertisers.

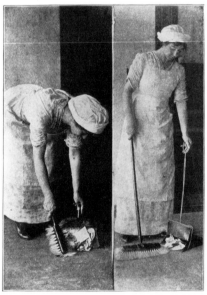

Above: *Using the short-handled and long-handled dustpan; from C. Frederick,* Household Engineering, *1915.*

Top: *Vegetable-preparing table; from C. Frederick,* Household Engineering, *1915. "A worker does neater, more careful work if she is neatly attired."*[10]

Above: *Christine Frederick in her model kitchen at Applecroft Experimental Station, Long Island; from C. Frederick,* Household Engineering: Scientific Management in the Home, *1915. Frederick recommended a small kitchen without a separate pantry and a special grouping of tools, equipment, and gadgets. The nearby "comfort corner" or "business corner" provided the "household manager" with an easy chair and a shelf for her books when she tired of the worker's drudgery.*

Left: *Step savers; from C. Frederick,* The New Housekeeping: Efficiency Studies in Home Management, *1912. "The modern woman is* chiefly a consumer, *and not a producer."*[11] *Another such observation comes from Henry James's "An International Episode" of 1878: " 'An American woman who respects herself,' said Mrs. Westgate, turning to Beaumont with her bright expository air, 'must buy something every day of her life. If she cannot do it herself, she must send out some member of her family for the purpose.' "*

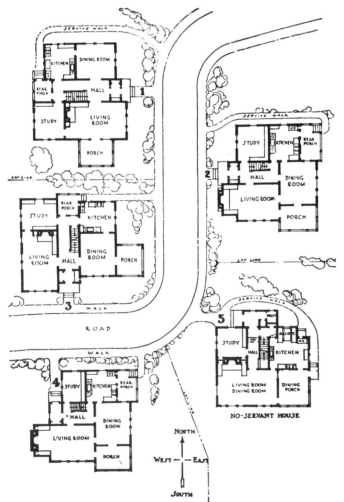

Above: A labor-saving cottage; from C. Frederick, Household Engineering, *1915. The facade Frederick admired was totally different from the efficient, sanitized interior she espoused. Brick, stone, stucco, and hollow tile were preferred because they gave a more "permanent" appearance. Smaller windows, placed near the ceilings with high interior sills, were preferable to wide plate glass because the occupants were less visible from the streets. Such a home would be a haven for the man: "His hours at home should be hours of recuperation, so that he can study his own work and become more proficient, and thus secure advancement or a better economic position."* [13]

Left: *Plans for a servantless house (with living room on the south, dining room east, kitchen north, porch east and south; from C. Frederick,* Household Engineering, *1915. As of 1910, 92 percent of the households in the United States had no live-in servants. Frederick encouraged her readers to view this shift in a positive light. The servantless house "offers the only real opportunity for a family to follow the exact standards it wishes."* [12]

Greta Gray

Greta Gray, a graduate of MIT in architecture and of Columbia in home economics, was the most progressive of the early popular writers on the domestic environment. Her *House and Home* of 1923 addressed women of all classes. Gray analyzed the home from the perspective of the woman who worked and lived there. Most of her suggested improvements were designed to ease the housewife's workload or her emotional strain. She contended that a woman's *experience* of the home, not her performance, was the most important issue to study, even though her problems might be difficult to calculate: fatigue from overwork, nervousness due to real or imagined dangers to one's children, depression from dreary surroundings, loneliness from isolation, "and others, equally as important, perhaps, but less tangible."[14] Gray didn't actively challenge the woman's traditional place in the home, but she did write about real women and their problems.

Exterior view and floor plans, two-family five-room house; from G. Gray, House and Home, *1923. Gray advocated local building standards that took into account the kind of family life prevalent in an area—large families, working parents, elderly people. "Houses to-day seem to be built and furnished almost exclusively for those who are in good health and for grown people."*[15]

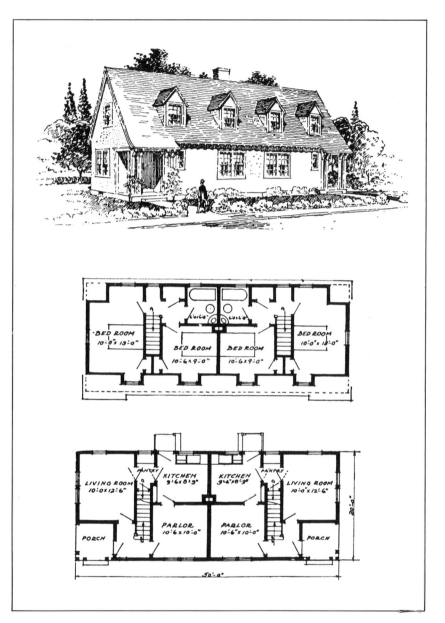

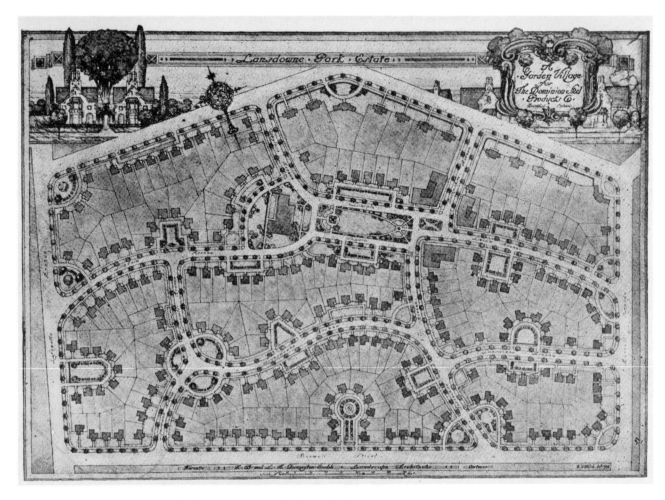

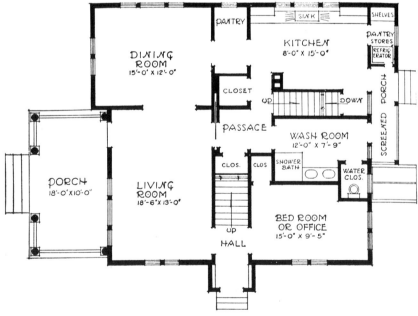

Above: Plan of the Garden Village of Dominion Steel Products Company in Bradford, Ontario; from G. Gray, House and Home, *1923. Like Catherine Bauer a decade later, Gray praised the concepts of the garden city. She argued against defining the family as a private institution or the home as a totally detached architectural problem.*

Left: First floor plan of concrete farm house; from G. Gray, House and Home, *1923. Gray taught her readers about the latest architectural innovations, including prefabrication. Note the spacious kitchen area, the screened kitchen porch, and the washroom for farmhands that is separate from the family's private spaces (and particularly from the kitchen where the woman worked). Gray suggested minute improvements: raising the wood floor 4 inches/10.2 centimeters above the cold cement slab in kitchens and laundries; providing chutes between floors for ashes, dust, garbage, and coal, as well as lifts for equipment; planning wide windows with pleasant views at the woman's main work areas.*

The Search for Order in the 1930s

Top: *Lilian Moller Gilbreth, demonstration kitchen of the Brooklyn Borough Gas Company, 1933; from* Architectural Record, *March 1934. Courtesy* Architectural Record. *Lilian Moller Gilbreth, an industrial engineer like her partner-husband Frank, pioneered in the field of "human engineering."* [16] *In 1933 the Brooklyn Gas Company commissioned her to do a series of efficiency studies in kitchen design. The architectural press gave much attention to the work of industrial research laboratories, hoping to promote renovations, and Gilbreth's model received wide coverage. Note the "planning desk" in the corner behind the refrigerator.*

Bottom: *View of kitchen-laundry spaces; from D. Field,* The Human House, *1939. The conflicts between the cults of efficiency and tradition came into sharper focus as houses became smaller. By the late 1930s, architects championed the "zoned house" as a way to resolve family tensions in a reduced space. Dorothy Field's* The Human House *explained the zones in terms of the different uses and meanings of the home for each family member as follows:*

Father's point of view:
  a place to rest up after work
  a place to entertain
  a workshop for a hobby
  a private study
  a store place for valuables —guns,
    fishing rods, collections, etc.
Mother's point of view:
  a place to work and to show
  a work place for cooking, sewing,
    washing, and ironing
  nursery space for teaching walking,
    talking, eating, climbing, hanging up
    clothes, dressing and undressing
  a habit-training center for school and
    adolescent children
  a family community center for fun
  a place for entertaining guests
    at meals
    at games
    conversation
  office space for correspondence,
    ordering, planning, accounts
  equipment for care of family's health
  storage space for family property
  storage space for personal property [18]

The mother is the selfless mediator without her own space, who helps the others find privacy and fulfillment.

26

Right: *Emily Post, "The Sort of House That Appeals to a Man." Copyright © 1930, 1933, 1939, 1948 by Emily Post, from* The Personality of a House. *With permission of Funk & Wagnalls Publishing Co., Inc. Emily Post, writing during the same period as Gilbreth, tenaciously defended traditional decoration and "homeyness." Her books accentuated the sexual division of labor and even portrayed a different esthetic and separate area for men and women within the home.*

Below: *E. Post, "A Delightful Man's Room." Copyright © 1930, 1933, 1939, 1948 by Emily Post, from* The Personality of a House. *With permission of Funk & Wagnalls Publishing Co., Inc. Although Post never acknowledged the repercussions of the Depression, her work reveals the deep longing for homes that offer images of security. She called for a special man's room in every home to provide comfort and reassurance. "The type of room the average man likes, and feels at home in, should not be easily spoilable. Chairs that look easily breakable, coverings light and perishable in color and texture, in short, are more or less unfitted to convey the feeling of 'home' to men."* [17]

Housing for Rosie the Riveter and GI Joe

During wartime, housing has always been built to be more practical and community oriented, as women are needed in factories—and in architectural offices of both private firms and governmental agencies. Housing that was quick to build and easy to keep up became a necessary part of the war effort. Women designed many of these houses. And they had other women workers in mind—not housewives.

There were two requirements for housing during each world war: that it accommodate women workers and that it not be abandoned after the war. The solution was to design simple, functional homes with adjacent neighborhood services—shops, schools, nurseries, playgrounds, clinics, and meeting rooms. Such services were provided, as Catherine Bauer duly noted, ''not at the instigation of social reformers (who have lit-

tle influence in wartime) but because employers and military authorities demanded it.'' However, as soon as the war ended, the commitment to such services became tenuous at best.

Many women wartime designers did assume that community values would continue to flourish after the war. As Elizabeth Kemper Adams prophesied in 1921:

With the housing experience gained during the war and the urgency of present housing problems, especially for industrial workers and other people of small incomes, there seems a new opportunity for women architects to direct their attention to building for these groups and to the problem of community centers.[21]

But after each war, there were massive campaigns to return women to the domestic sphere so that there would be jobs for men. Postwar ''dream houses'' were part of the package. If women wanted to stay on in offices, this is what they had to design.

Dorothy Rosenman, ''Housing to Speed Production,'' Architectural Record, *April 1942. Courtesy* Architectural Record. *''Men and women cannot work at the top efficiency our situation demands if they are not housed under circumstances that will assure their continuing ability to stay on the job.''*

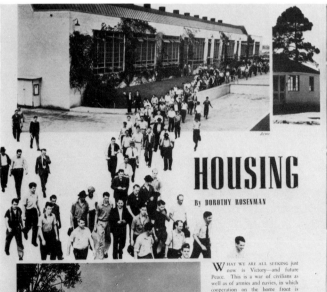

HOUSING to speed PRODUCTION

By DOROTHY ROSENMAN

The majority of readers (57.1 per cent) preferred this contemporary living room by architect Carl Koch to the traditional room below. Its spacious windows, good light and ventilation, reduced maintenance problems and adaptibility to active living were listed among its most important assets.

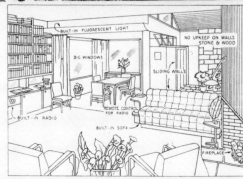

Living room contest put modern slightly ahead of traditional.

The traditional living room decorated by Lord & Taylor, was found to symbolize a comfortable, sheltered mode of living. Many women considered period furniture easier to combine and to rearrange. A number selected it on the ground that it would better fit their present or future homes.

George H. Van Anda

McCALL'S

13,539 women give reasons for disliking their LIVING ROOMS.

Too small	37%
Hard to entertain	32%
Furniture doesn't fit	30%
Not enough windows	29%
Everything old	27%
Hard to clean	22%
Color scheme ugly	18%
Everything shabby	14%
Uncomfortable	12%

SOFA STYLE PREFERENCE

	Sectional	47%
	Lawson	29%
	Camel Back	20%
	Ornate	4%

ARMCHAIR PREFERENCE

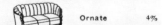

Lounge	53%	
Modern	26%	
Wing	17%	
Ornate	4%	

STORAGE UNIT PREFERENCE

	Sectional bookcase	58%
	Breakfront bookbase	27%
	Modern breakfront	15%

PORTABLE LAMP PREFERENCE

Plain	50%	
Oil base	20%	
Ornate	18%	
Modern Tube	12%	

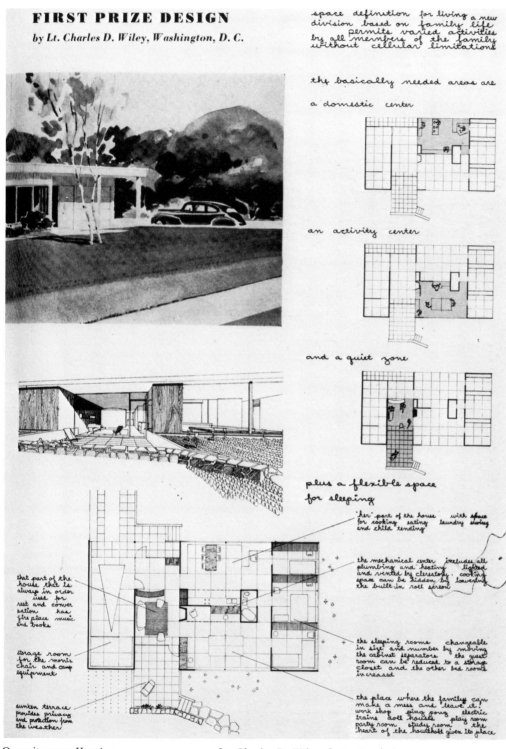

FIRST PRIZE DESIGN
by Lt. Charles D. Wiley, Washington, D. C.

space definition for living a new
division based on family life
permits varied activities
by all members of the family
without cellular limitations

the basically needed areas are

a domestic center

an activity center

and a quiet zone

plus a flexible space
for sleeping

"her" part of the house with space
for cooking eating laundry storing
and child tending

the mechanical center includes all
plumbing and heating lighted
and vented by clerestory cooking
space can be hidden by lowering
the built-in roll screen

the sleeping rooms changeable
in size and number by moving
the cabinet separators the guest
room can be reduced to a storage
closet and the other bed rooms
increased

the place where the family can
make a mess and leave it —
work shop ping pong electric
trains doll houses play room
party room study room the
heart of the household given its place

that part of the
house that is
always in order
used for
rest and conver
sation has
the place music
and books

storage room
for the movie
chair and camp
equipment

sunken terrace
provides privacy
and protection from
the weather

Opposite page: *Housing survey by Mary Davis Gilles (interiors and architectural editor of* McCall's), *"Mr. and Mrs. McCall Know What They Want,"* Architectural Forum, *April 1945. The housewife's "participation" in post-war housing design offered only a few conventional options.*

Lt. Charles D. Wiley, first prize design, Second Annual Small House Competition of Arts and Architecture, *sponsored by the U.S. Plywood Corporation; from* Architectural Record, *May 1945. Courtesy* Architectural Record. *Designers of the "Ideal Post-War Small House" tried to assure women that a well-designed house would help them produce a good family life.*

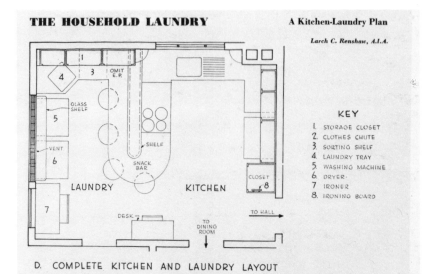

THE HOUSEHOLD LAUNDRY   A Kitchen-Laundry Plan

Larch C. Renshaw, A.I.A.

KEY

1. STORAGE CLOSET
2. CLOTHES CHUTE
3. SORTING SHELF
4. LAUNDRY TRAY
5. WASHING MACHINE
6. DRYER
7. IRONER
8. IRONING BOARD

D. COMPLETE KITCHEN AND LAUNDRY LAYOUT

By courtesy of Edison General Electric Appliance Company, Inc. of Chicago, Ill.

Right: *The household laundry, by Larch C. Renshaw, "Time-Saver Standards,"* Architectural Record, *May 1945. Courtesy* Architectural Record. *With the end of the war, housing articles focused on the woman's space in the home. Model laundries and kitchens became more spacious and pleasant environments in which to spend time.*

Below: *Kitchen views; from Elizabeth Mock,* If You Want to Build a House. *Copyright © 1946, renewed 1973, The Museum of Modern Art, New York. All rights reserved. Reprinted by permission. Mock's best-seller shows that there was always some skepticism and revolt against extravagant kitchen fetishism.*

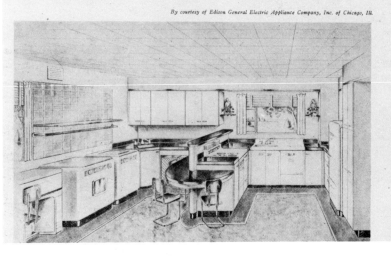

But we needn't settle for a vitamin laboratory and gadgetry . . .

Alternative Settings

There have been women who designed for groups other than middle class nuclear families. However, even socially innovative designs usually portrayed the woman at the hearth or in the nursery. This emphasis was a recurrent theme of American reformers, who often tried to solve larger social problems by perfecting the home—and keeping women there.

The Woman's Commonwealth

The Woman's Commonwealth originated in Belton, Texas, in 1866 under the leadership of Martha McWhirter (1827–1904). A group of thirty local women left their families to build their own houses and share domestic work. Soon their numbers increased, and they moved into a communal structure in the center of the town. They continued to plan and construct additions over the next 20 years. In 1886, they converted their residence into a hotel. Although it was boycotted for the first year, the Central Hotel did become a financial and social success, always filled with travelers and townspeople. When the group retired to Washington, D.C., in 1899, the people of Belton begged them to stay on.

In almost every way, the Commonwealth's buildings reflected an uncommon set of values. The facades were unpretentious, since the group favored extreme simplicity. The interiors were planned for interaction during work and leisure. Each room had several uses; each one opened into an adjoining space or an outdoor area. The women formulated these designs through group discussion, investigation of efficient methods and client preferences elsewhere, and an element of mysticism.

However, the Commonwealth didn't try to spread their new domestic order. They were cautious about sharing their ideas or taking in new members. Their private solution was workable, but they adamantly insisted on remaining an anomaly.[19]

Right: *Plan, the Central Hotel, operated by the Woman's Commonwealth, Belton, Texas, 1896. Courtesy Gwendolyn Wright. Note the open plan for communal work and social spaces in both main buildings. Private areas were scattered in small clusters.*

Middle: *Main Street elevation, the Central Hotel, 1891. Courtesy Gwendolyn Wright. The circulation system of three-story galleries provided wide, continuous porches. Here guests could visit and the Sisters could work.*

Bottom: *The Woman's Commonwealth, 1902; McWhirter is the second woman seated from the left. Courtesy Gwendolyn Wright.*

By Dolores Hayden

2. Challenging the American Domestic Ideal

The feminist economist, Charlotte Perkins Gilman, satirized home worship in a short poem:

Oh! the Home is utterly perfect!
    And all its works within,
To say a word about it—
To criticize or doubt it—
To seek to mend or move it—
To venture to improve it—
    Is the unpardonable sin!

Between 1898 and 1903 Gilman laid out the lines of an attack on the home that are still valid today: "The two main errors in the right adjustment of the home to our present life are these: the maintenance of primitive industries in a modern industrial community, and the confinement of women to those industries and their limited area of expression." A good number of 19th-century feminists had anticipated Gilman in these views; and contemporary feminists are still working

along these two lines: within the movement demanding wages for housework and the movement encouraging men to assume an equal share of housework. Ultimately these two contemporary political campaigns must converge with the demand for drastic changes in traditional "women's work" and drastic redesign of the environments in which domestic work is conducted.

This chapter surveys some of the results of agitation for domestic reform in the United States between 1800 and 1930, the designs, and buildings aimed at restructuring domestic work. They are not presented as solutions to the problems of women's work, but as architectural critiques of the traditional home, developed in built form rather than in words. In many respects they offer more significant social options than the ideal single family dwellings of the same period. Benevolent capi-

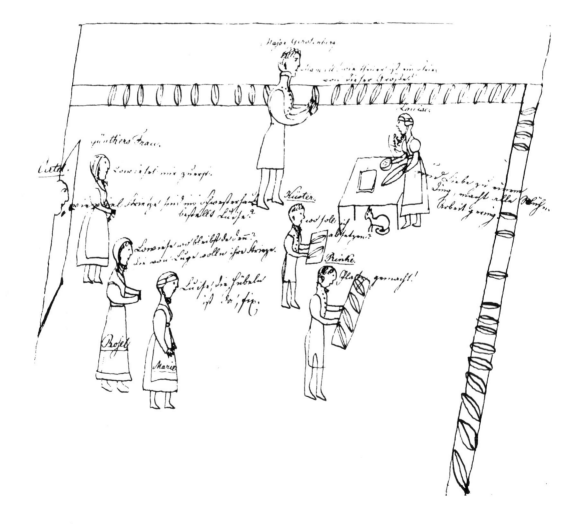

talists constructed idealized factories along with idealized workers' housing, demonstrating the role of the housewife and the house in keeping workers happy on the job. Urban and suburban social reformers also stressed the role of good housing in promoting social stability. In contrast with those who supported these causes, the advocates of collective housekeeping challenged the increasing separation of men and women, work and home, production and reproduction, all brought about by the development of American capitalism.

The plans and experiments of the collective housekeepers may not seem particularly practical now, but they are part of a long history of revolt against the single family home. They suggest women's power to imagine something better; they revive a sense of possibilities, urgencies, and priorities. After examining them, we can no longer take the housewife, or the house, for granted.

NEW YORK STATE.—THE BAKERY OF THE ONEIDA COMMUNITY OF FREE LOVERS.—FROM A SKETCH BY OUR SPECIAL ARTIST. SEE PAGE 38.

Top, right: *Women in communal kitchen, Oneida Community, Oneida, New York; from* Frank Leslie's Illustrated Newspaper, *Apr. 9, 1870. Women of the Oneida Community, which flourished at Oneida, New York, from 1848 to 1881, wore short hair, trousers, and sensible shoes of their own design. Here they are at work in their kitchen, which served 200 members living in the communal Mansion House.*

Right: *Communal Children's House, Oneida Community, Oneida, New York, 1848–1881; from* Frank Leslie's Illustrated Newspaper, *Apr. 9, 1870. Childcare at Oneida was a communal undertaking shared by both men and women. The communal Children's House replicated on a smaller scale the arrangement of sitting rooms in the adults' Mansion.*

Opposite page: *Moravian communal bakery, undated sketch. Courtesy Old Salem, Inc., Salem, North Carolina. Religious communitarian groups established dozens of experiments in communal living that included collective housekeeping and childcare during the 18th and 19th centuries. Here members of a Moravian community in North Carolina are shown at work in a communal bakery, surrounded by a border of loaves of bread.*

APRIL 9, 1870.] FRANK LESLIE'S ILLUSTRATED NEWSPAPER.

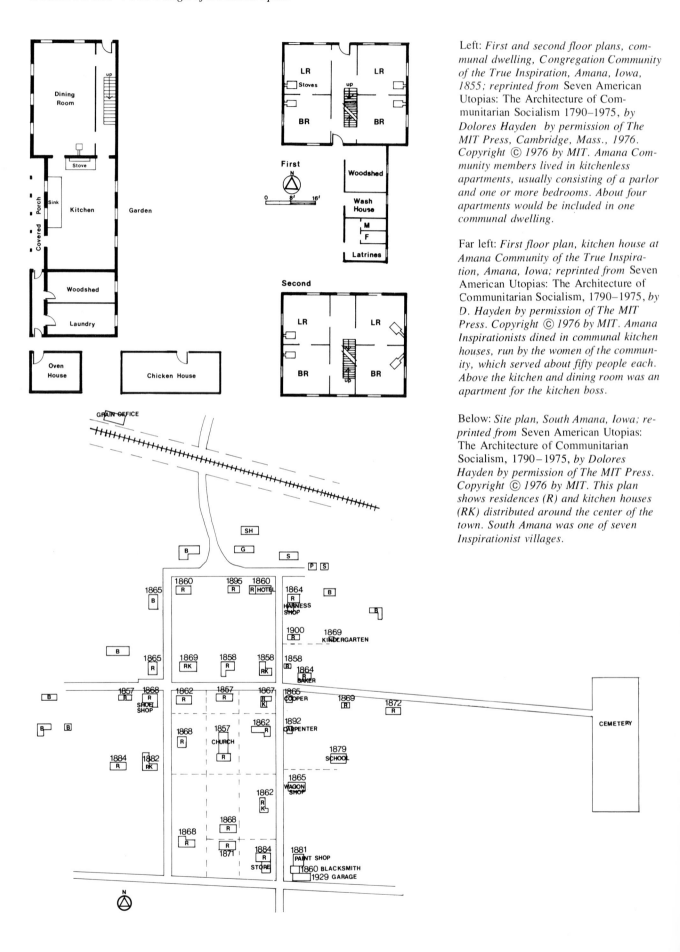

Left: *First and second floor plans, communal dwelling, Congregation Community of the True Inspiration, Amana, Iowa, 1855; reprinted from* Seven American Utopias: The Architecture of Communitarian Socialism 1790–1975, *by Dolores Hayden by permission of The MIT Press, Cambridge, Mass., 1976. Copyright © 1976 by MIT. Amana Community members lived in kitchenless apartments, usually consisting of a parlor and one or more bedrooms. About four apartments would be included in one communal dwelling.*

Far left: *First floor plan, kitchen house at Amana Community of the True Inspiration, Amana, Iowa; reprinted from* Seven American Utopias: The Architecture of Communitarian Socialism, 1790–1975, *by D. Hayden by permission of The MIT Press. Copyright © 1976 by MIT. Amana Inspirationists dined in communal kitchen houses, run by the women of the community, which served about fifty people each. Above the kitchen and dining room was an apartment for the kitchen boss.*

Below: *Site plan, South Amana, Iowa; reprinted from* Seven American Utopias: The Architecture of Communitarian Socialism, 1790–1975, *by Dolores Hayden by permission of The MIT Press. Copyright © 1976 by MIT. This plan shows residences (R) and kitchen houses (RK) distributed around the center of the town. South Amana was one of seven Inspirationist villages.*

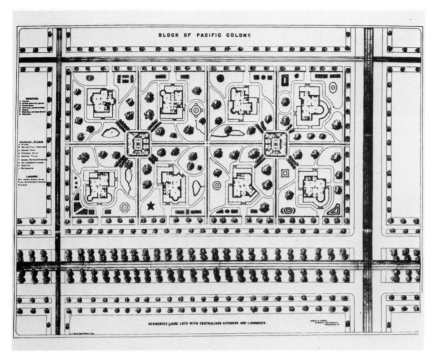

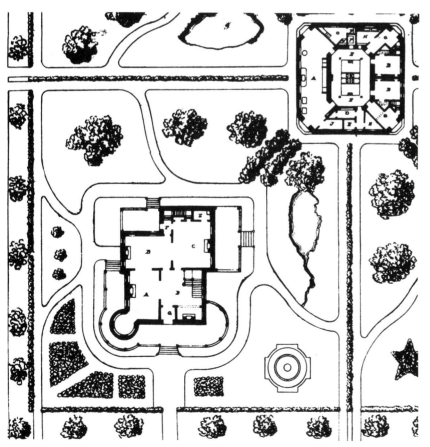

Above: *Marie Stevens Howland, feminist and utopian socialist; from Ray Reynolds,* Cat's Paw Utopia, *1972; drawing by Mary Reynolds. Howland resided at the Familistere established in Guise, France, during the 1860s and returned to the United States in 1866 to proselytize for collective housekeeping. She described collective domestic work in a novel,* Papa's Own Girl. *She assisted Albert Kimsey Owen and John Deery in the design of housing for the Pacific Colony of Sinaloa, Mexico, in 1885, which included resident hotels, row houses linked to communal kitchens, and picturesque suburban houses with cooperative kitchen facilities.*

Top, left: *Picturesque block design, Pacific Colony; from A. Owen,* Integral Cooperation, *1885. Each unit consisted of four private houses without kitchens but including dining rooms. These were linked to central kitchen and laundry facilities, with accommodations for servants of the four households.*

Bottom, left: *Detail of block, Pacific Colony; from A. Owen,* Integral Cooperation, *1885. House: A, parlor; B, sitting room; C, dining room; E, pantry; F, rear hall; G, vestibule. Kitchen building: A, kitchen; B, male and female dormitories; C, serving room; D, Steward's office; E, covered piazza; F, general pantries and store room; G, hall and stairs to laundry; H, scullery; J, refrigeration.*

Alice Constance Austin, feminist and utopian socialist; from Llano Viewbook, *1917. Courtesy Bancroft Library, University of California, Berkeley, California. Austin planned kitchenless patio houses for the Llano del Rio community established near Los Angeles in 1914. She was a self-trained architect influenced by Ebenezer Howard's* Garden Cities of To-Morrow. *Howard was an advocate of cooperative housekeeping himself, although this aspect of his work is rarely publicized. In 1935 Austin's* The Next Step: How to Plan for Beauty Comfort and Peace with Great Savings Effected by the Reduction of Waste *was published, which detailed her plans for a feminist socialist city.*

A. C. Austin, plan for kitchenless house, Llano del Rio, California; from A. C. Austin, The Next Step, *1935.*

A. C. Austin, view of kitchenless houses, Llano del Rio, California; from A. C. Austin, The Next Step, *1935. Note the underground tunnel at lower left for food delivery carts and small garages in front of houses. Dotted lines denote party walls.*

Above: *A* Ladies' Home Journal article, *"One Kitchen Fire for 200 People,"* detailed the successes of cooperative kitchens in operation in New York City and Montclair, New Jersey, in September 1918.

Right: *"Starting a Community Kitchen,"* The Ladies' Home Journal, *June 1919. Cooperative housekeeping became more popular as a cause during World War I. Myrtle Perrigo Fox and Ethel Lendrum published this article on how to begin such an enterprise.*

The Ladies' Ho

Starting a Community Kitchen
Just How it Can be Done With Little Outlay
By Myrtle Perrigo Fox and Ethel Lendrum, Home Demonstration Agent

HERE is a chance for a woman gifted with common sense, some business ability, and a fair knowledge of cookery, not only to release or relieve other women, but to add to the family income or even to earn her livelihood. You can start a community kitchen with three or four families as patrons. Serve two meals a week until you are asked to cook more. A modest beginning will enable you to gain your capital and experience at the same time.

The Cooked Dinner on the "Cash-and-Carry" Plan

The Community Kitchen Dinner Served at Home

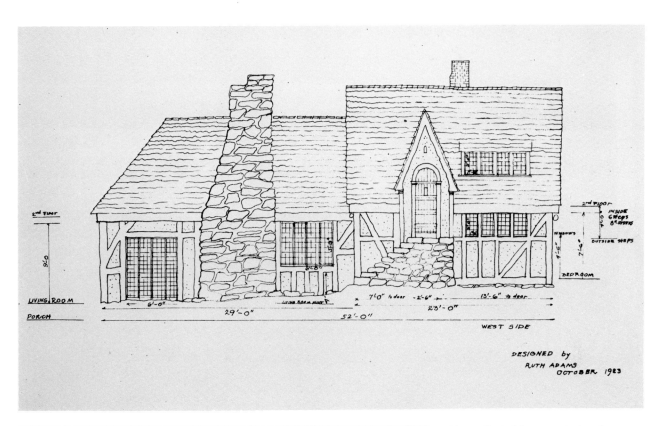

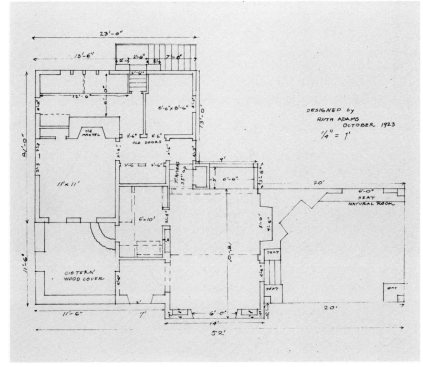

Above: *Ruth Adams, west elevation, kitchenless house, October 1923. Plan and elevation drawn by Margo Jones from originals supplied by Robert Beach of West Cornwall, Connecticut. Ruth Adams designed kitchenless houses for the summer community of Yelping Hill built in West Cornwall, Connecticut, beginning in 1922; a remodeled barn served as the community center, kitchen, and dining hall. She designed her own kitchenless house in an exuberant, eclectic style.*

Left: *R. Adams, ground floor, kitchenless house.*

By Dolores Hayden

3. Catharine Beecher and the Politics of Housework

Protection is the genius of your house
the pressure of the steam iron
flattens the linen cloth again
chestnuts pureed with care are
   dutifully eaten
in every room the furniture reflects
   you
larger than life, or dwindling

Adrienne Rich, "A Primary
Ground," 1972

Her forceful countenance dominates its frame of Victorian ringlets; her incisive prose holds up amid woodcuts of teakettles and bathtubs. Catharine Esther Beecher, a woman of overwhelming intellectual energy, confronted 19th-century America with an unusual talent for moral philosophy, but found society prepared to acclaim her chiefly as a domestic economist. Her life and her work exhaust one with paradoxes of sex and politics. She was the most influential woman designer of her century and the person who did the most to justify the exclusion of women from all professional careers. One must admire her guts and resourcefulness, as well as detest the ends for which they were employed: the idealization of female domesticity and the sex-stereotyping of household work.

Her vision of the home began with her definition of an ideal American woman as a self-sacrificing Christian wife and mother. This was conventional enough preaching, until she designed for this phantom female a concrete, replicable environment with which she could identify her religious obligations and in which she could develop her skills as a consumer. This fusion of Christian moral obligation and capitalist material culture became the bedrock of American gender socialization for over a century. Today consciousness-raising groups that struggle to extirpate female identification with housework (or male indifference to it) are still coping with her legacy—a synthetic vision encompassing the individual woman, the home environment, and the political economy, locked together in a system of personal and social values.

Very few architects or planners ever see such a transcendent social ideal realized. Frederick Law Olmsted is perhaps the only American designer of comparable importance in the 19th century. Yet for all her influence, Catharine Beecher has been largely ignored in architectural circles. As a woman, considered a domestic economist, her charismatic successes have been shared out among other domestic designers whose social and political analyses were much more superficial, such as Andrew Jackson Downing and Frank Lloyd Wright. A splendid and sympathetic biography of Beecher by Kathryn Kish Sklar, published in 1973, reveals the full extent of her career as a writer and educator[1]; "Women in American Architecture," exhibited in 1977, is the first major museum show to include her work as an architect.

Architectural critics who have looked seriously at Beecher's work have tended to regard her as a domestic technocrat, rightly enough, since 20th-century household management studies add little or nothing to her intuitive efficiencies. We cannot afford to admire the technical side of Beecher, however, and take for granted the sexism inherent in her moral philosophy of efficient, exclusively female domesticity. As Gwendolyn Wright demonstrates in Chapter 1, this domestic mythology demands the intellectual, economic, social, and political subordination of women. We can see Beecher struggling to overcome this sexism herself—at one moment, prescribing rigid roles for other women and at the next, trying to find ways to explore her own abilities and remain true to her own life experience as a woman. Beecher knew well the cost of sacrificing one's broader talents to a domestic world, and some of her very late work suggests an openness to less constricting definitions of womanly roles. A review of her life and writings reveals both her orthodoxy and her creativity in defining women's roles and devising domestic architecture to support them.

Author and Organizer

Catharine Beecher was born in 1800 in East Hampton, Long Island, a town founded by colonists from a Puritan covenant community in Connecticut.

Catharine E. Beecher, undated photograph. Courtesy Schlesinger Library, Radcliffe College.

Her father, the Reverend Lyman Beecher, represented this religious tradition in the town and was a spellbinding minister on his way to becoming a national figure. Her mother, Roxana Foote Beecher, bore eight children and was a model housewife who tried without success to interest Catharine in domestic skills. She preferred reading and writing, so it must have been a significant shock when her mother died in 1816, leaving Catharine to manage the household and the seven younger children. Her father remarried quickly, however, and Catharine was off to Miss Pierce's school in Litchfield, Connecticut. There her daily journals won prizes, developing what Sklar has called her skill in "private writing for public consumption," later the mainstay of her domestic books.[2] This was the end of her formal education. Her brothers, of course, went on to college while she was left to read privately with her sister, Harriet.

Some poetry she published led to courtship. She found her intellectual match in Alexander Metcalf Fisher, a young and renowned professor at Yale, but he died in a shipwreck before their marriage could take place. The tragedy left her immersed in his scientific papers. After teaching herself enough mathematics to understand them, she attempted to put grief aside and earn her living.

After a brief spell as a drawing instructor in New London, Connecticut, she opened her own school, the Hartford Female Seminary, in 1823. Daniel Wadsworth of Hartford, an amateur architect, provided her with a sketch for the facade of the seminary building, which enabled her to raise funds. He seems to have been the first person to stimulate the interest in esthetics and building that she developed throughout her career.[3] During this period, she taught and wrote energetically, producing her first book in 1831, *The Elements of Mental and Moral Philosophy, Founded Upon Experience, Reason and the Bible.* This book launched her lifelong argument for the moral superiority of women based upon their highly developed capacity for self-sacrifice.

In that same year, 1831, Catharine Beecher left her Hartford school and moved to Cincinnati, following her father's appointment there. She organized another school, the Western Female Seminary, and continued to write prolifically on doctrinal disputes, moral responsibility, abolition (which she more or less favored), and woman suffrage (which she opposed). She traveled extensively in 1836 to support a plan for the education and placement of female missionary teachers in the West, a project for which she later produced unusual domestic architecture. In 1836 she also wrote a long essay celebrating the differences between male and female character, introducing and elaborating now familiar stereotypes of gender.

She began work in that same year on her *Treatise on Domestic Economy, For the Use of Young Ladies at Home and at School,* which incorporated many of these ideas and was eventually published in 1841. Sklar estimates its effect: Beecher "exaggerated and heightened gender differences and thereby altered and romanticized the emphasis given to women's domestic role."[4] Unlike her philosophical writings that suffered the stigma of female authorship, her *Treatise* was an immediate, popular success, running through yearly editions, adopted as a school text, a classic succeeded only by her even more popular work, *The American Woman's Home,* co-authored with her sister, Harriet Beecher Stowe, in 1869.

The Minister and the Professional

The success of the *Treatise* and all Beecher's subsequent domestic publications centered upon her agile definitions of female dominance in the home. Earlier American works on domestic economy assume that men retain control of the typical middle class household, including women, children, and servants, but Beecher breaks with this tradition tentatively in the *Treatise* and decisively in *The American Woman's Home.* She proposes female supremacy in the home, enhanced by two metaphors of female authority: the "minister" and the skilled "professional," harnessing the imagery of religion and business, of power absolute in the colonial period and power just beginning to be felt in urbanizing America. These metaphors of ministerial and professional activity are supported by a most unusual economic rationalization. Domestic servants are to be replaced by women doing their own housework, but rather than indicating a diminution in status, this provides the opportunity for self-sacrifice (the ministerial role) and skill (the professional role). Thus zealous homemaking becomes an ideal for women of all classes, an activity that will confer purpose on the "aimless vacuity" of rich women, ennoble the "unrequited toil" of poor women, as well as improve the prestige of middle class women.[5]

The ministerial ideal transferred to the family many of the properties of the Puritan village of 17th-century New England. Beecher planned to recreate its hierarchy in miniature, describing the home as a Christian "commonwealth," where the woman is the "minister of home." As the head of the "home church of Jesus Christ," she can inculcate 10 to 12 offspring with the ideals of "work and self-sacrifice for the public good" and "living for others more than for self."[6] Exaggerated gender differences reinforce the notion of a worldly, competent male needing the spiritual presence of an otherworldly, domestic female. The woman establishing herself as minister of salvation in the home finds her parish, her office, and her life identically bounded. Borrowing polemic from the utopian socialists who were her contemporaries, as well as from Puritan leaders of covenant communities, Beecher avers that her model community—the family commonwealth—will be multiplied ad infinitum across the land, because this is "the true Protestant system . . . the Heaven-devised plan of the family state."[7]

Beecher supports the metaphor of traditional religious authority with quasi-religious rites that utilize the complementary professional metaphor and its associated technology. From drainpipes to Bible stands, folding beds to stoves, door knockers to andirons, she elevates a system of domes-

tic spaces, objects, and activities to a
level of frenzied holiness as the rites
of the ''home church'' of Christ.
Daily, weekly, and seasonal chores
provide a liturgy best expressed in the
proverbs that become its litanies: ''a
woman's place is in the home'' and
''a woman's work is never done.''
Beecher's famous technological innovations do not shorten the hours of
domestic work; they merely make an
obsessive domestic standard explicit.
Working class women can attain it;
middle class women, now deprived of
servants, can maintain it. Her most
technologically developed design, the
1869 American woman's home, is a
terrifyingly complete enclosure for
family life. Woman is installed as
both minister and professional in an
environment remarkably similar to
standard American suburban housing
today. To understand Beecher's design and its influence, it is necessary
to trace its development in her early
work, as well as her attempts to modify it in her old age.

The Marriage of Woman and House

Beecher's designs for her 1841
Treatise reveal her hesitation between
Gothic and Greek revival facades,
which she suggests should be painted
white to enhance the ''chief exterior
beauty . . . fine proportions.''[8] All
these designs are spatially and technically conventional: the houses are
boxes with a central core of fireplaces. The interior plans—a parlor
and dining room at the front of the
house, backed by a series of small,
unrelated spaces including ''bedpress-
es'' (tiny bedrooms), closets, and
kitchen—do not relate to the exterior
elevations and massing. The parlors
turn into bedrooms at night, but the
designs make few other concessions
to flexibility. Beecher does suggest a
plan for a dumbwaiter, and she men-
tions the best method of obtaining hot
water for bathing, but these are called
''back door accommodations.'' The
rest of the book is devoted to housekeeping instructions of a more traditional kind: such as recipes for
whitewash and advice on what china
to choose, how to make a bed, and
what upholstery materials wear well.

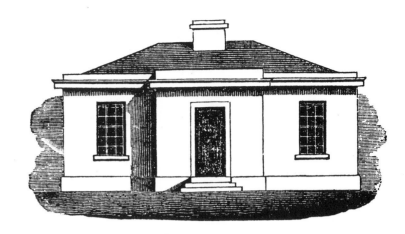

Fig. 18.

Ground-plan.

a, Porch.
b, Parlor, **15 by 16**
   feet.
c, Dining-room,
   15 by 16 feet.
d, d, Small Bed-
   rooms.
e, Stairs.
f, f, f, Closets.
g, Pantry.
h, Store-closet.
i, i, i, Fireplaces.
j, Kitchen.
k, Bedpress.
z, Cellar door.

*C. Beecher, floor plan and elevation for a
Greek Revival dwelling; from C. Beecher,*
A Treatise on Domestic Economy, For the
Use of Young Ladies at Home and at
School, *1841.*

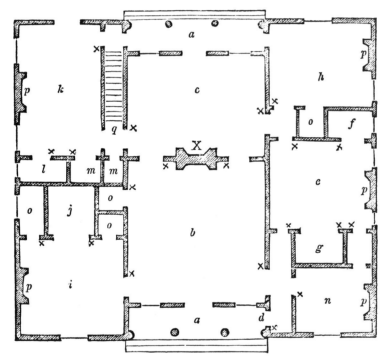

C. Beecher, floor plan and elevation of Gothic cottage; from C. Beecher, Treatise on Domestic Economy, *1841.*

By 1865, Beecher has broadened her concerns and her design skills. In the article "How to Redeem Woman's Profession from Dishonor," she presents an elaborate Gothic cottage full of mechanical equipment for the professional housewife, the minister of home. In this design, one can measure the growing correspondence between the woman's roles of caring for the family and maintaining the home environment by noting that names have changed for various rooms: the parlor has become the "home room"; the kitchen has become the "work room"; the dining room has become the "family room." Servants have been dispensed with. Instead of a "dark and comfortless" kitchen, she produces sunlight, air, and a "cooking form" that rationalizes food storage and preparation. The stove is enclosed. The work room opens into the family room, and Beecher suggests that women may wish to wear their good clothes in all areas. To illustrate the principle of the "close packing of conveniences," almost every household task is described step by step with the architectural arrangements that assist its convenient completion.

In *The American Woman's Home* of 1869, the marriage of woman and house is completed. The house plan is fully developed, interior elements simplified, elevations refined. The kitchen becomes a streamlined, single surface workspace, penetrating the center of the house with its mechanical core of water closets and heating and ventilating equipment. Flexibility is maximized with movable decorative screens hiding extra beds and dressing areas. These screens express both bourgeois consumerism and Victorian prudishness: tropical landscapes and elaborate finials conceal the utilitarian closets. Elsewhere in the house an aura of religious piety characterizes spaces arranged for the "minister of home," as niches with pointed arches make miniature shrines for the display of pictures, busts, madonnalike statues, and umbrellas.

Inventions proliferate so that the housewife will always have something more to worry about—such as hassocks that hide knitting or cabinets that store mending. There is a place

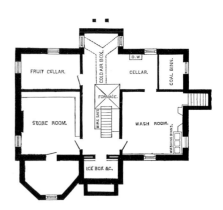

C. Beecher, first floor, second floor, and cellar plans of Gothic cottage; from Harper's New Monthly Magazine, *1865.*

Catharine Beecher and Harriet Beecher Stowe, view of a Gothic dwelling; from Beecher and Stowe, The American Woman's Home, *1869.*

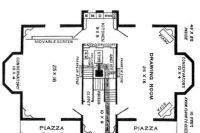
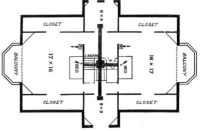

C. Beecher, ground floor, second floor, and cellar plans of a Gothic dwelling; from Beecher and Stowe, The American Woman's Home, *1869.*

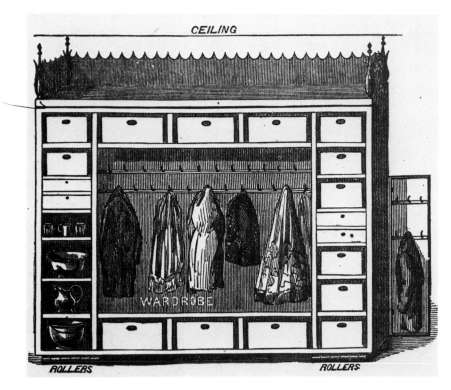

Above: *C. Beecher, domestic shrines: umbrella stand and stair detail; from Beecher and Stowe,* The American Woman's Home, *1869.*

Top: *C. Beecher, movable partition and wardrobe; from Beecher and Stowe,* The American Woman's Home, *1869.*

for everything, not unlike the ascetic Shakers' obsessive storage, but totally fussy and decorative, presaging the consumption fetishes of the 20th century. Indeed, Beecher was an advocate of household consumption from the time of her *Treatise,* where she argued that if Americans relinquished superfluous goods, then half the community would be unemployed: "The use of superfluities, therefore, to a certain extent, is as indispensable to promote industry, virtue, and religion as any direct giving of money or time."[9]

No longer an economic producer in the crude log house of the Puritan covenant community, the Christian woman is ennobled as a professional consumer promoting "industry, virtue, and religion." She now has the full equipment for endless, "efficient" activity in her role as "minister of the family state." The house is a church, the church is a house: the Puritan work ethic goes hand in hand with consumption and display. We are told that the Christian family and Christian neighborhood will be the "grand ministry" of salvation.[10] It will also be the mainstay of American bourgeois capitalism. A style of life has been conceived that will unify middle-American society.

Adaptations of the Ideal

Beecher is best known for her design of the "American woman's home," but there are several other projects she developed between 1867 and 1873 that are somewhat less conventional. A design for a tenement house published in 1869 reveals that the ideal unity of woman and home was not limited to the isolated Gothic cottage that provided its fullest expression. Indeed, the system of domestic spaces and rituals was so firmly established that the model Christian household could be compressed into the most minimal accommodations, while the ambition for display and consumption remained. In this way Beecher's middle class ideal was extended to suit working class families (called "the homeless, helpless, and vicious"), providing poorer women with aspirations sufficiently genteel to encourage upward mobility.

Yet another variation on the "American woman's home" is offered to middle class women: the prospect of a neighborhood where 10 to 12 families share a common laundry, bakehouse, and stables.[11] This is Beecher's only concession to the isolation and drudgery of domestic work, and it is never fully developed. Beginning in 1870, many middle class feminists were to take up this ideal as the basis of the Cooperative Housekeeping Movement, emphasizing women's professional rather than ministerial identity and hoping to share their domestic labors rather than do all the work in isolation.[12]

Both of these variations on the "model family commonwealth"—the tenement and the cooperative neighborhood—stress the professional tasks of the married housekeeper. Beecher's projects for single women emphasize the ministerial vocation rather than the efficient accomplishment of family chores. In 1869, Beecher recommends that women establish settlement houses as useful institutions, aimed at enriching the lives of immigrants and workers and assimilating them into Christian American life. In 1869, she also presents a special architecture for women missionary teachers in the West—a vocation she had begun promoting in 1836 in Cincinnati. She recommends this career for all classes of women as a means of bringing religious ideals and female influence to frontier communities that male ministers have not yet reached. Women in pairs are to settle in remote districts, perhaps caring for orphan children or training other women in domestic skills. Beecher designs a single building to serve as church, school, and home for these missionaries that includes a range of inventions and flexible partitions. In this building the church structure, hinted at in the crosses on the gables of her 1869 house, is expressed fully in a steeple. The pieties of family life are gone, and we see dedicated single women at work, very much ministers although not ordained, surely close to Beecher's own self-image. In her last book, published in 1873, her comments on the need for single women to make homes of their own are a reminder of her own situation. After a life of writ-

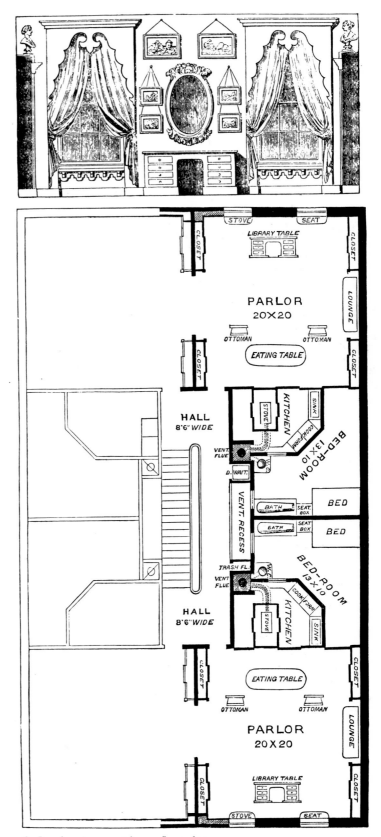

C. Beecher, tenement house floor plan and interior elevation showing window seats that can be used as beds, 1869, from Beecher and Stowe, The American Woman's Home, *1869.*

ing about other people's dwellings and family lives, she is single, with no home of her own and dependent on a kind-hearted niece until her death in 1878.

Above: *C. Beecher, view and elevation of dwelling, church, and school for missionary teachers in the West; from Beecher and Stowe,* The American Woman's Home, *1869.*

Right: *C. Beecher, second floor and ground floor plans of dwelling, church, and school for missionary teachers in the West; from Beecher and Stowe,* The American Woman's Home, *1869.*

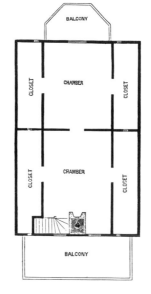

Pioneer and Policewoman

Catharine Beecher's rationalization of the structure and activities of the home is so skillful and well timed that she achieves her goal quite fully: the American home is henceforth consecrated as woman's province. Beecher anticipates the needs of the servant-less middle class, which are articulated by the end of World War I. She also anticipates the rise of domestic Taylorism—the scientific management of work propounded by such writers as Lilian Moller Gilbreth, who presents the homemaker as a manager, as an executive commanding dutiful daughters and even reluctant sons in the efficient performance of home tasks. She anticipates as well the spirit of the present-day British best seller *Superwoman* by describing a woman who dominates tasks with energy without ever raising any basic questions about women's roles.

At the same time, Beecher's influence sparked energetic protests by those women who could not accept the identification of woman and house that Beecher preached. Yet Melusina Fay Peirce's polemics against the isolation and drudgery of housewives, published between 1869 and 1884, still follow Beecher's line in that Peirce also sees housekeeping as women's particular sphere of expertise. She simply wants home management to be extended on a cooperative basis. It takes Beecher's own grandniece, Charlotte Perkins Gilman, in *Women and Economics,* published in 1898, and *The Home: Its Work and Influence* published in 1903, to develop a full repudiation of the identification of women with domestic life. Still, Gilman resembles her ancestress in that she too writes endlessly about the home, describing the weaknesses of its organization. Even the contemporary Italian feminist, Mariarosa Dalla Costa, in her campaign for wages for housework, echoes a bit of Beecher's argument when she claims that housewives should be recognized as true professionals. Although Beecher wrote of self-sacrifice in her time, she would probably support wages for housework now as an economic rec-

ognition of women's work in their own proper sphere.

Both Beecher's followers and her critics continued to work within the powerful framework of a female domesticity that she defined by developing one aspect or another of the paradoxical ideal she promoted. Arguments for female self-sacrifice or female dominance, for ministerial or professional identities, resound with her phrases, as do advertisements that portray the "little woman" ruling the "control center" of the kitchen. Only the most recent generation of feminist critics has succeeded in fully breaking down Beecher's identification of the home as a female workplace. Pat Mainardi's important essay of 1969, "The Politics of Housework," demolished male and female rationalizations of domestic self-sacrifice and "women's work."[13] In 1971, the Feminist Art Program exhibition, *Womanhouse,* took this argument further in its marshaling of material culture to mock sexist visions of domestic normalcy. New understanding of egalitarian relationships has emerged, along with new approaches to domestic organization. As our culture continues to free itself from restrictive stereotypes of domesticity, it becomes easier to understand Catharine Beecher and her influence.

In her long career she experienced all the problems women architects encounter today. Like many women in fields conventionally considered "masculine," Beecher could not resist proving that she had mastered the "womanly" arts of housekeeping as well. And like many architects, male and female, Beecher was willing to prescribe and design a domestic sphere for women that she would not accept for herself. Thus her work reflects her passionate crises of identity: the agile philosopher and the skillful architect alternate with the obsessive housekeeper and the militant opponent of "male" careers for women. She was a brave pioneer and a nagging policewoman, frustrated in her own aspirations while devising codes that frustrate other women—a talented, fearful, intense, indomitable, remarkable woman.

Sandra Orgel, Linen Closet; *from* Womanhouse, *a project of the Feminist Art Program, California Institute of the Arts, 1973. Photograph by Judy Chicago.*

Beth Bachenheimer, Shoe Closet; *from* Womanhouse, *a project of the Feminist Art Program, California Institute of the Arts, 1973. Photograph by Judy Chicago.*

Women in the Architectural Profession: A Historic Perspective

Angelica Kauffman (1740–1807), The Art-ist in the Character of Design Listening to the Inspiration of Poetry. *This is the only known painting in which both muse and creator are depicted as women.*

Women have been a part, however marginal, of the American architectural profession since its very beginnings. Architecture as a profession begins in the U.S. in 1857 with the foundation of the American Institute of Architects (AIA), the first organization created to define professional standards and responsibilities for architectural practice and to differentiate this practice from that of other professions related to building. Eleven years later, the Massachusetts Institute of Technology became the first recognized school of architecture in the country. In the period between the Civil War and 1900, 39 academically trained females graduated from the collegiate architectural system, and many women obtained their training as apprentices in architectural offices.

This section explores the life, work, and careers of women in architecture from the mid-19th century, when the architect's task was not yet professionally defined, to the 1960s, a decade marking the developmental peak of the corporate architectural office, as well as the increased questioning and redefining of architectural ideas on the international scene. Although statistics show that employment conditions for women architects remained quite unchanged during the 100-year period, a gradual transformation took place from the inconspicuous and reticent behavior of the first women architects to the public activities of the first women's professional organizations in the 1920s. The more recent part of this period includes the foundation of the Cambridge School of Architecture and Landscape Architecture for women and covers the effects on women's careers of the Depression, World War II, and the fifties' ''feminine mystique.''

This section shows that in spite of the meager educational and training opportunities available to them, women designed and built a large variety of building types. And it documents how women begin to transcend the confinement of domestic architecture, the only area of design which had been deemed proper for women. If in retrospect the design accomplishments of the individual pioneer women seem to us grander in scale and scope than those of contemporary women, this can only be attributed to the encouragement of other women, who, as clients and patrons, gave women architects the opportunity to demonstrate their competence and talent in the construction of public buildings.

By Judith Paine

4. Pioneer Women Architects

The general appreciation and commendation of the Woman's Building . . . and the exhibits contained within it of . . . architectural plans for the construction of houses, show that they are already alert and equipped to take possession of this newly acquired territory.

Bertha Honore Palmer, President, Board of Lady Managers for the Chicago World's Fair, 1893

Nineteenth- and early twentieth-century women architects are obscure. Seldom mentioned in histories of American architecture or even local guides, their achievements are more nearly unknown than forgotten. Prejudice nourished anonymity. Denied advancement and frequently employment by established architectural firms, women usually practiced alone or in small offices. Either way, thorough records of clients and work rarely survived. Since their commissions tended to be private buildings for individuals of modest means rather than public projects for large institutions, relatively few designs were published. Finally, like the first women to enter the professions of law and medicine, their abilities were questioned and their conduct scrutinized by a skeptical society. Those who departed from the Victorian code of babies, blushes, and bustles risked being labeled improper, peculiar, or both. These stigmas were especially dangerous to acquire in architecture, the practice of which depends upon securing commissions. Already twice removed from the acceptable feminine role by choosing to work outside the home and by daring to practice in a "masculine" field, women architects understood that reticence as well as competence was rewarded. Deliberately and consistently, women architects stayed inconspicuous so that their work would be judged on merit, not sex. This hesitancy to publicly promote their careers combined with the practical limitations women faced in the profession itself discouraged their contemporaries from seriously considering the work of women architects. Today most of their names are as faded as the facades they designed.

Background of Women Architects in America

Yet their accomplishments are remarkable. Expected to dabble in domestic work at best, women planned a wide range of buildings. Factories, hotels, churches, low-income housing, storeblocks, schools, and clubs were all designed by women before the turn of the century. They absorbed and applied the prevailing architectural vocabulary—Romanesque, Renaissance, classical, Queen Anne —with a stylistic eclecticism which matched that of their male counterparts. Moreover, the number of women who became architects during this period is surprisingly large. In 1880, the first woman we can identify as graduating from an architectural school received her degree from Cornell University.[1] Within a decade, another woman was not only a member but a Fellow of the American Institute of Architects, a measure of respect and honor from her colleagues. By 1910, more than fifty women were trained architects, although half the existing architecture departments still denied admittance to women.

These women, then, form the first generation who consciously sought and obtained the same formal education as men and therefore achieved identical professional qualifications. Some practiced architecture, some did not. All were unusual women— determined, talented, intelligent. And all the choices they made shaped, as those of pioneers inevitably do, the opportunities available to the generation of women who followed in their footsteps.

Women have always been active in planning domestic environments. Countless, anonymous women designed or built houses for their own families. In the 19th century, the writings of Catharine Beecher epitomized the movement that considered housekeeping a science and designed for that purpose. Occasionally isolated examples have become known of women who consciously designed for a public beyond their immediate family. For example, Harriet Warner of Wisconsin built the Lake Geneva

Seminary in 1884, Mary Nolan of Missouri exhibited a prototype house of interlocking bricks at the Philadelphia Centennial in 1876, and Emma Kimball earned her livelihood as a draftsperson during the 1870s in Massachusetts.[2]

One of the most interesting early figures is Harriet Irwin of Charlotte, North Carolina. In 1869 she applied for a patent for an "Improvement in the Construction of Houses." It consisted of a hexagonal building, a form that would, she believed, economize space, materials, and heat. The elimination of an entrance hall, the use of one central chimney, and the greater amount of floor space in lozenge-shaped rather than rectangular rooms would provide a better means of both lighting and ventilation. The patent was approved, and the house, capped with a mansard roof and surrounded by a traditional veranda, was built on West Fifth Street in Charlotte, North Carolina. Later, a few other hexagonal homes were constructed nearby. More than curiosities, they are evidence of the first dwelling plan patented by an American woman and indicate an initial, crucial step toward women creating a conscious identity as architects.

Harriet Irwin had no architectural training. Increasingly, however, women began to take course in architecture departments, newly established to legitimate the distinctions between architect and builder. In New York City, Cooper Union was open to women for courses in architectural design and engineering from its founding in 1859. Eleven years after the establishment of the American Institute of Architects in 1857, the Massachusetts Institute of Technology became the first recognized school of architecture in the United States. By 1890 two women had completed the special two-year course in architecture, and a third, Sophia Hayden, was the first woman to graduate from the full four-year program. Even before women entered the architecture program at "Tech," three state universities accepted women into their fledgling architecture departments: Cornell and Syracuse universities in 1871 and the University of Illinois in 1873.[3] Women had to pass rigorous

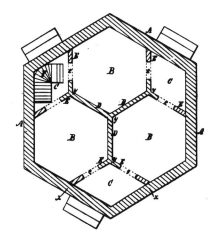

Above: *Harriet M. Irwin, sketch for hexagonal building, Charlotte, North Carolina, 1869. Courtesy Archive of Women in Architecture, New York.*

Left: *H. Irwin, patent drawing, plan and elevation for hexagonal building, 1869; from © Doris Cole,* From Tipi to Skyscraper, *i press, 1973. Reprinted by permission.*

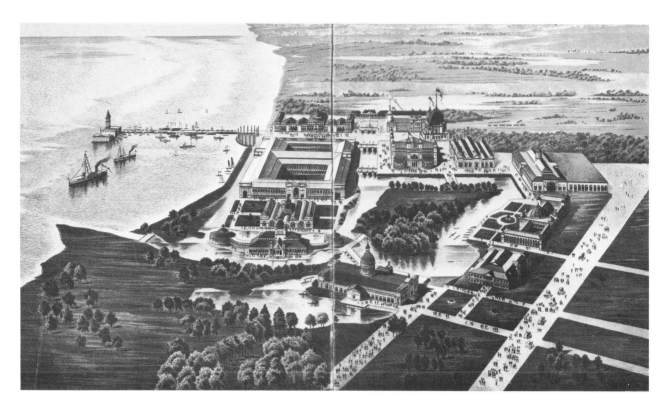

Above: *Artist's rendering, bird's-eye view of the World's Columbian Exposition, Chicago, 1893. Courtesy Judith Paine.*

Opposite page: *Sophia Hayden, the Woman's Building, the World's Columbian Exposition, Chicago, 1893. Courtesy The Hudson River Museum.*

entrance requirements. At Cornell, for example, an applicant was tested in "ordinary English branches, algebra, plane and solid geometry, physics, trigonometry, and a knowledge of the rudiments of French and German."[4] Meanwhile, a decade before the University of California officially founded its school of architecture in 1904, the most prolific architect of her generation, Julia Morgan, graduated from the department of engineering. She then continued her training at the École des Beaux-Arts in Paris, where she became the first woman to earn a degree.

In general, publicly supported schools were more open to women than private institutions. Offered federal land in exchange for providing industrial and mechanical education to residents under the Morrill Act of 1862, states were more concerned with qualifying for acreage than with the sex of the student population. Architecture departments founded at such schools as Harvard in 1895, the University of Pennsylvania in 1890, and George Washington University in 1893 had no incentive to admit women and consequently did not. Columbia University, for example, excluded women as a matter of policy

for a quarter of a century after its architecture department was founded in 1881. Even in 1910, the course bulletin announced that "Owing to the lack of suitable accommodations, women who desire to enter this school are advised to do the work of design elsewhere. . . ."[5]

However, not all women became architects by depending upon an approved academic program. Viable alternatives existed for those women resolute, lucky, or wealthy enough to use them. For example, Theodate Pope Riddle, excluded from architecture classes at Princeton in the 1890s, hired faculty members to tutor her privately. Others, at a distance from cities or educational facilities, enrolled in correspondence courses. Many continued the conventional system of apprenticeship in an office, sometimes taking over the practice when the architect retired or died.

At a time when more women began to study architecture, plans were underway for the largest exhibition held in America during the 19th century: the World's Columbian Exposition of 1893, commemorating the four-hundredth anniversary of the discovery of America. By drawing the most accomplished artists and sculptors to

Chicago and appointing the most noted architects to design buildings within a strict Beaux-Arts program, the fair has become a landmark in architectural history. It was also the setting for the most extraordinary and influential event of the century for women architects: the Woman's Building.[6]

The Influence of the Woman's Building

On February 3, 1891, Daniel Burnham, Chief of Construction of the fair, and Bertha Palmer, President of the Board of Lady Managers, circulated a sketch announcing a competition among women architects only for a Woman's Building. The competition would both publicize the fact that there were women in the profession and draw attention to the proposed building. Entrants had six weeks to prepare drawings and submit them with a statement of their architectural experience. The directions, prepared by Palmer, were specific:

A simple, light-colored classic type of building will be favored . . . the extreme dimensions not exceeding two

hundred by four hundred feet; exterior to be of some simple and definite style, classic lines preferred; the general effect of color to be in light tints. First story, eighteen feet high; second story, twenty-five feet high. .. . . The plans should show the outline desired, leaving all detail to the ingenuity of the competing architect.[7]

Thirteen entrants from around the country sent designs to be judged. On March 25, 1891, the winners of the $200,000 Woman's Building were announced: first prize, $1,000 plus expenses, Sophia Hayden; second prize, $500, Lois Howe, who had completed the special two-year architecture course at MIT; and third place, $250, Laura Hayes of Chicago.

Hayden's design was considered to be in the Italian Renaissance style. The first story is treated as a series of bays carried on Ionic columns; the second story consists of a broad ornamented frieze supported by coupled pilasters in a modified Corinthian order; and the third contains small rooms that open on either side to roof gardens that extend over the end pavilions and that were added under pressure from the Board of Lady Managers to meet additional exhibition requirements. Inside, the main

floor was dominated by a large exhibition hall, lit by a skylight and clerestory windows. In the tympanums were two large murals: *Modern Woman* by Mary Cassatt and *Primitive Woman* by Mary Macmonnies. Upstairs, an open central court was surrounded by rooms providing dormitory facilities for women visiting the fair, committee offices, and a library full of books by female authors, whose ceiling was designed by Candace Wheeler.

The existence of the Woman's Building itself began with Susan B. Anthony's quiet insistence that women share in the planning of the Columbian Exposition.[8] She and other notable women petitioned the Senate to that effect in January 1890 when Congress was considering the establishment of the fair. As a token gesture, a Board of Lady Managers was authorized, equal in number but not in responsibility to the Columbian Commission. Under Bertha Palmer's superb direction, the board enlarged its scope and purposes, developed a highly organized network of representatives in the United States and abroad, and weathered periods of severe frustration with the planning. The culmination of years·of effort was the

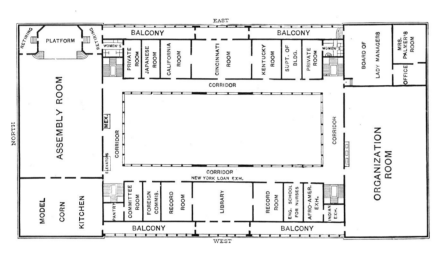

*S. Hayden, ground floor and gallery
plans, the Woman's Building. Courtesy
The Chicago Historical Society.*

Woman's Building. Originally it was intended to be simply the headquarters for the women connected with the fair, but its goals expanded to present ". . . a complete picture of the conditions of women in every country of the world at this moment, and more particularly of those women who are breadwinners."[9] Exhibits included records of women's progress in professional and economic status; reports from social, industrial, and cooperative associations; work from foreign countries such as lace and other handicrafts; and painting, sculpture, photography, and drawing. The library contained over 7,000 books encompassing scholarly and scientific subjects as well as poetry and fiction. The Woman's Building also served as a center for formal conferences, such as the World's Congress of Representative Women, which met in May 1893, as well as for informal discussions of social, political, and economic issues by such notable feminists as Susan B. Anthony, Elizabeth Cady Stanton, and Julia Ward Howe. Next to the Woman's Building was the Children's Building, for which the Board of Lady Managers raised $30,000 and which provided daycare facilities for the children visiting the fair.

Controversial from the start, the Woman's Building evoked a variety of responses. The Exhibition Jury awarded Hayden the artist's medal for "delicacy of style, artistic taste, and geniality and elegance of the interior hall."[10] Richard Morris Hunt, a noted architect, sent her a letter of commendation, and Daniel Burnham encouraged her to set up practice in Chicago. Above all, the building was considered "feminine." Henry Van Brunt, a well-known architect, wrote that it had ". . . a certain quality of sentiment, which might be designated as . . . graceful timidity or gentleness, combined however, with evident technical knowledge, which at once reveals the sex of its author."[11] Another critic looked at the building differently. "It is," he said, "neither worse nor better than might be achieved by either boy or girl who had two or three years' training in an architectural school."[12] And that was

Above: *Library interior, the Woman's Building; from* The World's Columbian Exposition, *The Rand Publishing Company, 1893.*

Top: *Mary Cassatt, mural, "The Modern Woman," the Woman's Building. Courtesy Ruth Iskin.*

Left: *Transept portal, the Woman's Building; from* The World's Columbian Exposition, *The Rand Publishing Company, 1893.*

Cover of catalog for the Woman's Building; from Maud Howe Elliott, Art and Handicraft in the Woman's Building of the World's Columbian Exposition, *1893.*

exactly what Sophia Hayden was, a 22-year-old graduate of MIT, who, like most of her classmates, had not yet supervised the construction of a building she had designed.

Yet the Woman's Building was inevitably compared with the other fair buildings designed by the most talented and experienced architects of the era, whose budgets were far beyond that allocated for the women's structure. To compound the issue, Hayden suffered an episode of what was termed "brain fever," known today as a nervous breakdown. The press, having reported her condition, then raised the question: Was architecture an unhealthy career for women?

It seems a question not yet answered how successfully a woman with her physical limitations can enter and engage in . . . a profession which is a very wearing one. If the building of which the women seem so proud is to mark the physical ruin of its architect, it will be a much more telling argument against the wisdom of women entering this especial profession than anything else could be.[13]

Would women's anatomy determine their architectural destiny? That idea was hardly new. What the Woman's Building did, because of its novelty and the personal circumstances surrounding it, was to bring into focus critical attitudes about the role of women as architects that had been blurred ever since women were first admitted to architecture schools and made it clear that they would seriously pursue that profession. Indeed, the arguments remain remarkably consistent through the years.

Weren't women as housekeepers and experts in household matters obviously suited to become architects? Not so! replied an editorial in 1876: "The planning of houses . . . is not architecture at all; and the ability to arrange a house conveniently does not in the least make an architect."[14]

Didn't women have a natural understanding of housing needs? Not at all. Domestic expertise was learned, not instinctive, and anyway, by the time women mastered a knowledge of

housekeeping, it was too late for them to study architecture.[15]

Was supervising construction a feminine pursuit? Certainly not. "The work of superintending would probably be found too laborious and inconvenient; and would . . . involve a change in fashion . . .; and the preparation of large working drawings would be almost equally awkward."[16] Fifteen years later, another architectural journal echoed this pervasive myth when it declared that "The physical difficulties of superintending and of acquiring that practical knowledge which only comes through superintending must constitute a permanent barrier to success in this line which will always confine the number of women architects, probably, within narrow limits."[17] The problem was, as Louise Bethune, an early woman architect, shrewdly observed, that those who shirk the "brick-and-mortar-rubber-boot-and-ladder-climbing period of investigative education remain at the tracing stage of draftsmanship."[18]

And that is clearly where they were supposed to stay — in the office as renderers and helpmates. The more talented the drawings, the more needed she might be, but her work, by its nature absorbed into the planning process, would be essentially invisible. What else would women do with their architectural training? One journal, prompted by the announcement of the Woman's Building, suggested that women architects design the following: artistic furniture, "for which the field is unlimited"; decorative detail for mantels and chimney nooks; and stair building, which would require new designs for balusters and railings.[19]

Some Examples of the Work of Women Architects

But some women had other ideas of their potential. How they used their skills in this era, in a less than supportive atmosphere, was crucial in defining both their personal image and their public role as architects. As part of a generation of women for whom

new educational opportunities inspired ambition and professional
commitment, the different ways in
which the individual woman, her
training, and circumstances interact to
create a career is especially intriguing.

Louise Blanchard Bethune
(1856–1913) received an ordinary
training as an apprentice in the office
of Richard Waite, a Buffalo, New
York, architect during the late 1870s.
But instead of staying in his office,
she had the temerity to open her own
at the age of 25. By the time the
Woman's Building opened in 1893,
she had already been practicing for
well over a decade. With her partner
R. A. Bethune, whom she later married, the firm built a $30,000 brick
and stone apartment house in
Bridgeport, Connecticut, and many
buildings in the Buffalo area: flats, a
block of stores for Michael Newall,
the Iroquois Door Company's plant
on Exchange Street, an Episcopal
Chapel in nearby Kensington, and the
Denton, Cottier & Daniels music
store—one of the first structures built
with steel frame construction and
made of poured concrete slabs to resist fire.[20]

Bethune was also responsible for
designing at least 18 schools in West-

UNION SCHOOL.

LAFAYETTE HOTEL, LAFAYETTE SQUARE, BUFFALO, N.Y.

Above: *L. Bethune, Hotel Lafayette, Buf-
falo, New York, 1898–1904. Courtesy
Buffalo and Erie County Historical
Society.*

Top: *L. Bethune, Lockport Union High
School, Lockport, New York, 1885. Cour-
tesy Buffalo and Erie County Historical
Society.*

*Louise Blanchard Bethune. Courtesy Buf-
falo and Erie County Historical Society,
Buffalo, New York.*

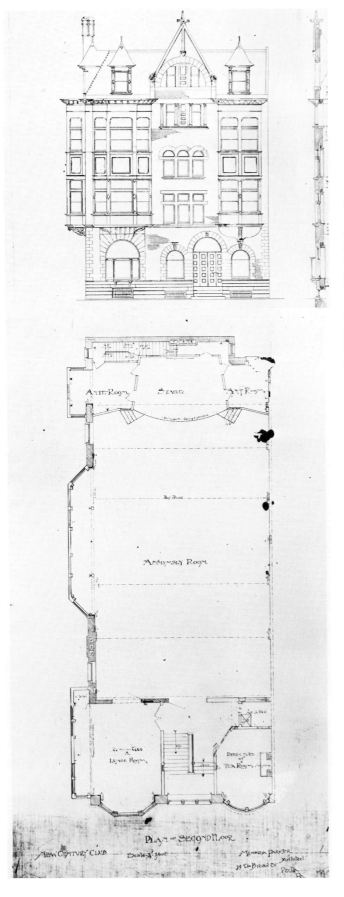

ern New York State, including the Lockport Union High School. The school, made of brick and rusticated sandstone, with a wide, arched entry way, lateral turret, and broad massing, is characteristic of the Romanesque revival style in which the firm usually worked. A departure from that mode was Buffalo's 225-room Hotel Lafayette planned in the French Renaissance style and completed in 1904.

Louise Bethune eagerly joined local architectural societies. In 1888, she was elected to the American Institute of Architects. A year later, when all members of the Western Association of Architects were made Fellows of the AIA, she became the first woman Fellow.

Self-confident and outspoken, Bethune was the best-known woman practicing architecture in the 1880s and 1890s. But she refused to enter the Woman's Building competition because the winner was not awarded an honorarium proportional to those given to the male architects at the fair. She believed that "women who are pioneers in any profession should be proficient in every department," and therefore would not confine her practice to domestic work.[21] Indeed, she said that designing homes was the worst paid work an architect ever does (which it is) and that as a special branch for women it should be "quite out of the question."[22]

Minerva Parker Nichols (1861–1948), however, devoted most of her career to domestic architecture because she felt that "specialists in architecture, as in medicine, are most assured of success."[23] After she trained with Frederick Thorn, Jr., in Philadelphia as a draftsperson, she took over his practice at 14 South Broad Street in 1888. In Philadelphia and its suburbs of Radnor, Cynwood, Berwyn, Germantown, and Overbrooke, she designed homes in a variety of styles. In the early 1890s, she built two New Century for Women clubs—one in Philadelphia in the Renaissance style, recently demolished; another in Wilmington, Delaware, still extant.

Not all her work, however, was residential. She planned two factory buildings for the Philadelphia spa-

Julia Morgan, James Lombard House,
Piedmont, California, 1915. Photograph
by James H. Edelen.

Opposite page: *Minerva Parker Nichols,*
front elevation and second floor plan,
New Century Club for Women, Philadel-
phia, Pennsylvania, 1893. Courtesy The
Schlesinger Library, Radcliffe College.

ghetti manufacturer Geano and Raggio, and a year after her marriage, in 1894, she designed the Browne and Nichols School in Cambridge, Massachusetts. Her chief obstacle, she believed, was not how to practice architecture, but how to obtain the technical and architectural training necessary to do her work well.[24]

Marion Mahony Griffin (1871–1961), one of the three women in the class of 1894 at MIT, received an excellent architectural education. As an extraordinarily talented designer, her association with Chicago avant-garde architects at the turn of the century was both stimulating and productive. From 1895 to 1909, when he departed for Europe, she worked with Frank Lloyd Wright in his Oak Park studio and became his chief draftsperson. Not only did Wright respect her ability, he even acknowledged her drafting superiority.[25] In 1907, an exhibition of Wright's designs held at the Chicago Architectural Club became the basis for the folio of work published by Ernest Wasmuth in 1910, known today as the Wasmuth drawings. Mahony was considered the most talented of the Wright associates who contributed to the book. Her distinctive style— carefully, delicately outlined plants and trees silhouetted in the foreground, with the building viewed from a low angle of perspective as in a Japanese print—has led one authority to attribute nearly half the plates in the folio to Mahony's hand. Mahony was also involved with her own architectural commissions throughout her long life.

If Marion Mahony was the most imaginative of the pioneer women architects, then Julia Morgan (1872–1957) was the most prolific. She designed nearly a thousand buildings, most of them located in California, including residences, churches, schools, clubs, and institutional buildings. Best known for her least typical work—the estate of San Simeon designed for William Randolph Hearst —she was also the chief designer for the western branch of the YWCA, including the Asilomar Conference Grounds at Pacific Grove, California. The range of styles that she used in her residential designs reflects the ec-

Above: *Hazel Wood Waterman, Administration Building, the Children's Home, Balboa Park, San Diego, California, 1912–1925. Courtesy The San Diego Historical Society Library.*

Top: *J. Morgan, Allen Chickering House, Piedmont, California, 1911. Photograph by James H. Edelen.*

lectic approach of her Beaux-Arts training, as well as the tastes of the day. Although the styles vary, underlying the differences are a great attention to detail, understated ornament, and a casual flow of interior space. Morgan was modest, diligent, and extremely thorough in her work. She refused to give interviews or have her work published in architectural journals. When she retired in 1952, she carefully destroyed her office records.

While Morgan was headquartered in San Francisco, another California woman, much less known, was working in San Diego. Hazel Wood Waterman (1865–1948) became interested in design as an art student at the University of California at Berkeley in 1882–1883, and her concern continued when she hired Irving Gill to plan the Waterman family home in 1901. Impressed with the creativity of her ideas and esthetic values, Gill suggested that she consider architecture should she ever need to make her own living. When her husband died suddenly in 1903, she remembered Gill's advice and enrolled in an International Correspondence Course. Within two years she was working as one of Gill's chief draftspersons. Her first major work was a series of three residences for Alice Lee in San Diego. In 1906, Lee, after meeting Waterman, asked Gill to have her design the houses, with the stipulation that the contract be under Gill's supervision. Although recognized as an important development in Gill's career, Waterman's design contribution was not acknowledged at the time.[26] In 1910, she received the commission to design the Wednesday Club, a woman's club in San Diego, and from 1912 to 1925 she worked on a series of buildings in Balboa Park, San Diego, that make up the Children's Home. The Administration Building, now destroyed, showed her concern for a cubic mass punctured by stark openings, which celebrate the use of reinforced concrete and geometric form. Waterman's work with Gill, together with her efforts to train younger women in her office such as Lilian Rice, make her an important figure in the history of women's accomplishments in the built environment of southern California.

At the same time across the continent, Theodate Pope Riddle (1868–1946) was planning highly distinctive structures in Connecticut. Riddle became a registered architect in New York and Connecticut in 1910, a member of the American Institute of Architects in 1918, and a Fellow in 1926. Independently wealthy, she collaborated in 1901 with Stanford White of the firm McKim, Mead, & White in the design of Hill-Stead, the family home. Now a museum open to the public, Hill-Stead is a white clapboard, balconied country house reminiscent of Mt. Vernon. Although Riddle planned other residences, her first large commission was the Westover School in Middlebury, Connecticut, of 1909. It consists of a large building shaped in the form of a quadrangle. Cass Gilbert, the well-known architect and severe critic, considered it to be "the most beautifully planned and designed . . . girls' school in the country."[27]

Riddle's main goal, however, was to design both the architecture and the curriculum of a boys' school. She fulfilled the architectural ambition at Avon Old Farms, which was founded as a protest against conventional educational policies by offering courses

Above: *Theodate Pope Riddle; from Phyllis Fenn Cunningham, Hill-Stead Yesterdays, 1973. Courtesy Hill-Stead Museum.*

Top: *Theodate Pope Riddle, aerial photograph, Westover School, Middlebury, Connecticut, 1909. Courtesy The Westover School.*

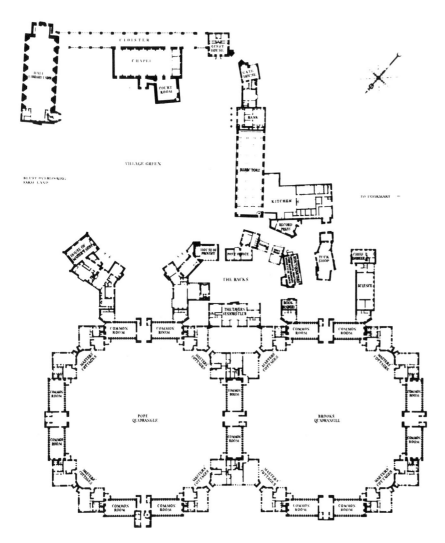

Above: *T. Riddle, plan, Avon Old Farms
School Building, 1909; from Brooks
Emeny,* Theodate Pope Riddle and the
Founding of Avon Old Farms, *1973.
Courtesy Avon Old Farms School.*

Right *T. Riddle, detail of the Pope Quadrangle, Avon Old Farms School. Photograph by Laura Rosen.*

that emphasized progressive theories
and manual labor. The school included a forge, carpentry shop, and
wheelwright shop as well as the traditional assortment of dormitories and
school buildings. Modern construction methods were shunned; instead,
16th-century tools were used by English workers who gauged levels ''by
the eye.'' The result is a series of
reddish brownstone buildings with
slate roofs, influenced by the popular
turn-of-the-century craftsman movement that stressed the appropriate use
of natural materials.

Most of the women described so far
worked alone or with male architects.
But with the increasing number of
women graduating with degrees in architecture, women began to form their
own firms. One of the earliest partnerships was that of Florence Luscomb (b. 1888), an MIT graduate
of 1908, and Ida Annah Ryan
(1883–1960), an MIT graduate of
1905. Ryan, who won the prestigious
Travelling Fellowship from MIT for
the year 1906 for her Pantheon and
Home for Soldiers and Sailors, established a practice in Waltham, Massachusetts, and invited Luscomb to
join her in 1909. That office continued until the outbreak of World
War I.

Another firm in the Boston area
that lasted for many years was formed
in 1913 by MIT graduates of 1906
Lois Howe (1864–1964) and Eleanor
Manning (1884–1973). Thirteen years
later, Mary Almy (1883–1967), an
MIT graduate of 1917, joined the office, which continued for another decade. One of the firm's special interests was low-income housing. In
1924, they were invited to build a
series of homes in Mariemont, Ohio,
a Cincinnati suburb known as the
''National Exemplar in Town
Planning.''[28] Manning designed the
first low-income public housing in
Boston—Old Harbor Village—while
Howe preferred to concentrate on
suburban residential work such as her
house for A. A. Burrage in Brookline, Massachusetts. Although the
partnership dissolved in 1936 during
the Depression, individual members
continued to build, design, and teach

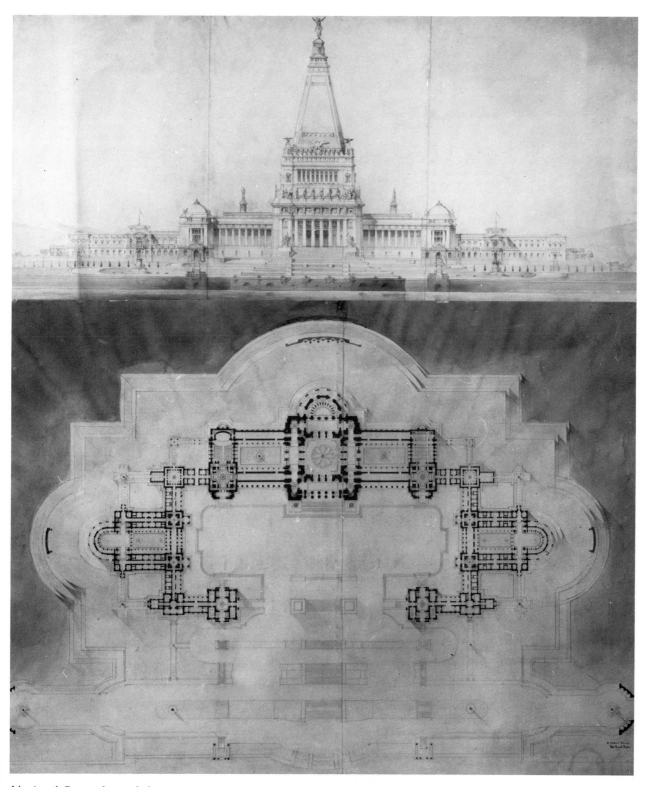

*Ida Annah Ryan, plan and elevation,
project for A Pantheon and Home for Soldiers and Sailors, winner of the Traveling
Fellowship for 1907, MIT. Courtesy MIT
Historical Collections.*

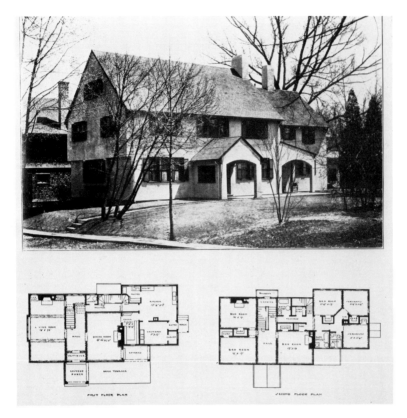

in the metropolitan Boston area.

The earliest known women's firm in the New York City area is Schenck & Mead, formed about 1912 and lasting until Schenck's death in 1915. Little is known about Anna Schenck, but Marcia Mead (1879–1967) had a long and active architectural career. Mead spent an extended apprenticeship in various architectural offices before entering Columbia's School of Architecture at the age of 32. During World War I, she planned housing for black war workers in Washington, D.C., as well as a series of projects for the Bridgeport Housing Company. She also designed YWCAs in Jersey City, New Jersey; Buffalo, New York; and Bridgeport, Connecticut. She was the author of *Homes of Character,* which described various architectural styles that could be adapted for small houses; a member of the United States Housing Commission; and a part-time professor at Columbia University's School of Architecture.

Top, left: *Lois Howe, photograph and floor plan, Burrage House, Boston, Massachusetts, 1906; from* The American Architect and Building News, *1906.*

Left: *Anna Schenk and Marcia Mead, community plan and unit house plan, "Connecticut Development" for the Bridgeport Housing Company, Bridgeport, Connecticut, 1918; from* Architectural Record, *November 1918.*

Alternatives for Women Designers

Frustrated in their plans to practice architecture, many women devoted their training to other related interests. Some became teachers. For example, Mary Wardwell (1866–1935), a Cornell graduate of 1888, taught mathematics at Buffalo High School and Eliza Newkirk (1877–1966), an MIT graduate of 1904, became an instructor of architectural history at Wellesley College. Other women became journalists or writers. Ethel Bartholomew (1867–1937), an MIT graduate of 1895, became editor of *Construction Details,* a monthly architecture magazine published in St. Paul, Minnesota. Esther Stone (1872–1950), an MIT graduate of 1896, and Katharine Budd (born 1860, no trace after 1932) of New York City were among those who published articles on household management in general and kitchen efficiency in particular. Women also developed an interest in landscape architecture, and MIT began to offer courses in that field for women already studying architecture. Before 1920, this concern helped create the first architecture school solely for women, the Cambridge School of Architecture and Landscape Architecture, in 1917.

Certain patterns emerge during this 30-year period. Women, defined as homemakers, were directed toward designing, altering, or renovating houses. But women turned this inevitable type casting to their advantage. They combined their domestic knowledge with social reform issues to become experts in housing for low- and moderate-income groups. For example, the first known published sketch by a woman in an American architectural journal was a workman's cottage by Margaret Hicks (1858–1883) of Cornell in 1878.[29] Three decades later, Ida Annah Ryan wrote that she was "... giving much time and study to the model tenement idea which represents sanitary, economic, up-to-date housing and ... had just finished one building for nine families."[30] In the twenties and thirties, firms such as Schenck & Mead and Howe, Manning, & Almy continued this tradition in public housing.

The rise of the Woman's Club movement also had important implications for women architects. Most clubs deliberately sought to commission a woman to design their buildings. Later the YWCA organization did likewise. Since most work done by women was residential, the local YWCA buildings offered women architects the opportunity to execute public projects.

Another continuous thread is the crucial role of the patron in the careers of several women architects. For example, it was Mary Hilliard who offered Theodate Pope Riddle her first chance to design independently when she commissioned her for the Westover School, and it was through Phoebe Hearst that Julia Morgan first gained an entree into wealthy San Francisco society.

The first generation of women architects did far more than design quaint chimney nooks. From stores to chapels, from Italian Renaissance to colonial, women explored a range of typologies in a variety of styles. Waterman's and Morgan's experiments in reinforced concrete and Howe's use of exterior plaster construction indicate an adventurous approach toward building materials. Their refusal to accept narrow stereotypes of what their work should be forced a broader definition of their architectural abilities. And finally, their work established a solid foundation on which the next generation of women could, and did, develop innovative ideas and designs that continue to enrich American architecture.

Margaret Hicks, workman's cottage, student project, Cornell University, 1878; from The American Architect and Building News, *1878. This is the first published project by an American woman architect.*

5. Some Professional Roles: 1860–1910

Like most pioneers, the architects described in this chapter can be considered "exceptional women." They were certainly exceptional for their time. All three—Sophia Hayden, Marion Mahony, and Julia Morgan—had excellent academic and technical training. Their artistic talent received recognition while they were still students; they were determined in their pursuit of professional goals; their work was encouraged by mentors and powerful patrons; and the buildings they built were of public significance.

The difference among them is one of degree in the fulfillment of the exceptional woman's role: Hayden's professional career ends with her first and last building; Mahony's wanes after her marriage; and Julia Morgan's attains full expression and success at the price, however, of an unrelentingly absolute commitment to her professional work.

The following essays relate their lives and careers, discuss the contexts that permitted or hindered their development, and present representative examples of their architectural work.

Sophia Hayden. Courtesy MIT Historical Collections.

Sophia Hayden and the Woman's Building Competition
By Judith Paine

It is ironic that more is known about a building which stood for six months than about its architect who lived for 87 years. Sophia Hayden's foreign birth, her dark, exotic beauty, and the almost complete obscurity that followed her sudden fame have made her a mysterious individual. Her transformation from a talented architectural student to a public figure subject to criticism, her experience defending the integrity of her design to a board of some of the most powerful women in America, and her subsequent breakdown make her a sympathetic, if not poignant, pioneer in the history of women in architecture.

Sophia Hayden was born about 1868 in Santiago, Chile, the daughter of a Spanish woman and a New England dentist, Dr. George Henry Hayden. When she was 6 years old, she returned to America to live with her grandparents in Jamaica Plains, Massachusetts, where she attended local schools and graduated from West Roxbury High School. Later her family, which included three brothers and one sister, moved to Virginia. Hayden, already conscious of women's contributions to the arts and the possible consequences to their personal lives, delivered her graduation essay on "Our Debt to George Eliot," the prominent English novelist whose real name was Marianne Evans.[1] In 1886, she entered the Massachusetts Institute of Technology and four years later became the first woman to complete the 4-year course in architecture. Described as gifted, with a tremendous perseverance and fondness for her work, she said that it had always been her intention to practice architecture.[2]

Reserved, modest, and talented, she pursued her studies with "quiet determination" as one of the few women enrolled in architecture classes and earned her degree with honors. As her senior thesis, she submitted a design for a Fine Arts Museum, a "classic" plan that reflected the Beaux-Arts training she received at MIT.[3] In 1891, she heard about the competition for the Woman's Building through friends in Chicago, as well as from Lois Howe, a student who completed the special two-year course in architecture in 1890. Both young women decided to enter the competition to "see what fortune would attend two institute girls."[4] On March 25, 1891, she was teaching mechanical drawing at the Eliot School in Jamaica Plains when she received word that she had won the $1,000 first prize. For the next two years, Hayden was busy traveling to Chicago to prepare working drawings for the building and discussing numerous alterations demanded by the Board of Lady Managers to meet a variety of unanticipated needs. The pressure to please too many, the unaccustomed criticism she received, and the physical demands she underwent took their toll. Soon after she attended the informal dedication of the Woman's Building in October 1892, she suffered an episode of "brain fever," or a nervous breakdown. When the fair opened in May 1893, she was conspicuously absent.

The following year she planned a Memorial Building for the Women's Clubs of America. But it was never built. Soon afterwards she married an artist, William Bennett. When she died in 1953, her short obituary did not mention her profession.

In contrast, Lois Howe, who received the $500 second prize, had a long and active career in architecture. She died in 1964, only a few months short of her 100th birthday. Buildings she designed or renovated, particularly residences, dot the Boston suburbs of Cambridge, Concord, Arlington, and Wellesley. She began working in the office of Francis Allen immediately after graduation from MIT in 1890 and designed her first house in association with Joseph Prince Loud in 1894. The following year she opened her own office on Clarendon Street in Back Bay Boston. Her experiments in using plaster as an exterior finishing material received widespread publicity and her interest in architectural history led her to take measured drawings of New England vernacular architecture, which she published in collaboration with Constance Fuller in 1913.[5] When she took Eleanor Manning, MIT class of 1905,

MRS. SUSAN G. COOKE,
Secretary Board of Lady Managers.

MRS. V. C. MEREDITH,
Vice-Chairman Executive Committee,
and Chairman of Committee on Awards.

MRS. POTTER PALMER,
President Board of Lady Managers.

MRS. RUSSELL B. HARRISON,
Vice-President at Large.

MRS. JOHN A. LOGAN,
Vice-Chairman Committee on Ceremonies.

Members of the Board of Lady Managers, the World's Columbian Exposition, Chicago, 1893; from Maud Howe Elliott, Art and Handicraft in the Woman's Building of the World's Columbian Exposition, 1893.

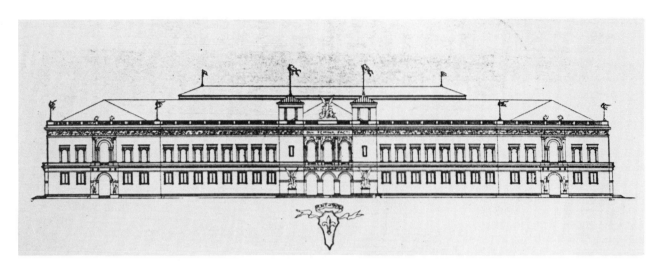

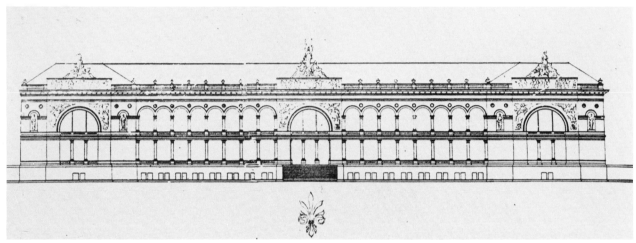

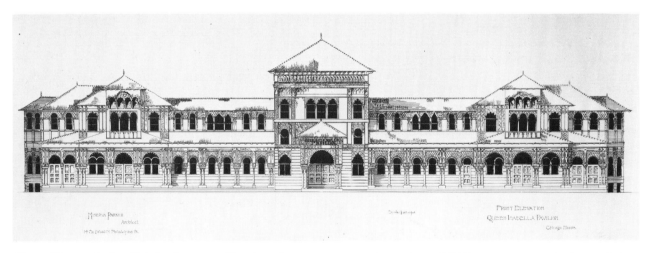

Above: *Minerva Parker Nichols, Queen Isabella Pavilion, commissioned by the Isabella Society for the World's Columbian Exposition, 1891. Courtesy The Schlesinger Library, Radcliffe College.*

Top: *Lois Howe, second prize design for the Woman's Building, from* Inland Architect and News Record, *September 1891.*

Middle: *Laura Hayes, third prize design for the Woman's Building; from* Inland Architect and News Record, *September 1891.*

into practice in 1913, she founded one of the longest lasting and most prolific women's architectural partnerships, which continued until 1937.[6] Howe became a member of the American Institute of Architects in 1901 and a Fellow in 1931.

Unlike the other two winners, Laura Hayes, who won the $250 third prize, had no formal training in architecture. She was born in 1870, the daughter of a one-time member of the Ohio State Legislature who helped plan the park system in Chicago.[7] After graduating from St. Mary's Episcopal Church School in Knoxville, Illinois, she worked as a bookkeeper until Bertha Palmer hired her as a private secretary. Hayes was an astute observer of people and her surroundings. Familiar with the Woman's Building Competition announcement, which included a general plan of the proposed structure, as well as with Palmer's preferences, she spent nights and weekends preparing her entry. When the winners were announced, Palmer immediately explained that all submissions had been anonymously entered and selected. Although Palmer hoped to have her secretary pursue the profession Laura Hayes disappeared into obscurity.

Of the ten other entries for the Woman's Building, one more deserves mention. Prior to the Board of Lady Managers' decision to have a competition for a Woman's Building, the Isabella Society commissioned Minerva Parker Nichols to design an Isabella Pavilion to honor the Spanish Queen who supported Columbus in his explorations of the New World. Nichols completed a design for an ornate Moorish building.[8] However, when Palmer assumed control of women's activities at the fair, the rules for the Woman's Building Competition stressed a classical, Beaux-Arts form. Minerva Parker Nichols submitted her Isabella Pavilion plan anyway, but it did not place among the winners. A generous woman, Nichols came to Hayden's defense after her breakdown. Writing in *American Architect and Building News,* she argued that one woman's illness under unusual circumstances would not deter women from becoming architects then or in the future.[9]

Report Presented by Sophia Hayden to the Board of Lady Managers in 1894

In presenting my report, as architect of the Woman's Building, it may be of interest to review the method that was adopted in the selection of an architect.

When the Board of Lady Managers, through their honored President, had succeeded in obtaining a certain definite appropriation, from the Chicago Directory, for the purpose of erecting a building for the use of their Board, the bold and novel idea was conceived of having it designed by a woman. Mr. D. H. Burnham, Chief of Construction, was appealed to, who although at first deprecating the idea, finally consented to try a scheme of obtaining designs from women. He departed from his plan, adopted for the other World's Fair buildings, of selecting an architect outright, for the simple reason that there were no women practicing architecture who had a sufficiently established reputation to warrant him in making a choice.

A competition was consequently called for, and an advertisement was issued by the Department of Publicity and Promotion, from which I quote:

Sketches are asked for on or before March 23rd, 1891, for the Woman's Building of the World's Columbian Exposition.

None but those made by women will be considered. Applicants must be in the profession of architecture, or have had special training in the same, and each must state her experience, in writing, to the Chief of Construction. . . .

All sketches must be sent in sealed, with only a motto on the envelope, which must contain a second envelope enclosing name and address of designer. . . .

The selected design will carry with it the appointment of its author as Architect of the building in question. The Architect in question will make her working drawings in the Bureau of Construction, and receive an honorarium of $1,000, besides expenses.

A prize of $500 and one of $250 will be given for the next two best drawings.

A simple, light colored classic type of building will be favored.

All drawings to be sent to D. H. Burnham, Chief of Construction, . . .

The general outline of the building must follow closely the accompanying sketch plans, the extreme dimensions not exceeding two hundred by four hundred feet; exterior finish to be of some simple and definite style, classic lines preferred; the general effect of color to be in light tints.

Staff, stucco, wood, iron and equivalents to be freely used as building material, with discretion as to the disposition and ornamentation, so as not to render the building too costly. First story eighteen feet high, second story, twenty-five feet high.

These dimensions not obligatory, but suggest what would answer both the practical requirements as well as to come within the limit of sum appropriated, vis: $200,000.00.

The plans show the outline desired, leaving all detail to the ingenuity of the competing architect, who is expected to give them a thorough study, locating openings, etc., so as to give easy access and exit to the constant flow of passing crowds.

The main entrance will lead down a series of steps to the water landing, and should be equal in importance and beauty to the one towards the west. . . .

Drawings must be made to a scale of one-sixteenth of an inch to the foot. They must include elevations of one front, one end, as well as one perspective.

Signed, D. H. Burnham, Chief of Construction, World's Columbian Exposition, Chicago, Feb. 3rd, 1891.

This advertisement was brought to my notice, and I made drawings in accordance. As I was not established in an office at the time, I made the drawings in my own home, and it may be of interest to state that they passed no one's inspection, until they were opened in Chicago. I stated in my sealed letter that I was a graduate of the Architectural Department of the Massachusetts Institute of Technology. Mr. Burnham considered this, in connection with my plans, a sufficient warranty of my ability, to call me to Chicago, for March 25th, 1891, I received the following telegram: ''I have the honor of informing you that your design for Woman's Building has taken first place. Please come here at once for consultation at our expense." I returned a telegram stating that I would start for Chicago on the 29th.

The second and third prizes were awarded to Miss Lois Howe of Boston, and Miss Laura Hayes of Chicago. Thirteen designs were submitted.

In designing the building I kept very closely to the sketch plans. The principal deviation, in the original drawings, was the addition of an open arched arcade with balcony over. These were added to the east and west side. Subsequently I added a third story, with roof promenade, to the north and south wings, to meet new requirements that had arisen.

The main feature of the plan is the large exhibition hall, 65 by 120 feet. Around this the smaller rooms are grouped, the wings forming large exhibition rooms, on this floor. The entrances are placed north, south, east, and west, on the axes of the building. At the four corners of the large hall, staircases lead up, from corridors, to the second story. In the second story, the rooms are arranged around the main hall, intercommunication being obtained by means of a gallery overlooking the hall. In the north wing a large assembly room was placed. The third story was planned to extend only over a portion of the north and south wings. At first, this part was subdivided into smaller rooms, designed for committee rooms. Subsequently the partitions were removed, in the south wing, as it was used for a different purpose.

On the exterior, the subdivision of the stories is plainly marked in treatment. The building rests on a continuous base five feet in height. The first story is treated with an order of round arches, carried on Ionic columns, and corresponding blank arches, carried on Doric pilasters. In the second story, a modified Corinthian order is used, with coupled pilasters, which carry a broad frieze, which is developed, over the east and west entrances, into a low pediment. The third story additions and roof gardens are surrounded by an open screen of small columns and cary-

atides, which support a light entablature.

Thus the exterior expression of the building is evolved quite naturally from the interior conditions. It is not modeled after any precedent. In style it may be called Classic or Italian Renaissance, although it follows strictly speaking, neither style. It is the result of careful training in Classical design and is the expression of what I felt and liked.

According to the conditions, under which I had been called to Chicago, I commenced upon my working drawings, as soon after my arrival as I could get established in a room connecting with the Construction Department.

The design was first remodeled, to meet new requirements that had arisen. Under these new conditions, the third story rooms and colonnades were added to the two wings. I also made some changes in one or two minor details at the suggestion of Mr. Atwood, who was chosen, at this time, Consulting Architect. Finally I made one quite notable deviation from the original drawings, in the treatment that I desired, for the upper portions, would add materially to the cost, as that portion would be out of sight, being so far back from the facades. I deferred to their wider experience and left the clerestory practically unstudied. I think now that the work was unduly hurried at this point, and that some mistakes might have been avoided if I had been able to give the drawings more careful study. Naturally your President wished to see the work progress, consequently the Woman's Building was the first one commenced and the first one finished, in construction.

I completed one eighth of an inch to the foot scale working drawings, including elevations, plans and sections, with the aid of two draughtsmen under my immediate supervision. I judged then that my obligations, under the rather vague conditions that I had undertaken the work, were discharged, as the Construction Department had charge of all constructional details of the World's Fair buildings. When the half inch to the foot scale working drawings were

completed, I returned to Boston, May 26th, 1891.

My official connection with the Exposition was not resumed until December, 1891, when I received a letter from Mr. Burnham, from which I quote: "I am having prepared and it will be my pleasant privilege to send you in a day or two, photographic views of the work to date upon your building. In forwarding these to you I desire to again sincerely congratulate you upon the success of your plans, which is further evidenced by the construction. I would in addition to this suggest that if it may be convenient to you, it would be of great advantage to have you here for a few days at least to inspect the work, and give us any further ideas you may desire carried out." In compliance with his request, I returned to Chicago. I found that the exterior of the building was about completed, and judged it to be satisfactory, with the exception of the clerestory, which I had left in such an unfinished condition. I also saw for the first time, the models for sculpture work, for the building. The contract had been awarded to Miss Alice Rideout, of San Francisco.

While studying the changes, that I contemplated, in the building, I tried to help the office of the Board of Lady Managers, in disposing of some of the materials that had been generously offered, by members of the Board, towards the construction and decoration of the building. I found that very little could be done to advantage with these, as the temporary nature of the construction and materials of the building would not permit it, besides it was too late to give these details the study that would have been necessary in any case. I also wished at this time to undertake the interior decoration but as it was determined to have the decorations a part of the exhibit, I gave the idea up as it was practically impossible to separate the two, in this building. After some delay the changes that I desired were finally carried out by the Construction Department.

Financial

Cost of Woman's Building, taken from Report of Auditor

Plaster Modeling	$ 3,100.00
Exterior Covering	24,583.73
Lathing and Plastering	6,588.00
Painting and Glazing	6,783.21
Roofing and Skylights	5,904.67
Carpentry and Iron Work	74,680.26
Inspection	60.86
Plumbing and Sewerage	4,107.75
Elevators	5,252.00
Repairs, Pre-Expo. Period	1,810.45
Miscellaneous	5,752.97
Total	138,623.90
Coloring and Decorating	12,368.41
Sculpture, Modeling and Statues	7,809.37

Amounts Paid by Exposition Company to Miss Sophia G. Hayden

Original Fee	$1,000.00
Extra Fee (Services)	450.00
Expenses	527.60
Total	1,977.60

Finally, I have to report that the building has received an Award,—"For delicacy of style, artistic taste, and geniality and elegance of the interior hall." Signed, Giuseppe Spera, Individual Judge. Approved, Dr. K. Buenz, President Departmental Committee, and John Boyd Thacher, Chairman Executive Committee on Awards.

Also, your architect has received the Artist's Medal presented by D. H. Burnham, Chief of Construction, in behalf of the Exposition, at the Dedicatory Exercises, October 21st, 1892.

Also, from your Honorable Board, a gold medal, bearing on the front the head of the President of your Board, and on the reverse, the Woman's Building.

Architect of Woman's Building
Boston, April 28th, 1894

Marion Mahony Griffin
By Susan Fondiler Berkon

American university training in architecture was no longer a unique practice among women when Marion Mahony (1871–1961) received her Bachelor of Science degree from the Massachusetts Institute of Technology in 1894. In fact, in the years between 1878 and Mahony's graduation, eight women in three different collegiate departments had completed a four-year academic program in architecture.[10] Yet unlike many of these early graduates, Marion Mahony did not renounce ambition with the attainment of a degree. Nor was she forced into extraneous work as a result of discrimination by the existing firms.[11] Although evening school teaching and miniature portrait painting became eventual part-time necessities,[12] Mahony returned to her native Chicago in the summer of 1894, became the first woman licensed to practice architecture in Illinois,[13] and was hired by her cousin, architect Dwight Perkins, as a draftsperson.

Glossing over the apparent nepotism, Mahony wrote the following class letter in 1898:

I felt right proud when I obtained a position as draftsman one week after leaving Tech, and prouder still to be earning the lordly sum of six dollars a week, my employer's estimate of the value of my service far exceeding my own. (Chicago men welcome women into the profession with open arms.)[14]

Marion Mahony Griffin. Courtesy The Art Institute of Chicago.

Less than scrupulous about her own limitations, she was curiously heedful of her male colleagues'. Was Mahony's diffidence a factor that militated against a future independent architectural practice? Or was her subsequent career as a design collaborator with three male architects (Frank Lloyd Wright, Hermann von Holst, and Walter Burley Griffin) merely shaped by circumstances rather than premeditation? The answers are not easily discernible.

Since the Perkins office suffered a cutback in work in 1895, Mahony spent two months in the employ of two male architects whom she identifies as "two classmates who had left Tech before graduating."[15] Later in that year she entered Frank Lloyd Wright's office, where she recalls her salary was reduced from $15 to a meager $10 per week. However, Marion claims she was compensated and "consoled" for the unfair dispensation by receiving the title of superintendent of the office force.[16] During this early professional period she also acknowledges having signed "Marion Mahony, Architect" to the drawings of one house—a mountain cottage.[17]

At Wright's Oak Park Studio, Mahony functioned in a variety of capacities. Primarily she was an artist-architect, designing minor parts of the Wrightian earthbound "organic" residence—the mosaic fireplaces, the landscape murals, the interior furniture, stained glass, and rugs. All, she later claimed, were kept by Wright for future use.[18] Mahony's greatest single contribution to Wright's career was her virtuoso drawings of the studio's domestic designs for the monograph *Ausgeführte Bauten und Entwurfe von Frank Lloyd Wright,* published in Berlin by Ernst Wasmuth in 1910. Since Wright's work was virtually unknown outside the United States, the portfolio served as a source of study for modern European architects, thus influencing the designs of the Bauhaus in Germany and the De Stijl movement in Holland.

Mahony's second known independent commission, the All Souls Unitarian Church in Evanston, Illinois, was designed in 1902 and executed in

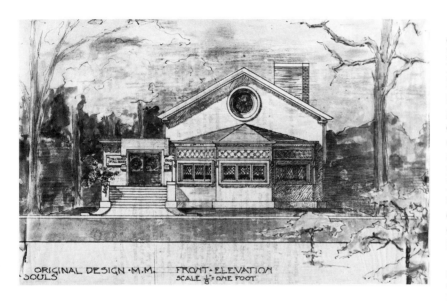

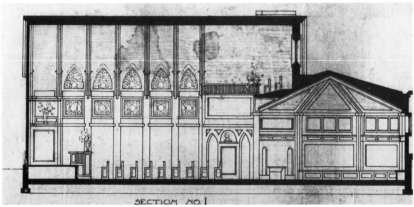

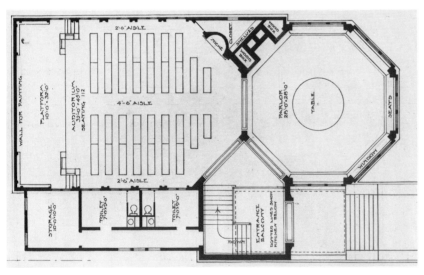

Above: *M. Mahony, section and plan of auditorium and parlor, project for All Souls Unitarian Church, Evanston, Illinois, 1902 (design never executed), from M. Mahony Griffin,* Magic of America. *Courtesy The New York Historical Society.*

Top: *M. Mahony, front elevation rendering, project for All Souls Unitarian Church, Evanston, Illinois, 1902 (design never executed). Courtesy The New York Historical Society.*

1903. James Vila Blake, the minister of the church, was a friend of the Mahony family and suggested that Marion be the architect. The project, by her own account, did not go smoothly, and the original avantgarde octagonal design was abandoned in favor of the building committee's preference—a Gothic stone church with a traditional meeting house plan.[19] The only creative Mahony touches left intact were the art glass ceiling skylights at the entrance of the church and in its chancel.[20] The church was demolished in 1960.

Mahony attempted to augment her designer status with her second major professional collaborator, Hermann von Holst. In 1909, when Wright hastily departed for Europe, he desired that his work be carried on by a fellow studio member. However, von Holst, Wright's eventual successor, was a Beaux-Arts classicist and had no direct design relationship to Wright by either training or design philosophy. It is said that von Holst took over the Wright studio solely on the condition that Marion Mahony would come into his office as a designer.[21] Although she had refused Wright's offer to head the studio practice, she accepted the position with von Holst, insisting on "full authority and final decision on all matters of design and construction."[22] Despite this agreement, most subsequent architectural drawings bore the label "Hermann von Holst, Architect, Marion Mahony, Associate." She received little public recognition for her role as chief designer of many of the Wright-inherited commissions as well as other independent office works.[23]

Design accreditation in this period, 1909–1913, has been a formidable task for historians. Although Mahony's "prairie"-styled houses did not always adhere to the predominant horizontals of a Frank Lloyd Wright residence, her designs did possess other prairie house forms, that is, a fully spreading ground plan with rooms opening up into one another; the interweaving of exteriors and interiors by means of terraces and cantilevered roofs; the use of long window bands. More easily identifiable

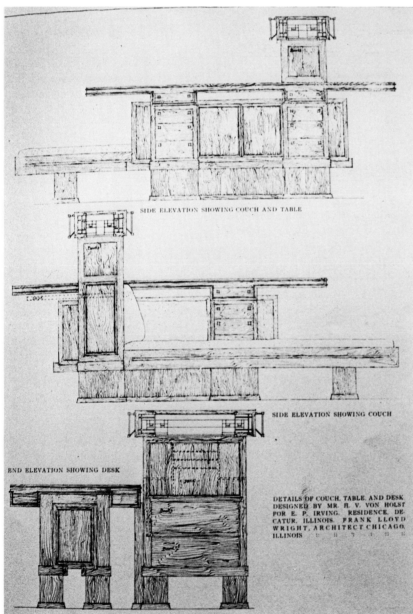

SIDE ELEVATION SHOWING COUCH AND TABLE

SIDE ELEVATION SHOWING COUCH

END ELEVATION SHOWING DESK

DETAILS OF COUCH, TABLE, AND DESK
DESIGNED BY MR. H. V. VON HOLST
FOR E. P. IRVING. RESIDENCE, DE-
CATUR, ILLINOIS. FRANK LLOYD
WRIGHT, ARCHITECT CHICAGO,
ILLINOIS

Above: *M. Mahony, perspective, C. H. Wills Residence, Detroit, Michigan, December 1909 (design never executed). Courtesy The New York Historical Society. In this rendering Mahony has typically enframed the geometrical architectural mass within a natural setting of fluffy foliage and twining tree trunks. The use of dramatic tonal contrasts between the foreground and background enhances the picturesque quality of the composition. In this copy, from the* Magic of America *"Herman V. von Holst, Architect" has been crossed out and "M. M. and von Holtz (sic) Arcts. Detroit" substituted.*

Left: *M. Mahony, drawing, combination table, couch, and lamp, E. P. Irving House, Decatur, Illinois, 1910; from* The Western Architect, *May 1913. Wrongly attributed to Hermann V. von Holst in* The Western Architect. *This oak piece is more complex than any Wright design, yet still adheres to the absolute design integration philosophy of the Prairie architects where every facet of the building contributed to the total environment. The piece retains a "craft-style" spirit in its straight line and rectilinear character, its robust, sturdy forms and functional usefulness.*

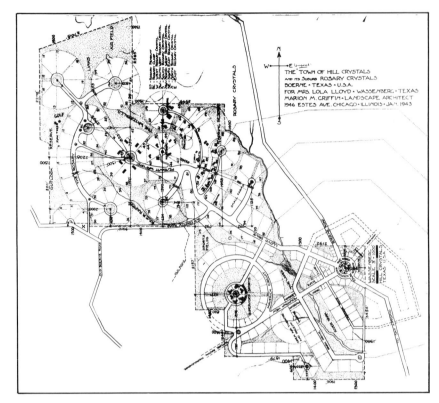

Above: *M. Mahony, site plan, project for the town of Hill Crystals and its suburb, Rosary Crystals, Boerne, Texas, commissioned by Mrs. Lola Lloyd, Wassenberg, Texas. Courtesy The Art Institute of Chicago. Since the whole district of approximately 2 square miles was naturally terraced, the houses were designed one tier overlooking another, thus giving each wide unobstructed views. The plan retained the rural advantage of long and varied walks and included a system of parks interlacing with the housing and the larger open spaces. A number of radial thoroughfares were established for present transportation needs and future business expansion.*

Left: *M. Mahony, site plan, project for World Fellowship Center, Conway, New Hampshire, commissioned by Mrs. Lola Lloyd, Winnetka, Illinois, October 1942 (design never executed). Courtesy The Art Institute of Chicago. The plan as designed by Marion M. Griffin incorporated the natural slopes of the land (ranging from 800 to 1,100 feet above sea level) and opened the hillside out to the views of Mt. Chokorua in the White Mountains. The interior park with the Community Social Center was to be preserved in its natural state and surrounded by land allotments for other educational and social buildings. The entire circuit of the 320-acre property was to be removed from all speedways.*

were specific Mahony features such as cubic planters, driveway lights, or gold ceramic tiles grouped along a band of windows or embedded in a plaster gable. Wright himself claimed some of the so-called "von Holst–Mahony" designs as his own.[24] Also the contemporary architectural journals compounded misattributions. For example, the April 1913 *Western Architect* credited von Holst with the interior combination couch-desk-lamp that was later proven to be a Mahony integrated functional piece.[25]

Von Holst was also guilty of design piracy. In his own written account of the building of the 1913 D. M. Amberg house in Grand Rapids, Michigan, von Holst omitted any mention of Mahony's design influence.[26] Ironically, an editor in an earlier issue that year, observing the absence of women practitioners, thought it neither logical nor necessary "unless there is one underlying law of sex governing architectural practice as yet undiscovered."[27]

Mahony never mentioned von Holst's impropriety; she was too preoccupied in later years with Wright's "injustices" to her husband and herself. In June 1911, she married Walter Burley Griffin, a former Oak Park Studio apprentice whom von Holst occasionally employed for landscape plans. There have been many interpretations of the Griffin marriage; the most popular was that the union was a trade-off of architectural drawings for domestic security.[28] Although not a feminist, Mahony was certainly not the desperate old maid she has been portrayed as being. Her professional life-style was not altered after her marriage. Mahony herself described the early phase of her relationship as an "equitable partnership together," making "each individual independent and responsible."[29] Some architectural critics felt that the Griffins' careers became impossible to separate at this juncture. Although Marion took a backseat in terms of overall design, she was ever present in her contributions to Walter's projects, be it interior design or renderings of his numerous residential and community plans in the United States and abroad.

Winning the competition for the Australian capital of Canberra in May 1912 marked the turning point in their collaborative career. Although Walter Griffin is credited with being the first Chicago architect to win an international competition, distinction was also granted to Marion, since it was recognized that the beauty of Walter's plan was enhanced by Marion's perspective drawings executed in photodyes and watercolor upon satin. About this event Marion later wrote:

I was proud to have the prize come our way. Proud for my husband's sake. I can never aspire to be as great an architect as he but I can best understand and help him and to a wife there is not greater recompense.[30]

Close outsiders differ somewhat in their architectural appraisal of the Griffin team. Most felt that Walter's maturity in architectural design benefited from Marion's influence. Roy Lippincott, Walter's brother-in-law and draftsman, stated that the success of at least two of Griffin's major projects in Australia was due to Marion— namely the designs of the Australia Cafe of 1914 and the Capitol Theatre of 1922–1924, both in Melbourne.[31]

That is not to say that the influence was one way between Marion and Walter. On the contrary, Walter's intense interest in landscape architecture became Marion's as well. In the early 1920s while in Australia, Marion helped design the romantic, self-contained community of Castlecrag on the banks of the Sydney harbor. Both Griffins shared the ideal of a civilization in which everyone lived at home with nature and each other, which explains their close involvement (especially Marion's) with the Christian occult Anthroposophical Society where humanity's creative force and not destruction of nature was stressed. In addition, they were both cataloguing horticulturists and botanists, and they each eventually specialized in the native flora and fauna of Australia.

Years later, upon her return to the United States, Marion applied this training to two major community planning projects. The first was the World Fellowship Center in Conway, New Hampshire, which Marion designed in October 1942 for Mrs. Lola Lloyd of Winnetka, Illinois. Lola Maverick Lloyd (1875–1944) was an international pacifist, feminist, and a cofounder with Jane Addams of the Women's International League for Peace and Freedom.[32] Her activity as chairman of the Campaign for World Government probably led to membership in the World Fellowship movement, a group concerned with achieving a fuller realization of worldwide human unity. She purchased a 320-acre property in Conway, New Hampshire, with the hope of developing a World Fellowship Center there. (The center exists today—minus the Mahony design input.)

Marion Griffin's own personal interest in the Single Tax and Anthroposophy likely created an interest in World Fellowship. The commission for the center and for a second Lloyd project for the town of Hill Crystals and its suburb Rosary Crystals, near Boerne, Texas, in January 1943 might be traced to a membership in this organization. Although they were never executed, both projects were planned in keeping with an environmental approach to design where the physical aspects of the design were dictated by the terrain rather than a superimposed gridiron plan.

The symbiotic nature of the Griffin professional partnership makes it difficult to discern Marion Mahony Griffin's design hand. Her allegiance to her husband's professional reputation rather than her own hindered her professional advancement. After Walter's death of peritonitis in February 1937 in India, Marion turned down an offer of partnership and a teaching position at the Technical School in India in order to finish his work. Aside from the two community projects discussed previously, the last known Marion Mahony Griffin design was a plan for South Chicago,[33] an unexecuted project designed in 1947 some 14 years before her death. Her last projects indicate her concern for the larger design environment and her ability to solve the humanistic problems of design on both a small and a large scale.

Julia Morgan

By Sara Boutelle

Julia Morgan (1872–1957), our most prolific pioneer woman architect, emerged on the American scene at the turn of the century. She designed more than 800 buildings in a career that spanned half a century.

A native of San Francisco, but longtime Oakland resident, she was accepted into the rigorous Engineering School at the University of California at Berkeley, the only woman student at the time. She received an engineering degree in 1894. During her 4-year study she attended informal discussion seminars on architecture at the home of Bernard Maybeck. With his encouragement and that of her family— especially her architect-cousin Pierre Lebrun of New York—she firmly resolved to pursue an architectural career.

After a year's work experience building with Maybeck, Morgan decided to further her training at the École des Beaux-Arts in Paris, then the center of architectural education. Women, however, were not eligible for entrance into the school. Nevertheless, Morgan set out for Paris and the atelier of Marcel de Monclos,[34] where she endured 2 years

Julia Morgan, 1928 or 1929. Courtesy Estate of Julia Morgan.

Above: *J. Morgan, Alumnae Hall, Mills College, Oakland, California, 1916. Photograph by James H. Edelen.*

Top: *J. Morgan, library, Mills College, Oakland, California, 1906. Courtesy Mills College.*

of grueling tests and competition before being accepted at the École, the first woman in the world to study there. For the next 4 years she studied at the Atelier Chaussemiche, where she won many awards and medals. In 1902 she received her Certificat d'Étude.[35]

Morgan returned to the San Francisco Bay Area in 1902 and became a licensed architect—probably the first woman in California history to do so.[36] She joined the office of John Galen Howard, who was then developing a master plan for the University of California at Berkeley. Morgan worked with him on the Hearst Memorial Mining Building and is said to have designed the campus's Greek Theatre.[37] Howard is said to have boasted of possessing "the best and most talented designer, whom I have to pay almost nothing, as it is a woman."[38]

Late in 1904, "J.M.," as she was known to her staff, started a firm of her own in San Francisco. Between 1907 and 1910 she had a partnership with a former Howard draftsman, Ira Hoover, but she reestablished her office as an independent practice late in 1910.[39] Her first commissions included numerous informal residences for private clients like her sister Emma North in Berkeley in 1909, as well as college buildings like the Mission Revival Campanile of 1904 and library of 1906 at Mills College, a women's college in Oakland. Possibly because the reinforced concrete Mills Campanile withstood the 1906 earthquake, J.M. was given the commission to rebuild the structurally damaged Fairmont Hotel in San Francisco. From this point on her reputation was made.

Perhaps the most important Morgan client was Phoebe Apperson Hearst, the arbiter of Bay Area taste, whom Morgan had known during her Paris school days.[40] Soon after establishing her own practice, J.M. was given the job of building an addition to the Hearst Hacienda in Pleasonton. It was considered a success and led to further commissions from the Hearst family, culminating in the famous San Simeon (begun in 1919, with work continuing through the 1930s) for William Randolph Hearst.

J. Morgan, San Simeon, San Luis Obispo,
California, 1920–1937. Photograph by
Walter Steilberg.

Above: *J. Morgan, Roman pool, San Simeon, San Luis Obispo, California, 1920–1937. Courtesy Pana-Vue Slides.*

Right: *J. Morgan, child's playhouse, San Luis Obispo, California, 1920s. It was designed for daughter of Steve Zagar, who drove the taxi between San Luis Obispo and San Simeon. Photograph by Will Boutelle.*

Opposite page: *J. Morgan, interior, YWCA, Oakland, California, 1915. Photograph by James H. Edelen.*

The importance of Phoebe Apperson Hearst to Julia Morgan's career has been variously argued. Although Asilomar, the great seaside conference center begun by Morgan in 1913 for the YWCA, was a pet project of Hearst's, there is evidence that the YWCA in Oakland of 1915, the first of a national chain of commissions built by Morgan for the women's social service organization, had been planned with Grace Merriam Fisher, a Berkeley sorority sister of Morgan's, who became an important board member of the YWCA in 1910.[41]

Institutions—especially for women's use—played a major role in Morgan's practice. Aside from the previously mentioned YWCA buildings, Morgan served as consulting architect for the organization's hospitality houses built during World War I. A surge of interest in women's clubs gave J.M. the opportunity to build both the simple redwood Saratoga Foothill Club in 1915 and the very elaborate Romanesque-Gothic reinforced concrete Berkeley Women's City Club in 1929. Work also came from women's hospitals and retirement homes.

Julia Morgan's buildings reveal an eclectic approach to design. Although the larger share of her work suggests a loose historicism influenced by her École training in Paris, her architectural practice among the so-called California School familiarized J.M. with the avant-garde interest in structural honesty and the use of indigenous materials. Her most notable early commission of 1908–1910, the St. John's Presbyterian Church in Berkeley, used the Craftsman style, which allowed the structural materials to become part of the design by leaving the interior wooden studs and trusses exposed. If Morgan's side-entranced house designs in city and suburb seem derived from the same general plan, it is not obvious in the finished product.[42] The interiors, consisting downstairs of entry hall and staircase placed between living and dining rooms with a kitchen and pantry placed behind them, were varied in size and character so as to accommodate both the Piedmont tycoon and the middle class Berkeley or Oakland professional.

Above: *J. Morgan, interior, YWCA, Berkeley, California, 1919; demolished in campus expansion. Courtesy Documents Collection, College of Environmental Design, University of California at Berkeley.*

Right: *J. Morgan, YWCA, Oakland, California, 1915. Photograph by James H. Edelen.*

Left: *J. Morgan, interior, Berkeley City Club, Berkeley, California, 1928. Photograph by James H. Edelen.*

Below: *J. Morgan, the King's Daughters of California Home for Incurables, Oakland, California, 1912. Photograph by James H. Edelen.*

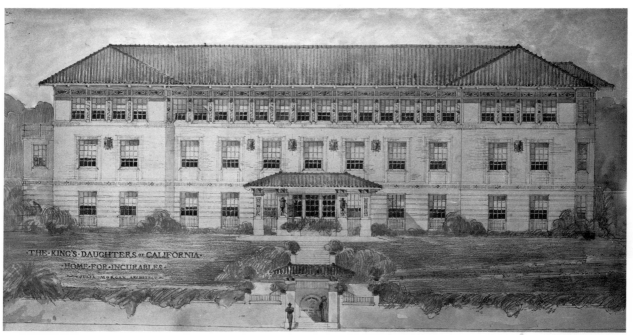

Above: *J. Morgan, exterior, St. John's Presbyterian Church, Berkeley, California, 1909–1910. Courtesy the Documents Collection, College of Environmental Design, University of California at Berkeley.*

Right: *J. Morgan, octagonal hall, Ben Reed House, Piedmont, California, 1926 Photograph by James H. Edelen.*

Julia Morgan's role as patron or director of her office's architectural commissions was never in question. Her suite of offices, located in the Merchants Exchange Building in San Francisco from 1906 to 1952, contained a complete library of rare books and periodicals and operated as an atelier or workshop.[43] Morgan was the one who saw or dealt with clients, and all her engineers and designers carried out her projects without deviation from her small sketches. The staff became her family, shared in her successes, and were always carried during illness or slow times. Thaddeus Joy, Walter Steilberg, James LeFeaver, Bjarne Dahl, Ed Hussey, Camille Solon, and others were with her for years. At least two women who worked for Morgan became certified architects: Dorothy Wormser and Elizabeth Boyter.[44] In fact, by 1927 there were 6 women among an office staff of 14, an unusual ratio for that time, as well as for the present.[45]

Julia Morgan's architectural career was a full-time, lifelong endeavor. Her last major project, in the 1940s, was a Museum of Medieval Art for San Francisco. William Randolph Hearst had bought the abandoned Spanish monastery of Santa Maria de Ovila in 1931 with the idea of reassembling the structure in his northern California mountain retreat. Because of the costly nature of the project, he donated the monastery instead to the city of San Francisco, stipulating that the structure be incorporated into a Julia Morgan design for a medieval art museum. Ultimately much of the disassembled structure was destroyed in a fire, and the project was never completed. Nevertheless, despite this last fiasco, as well as her willful destruction of nearly all her office's records in 1952, Julia Morgan's legacy —in redwood, concrete, and brick— survives.

Julia Morgan's associates, 1920: left to right, *Schalk, Walter Steilberg, Dorothy Wormser, Thaddeus Joy, Clifford. Courtesy Dorothy Wormser Coblentz.*

By Mary Otis Stevens

6. Struggle for Place: Women in Architecture: 1920–1960

In 1921 a news item bearing the following headlines was published in a Chicago newspaper: "Only Girl Architect Lonely: Wanted—To meet all of the women architects in Chicago to form a club." Inspired by this, a small group of women draftspersons met with Elizabeth Martini, the only woman architect in Illinois at that time, and formed a club known as the Chicago Woman's Drafting Club.[1]

The ad placed by Elizabeth Martini was probably insignificant news then, but it was correctly perceived 17 years later by members of that organization, subsequently reconstituted as the Women's Architectural Club, Chicago Chapter, for being what could be termed "a fertile idea." From the perspective of the 1970s, even more meanings are discernible. That lonely cry is evidence that women architects had finally realized that until they drew together into a sisterhood, they could hardly expect the brotherhood that held all the strings of power to admit them as equals into the profession.

Early Organizations

Not only did this consciousness begin to unite women practicing architecture and its related disciplines in the Chicago area, but even earlier, in 1915, a small group of women students at Wsshington University in St. Louis and another at the University of Minnesota formed local organizations. These two initiatives date the first efforts of women architects to associate professionally during the First World War. They can be viewed as well in the broader context of the general labor movement to form unions and press for a fairer position at the collective bargaining table. Although not aware, because of their middle or upper class backgrounds, that their status in society linked them with other groups dispossessed for one reason or another of merited rights and opportunities, these remarkable women in architectural practice during the early decades of this century were coping in the most effective way they could to win their struggle for place in American society.

In 1922 the Midwestern women held a convention in St. Louis and decided to make their organization national, calling it Alpha Alpha Gamma. Four chapters formed the original nucleus: Alpha at St. Louis, Beta at Minnesota, Gamma at Texas, and Delta at the University of California. During the next three decades five more chapters were added, but by then the alumnae by far outnumbered the undergraduate members. For that reason, at the 1948 convention held in San Francisco, Alpha Alpha Gamma was reorganized as the Association of Women in Architecture (AWA), with Alpha Alpha Gamma continuing as the undergraduate affiliate. The AWA is still in operation to serve, as Alpha Alpha Gamma proposed to do, as "an avenue of contact between women of similar backgrounds with common problems, ideals and interests."[2] The image of a professional sisterhood is clear in the intentions of Alpha Alpha Gamma's founding members. They advertised that their organization provided "a backlog of experience which is shared with younger members"[3] and in recognition of the problems women face due to family mobility, "a readymade group of friends for women moving to new communities."[4]

Alpha Alpha Gamma, as well as the AWA, was a national organization from the start, and its intent was to attract an equally broad membership. Architectural engineering, interior, industrial, landscape, and textile design, as well as ceramics, sculpture, mural painting, "and such other arts as the chapter shall deem allied to architecture" were all listed among its member disciplines. By contrast, the Women's Architectural Club in Chicago was a local organization that by 1932 had only 14 members, all the female practicing architects in the area. With such a narrow constituency, the club was eventually absorbed within the AIA and became known as the club of architects' wives.

However, the activities of the club's founders won recognition at the series of Women's World Fairs that were held in that city in the late twenties and early thirties. At the 1927

Fair, the Chicago Women's Drafting Club was offered space for a small exhibit "on one side of the booth given to science and the allied arts."[5] This prompted the members not only to change the club's name, to the Women's Architectural Club, Chicago Chapter, but to extend its membership to "women architects, architectural draftsmen, architectural students, architectural renderers, and landscape architects at the discretion of the membership committee."[6] Although initiated by less than a dozen founders and never attracting a great many more because of its elitist structure, the club was remarkably effective in its promotional activities due to the outstanding women architects who joined. Among them were three University of Michigan graduates—Juliet Peddle, AIA, who opened her own office in Terre Haute in 1939; Bertha Yerex Whitman, who worked in a number of recognized firms without being made a partner or associate in any, and Ruth H. Perkins, AIA, who is distinguished for designing the club's logo identifying the *Architrave*.

At the second Women's World Fair held in the spring of 1928, the Women's Architectural Club "had a very fine exhibition including drawings, photographs of executed work, renderings, a wood carving of an English Chapel, and a Model Nursery."[7] An honorary membership was given to Elizabeth Scott, a London architect, who had won the English competition to design a Shakespeare Memorial Theatre. However, by 1932 the spotlight shifted to this side of the Atlantic with the exhibition that year of the Scheid House by Bertha Yerex Whitman.

Such club activities were probably the most professionally rewarding involvements open to women in practice between the two world wars because it was through the clubs rather than as individuals that women architects could expect to receive public recognition for their work. During the Depression years especially, the prospects for women were bleak. Their already precarious situation was further undercut by the scramble for any work available. There were no spaces reserved for women in whatever architectural lifeboats floated around. Not surprisingly, therefore, only a token number of women architects survived in practice.

THE ARCHITRAVE

JULY 1938

Above: *Cover,* Architrave, *magazine of the Women's Architectural Club, Chicago, July 1938; designed by Ruth H. Perkins. Courtesy Bertha Yerex Whitman.*

Left: *Bertha Yerex Whitman, Scheid House, Hubbard Woods, Illinois, 1932; exhibited at the Chicago World's Fair, 1932. Courtesy Bertha Yerex Whitman.*

"A Thousand Women in Architecture"

Up to 1929 there were only nine registered architects in the state of California. Among them were Julia Morgan, architect of William Randolph Hearst's San Simeon, and Lilian J. Rice, described as "a wonderful woman, fine teacher and good architect" by her colleague, Rose Connor, AIA, who compiled the 1958 survey from which the following data are taken. Using "lists of women architects sent by the Architectural Examining Boards of the various states,"[8] Rose Connor found only 320 women architects registered in the country in 1958. Relative to the number of all registered architects for that year, this figure represents 1 percent of the total. The same percentage applied to women members of the American Institute of Architects.

Rose Connor stated that "The following states had no women architects: Kentucky, Mississippi, Nevada, N. Dakota, S. Dakota, Utah and Wyoming."[9]

The employment status of these 320 women in 1958 is particularly telling of the options open to qualified women architects until the rise of feminism in the 1960s. Thirty-five, or 10 percent, had their own offices— "including those whose office is in their home"—29 were "partners with architect-husbands," and 13, or 4 percent, were "partners or executives in architects' offices." Women in these three categories comprised 24 percent of the total; the remaining women, in fact three out of four, were employed, if at all, in "undefined architectural capacities."[10] Their marital status reveals similar constraints. Less than half of these 320 women architects had married, three were

"A Thousand Women in Architecture," projects: top right, S. W. Thayer School, Burlington, Vermont, by Ruth Reynolds Freeman; bottom right, proposed oil refinery, Mexico, by Lavone Dickensheets Scott; bottom left, Eleuthera House, Bahamas, by Eleanor Raymond; top left, apartment house, Tel-Aviv, by Elsa Gidoni; center, stairway in Swiss Life Insurance Building, Berlin, by Marie Frommer; from Architectural Record, March 1948. Courtesy *Architectural Record.*

widows, and four were divorced. One out of four was a college graduate.

The 1958 profile of women in architecture shows no significant improvement over the statistical survey done 10 years earlier by the editors of *Architectural Record* for their 1948 two-part article, "A Thousand Women in Architecture." How discouraging this news was is revealed in letters from Lucille B. Raport, AIA, and members of her committee of the AWA to one another and to David McCullough, then Associate Editor of the *Architectural Forum,* who was working on an update of the *Record's* 1948 survey. These letters include such notations as "Architecture is a man's world, well almost, anyway,"[11] and "In the 98 years of the American Institute, only three lady Fellows, if you'll pardon the expression, have been named."[12]

The 1948 and 1958 surveys both show that only one woman in four trained to practice architecture succeeded in doing so. Since only 18 of the 1,119 women on the list compiled by the Women's Architectural Association and the deans of architectural schools across the country were featured in the *Architectural Record's* 1948 article, it is not surprising that "not a single one indicated any disappointment whatever in her chosen career."[13] Among those singled out by the editors were Eleanor Raymond, Elizabeth Coit, Lucille B. Raport, Rose Connor, and Victorine Homsey, all AIA members.[14] Looking back now, three decades later, they still seem as a group to represent a cross section of professional practice—male or female—at the time.

Male perceptions of women architects are not concealed in the article, as this editorial remark makes clear: "Logically enough, most of them stress residential work as the easiest to obtain and, on the whole, the most satisfying and natural for women to engage in."[15] However, the unequal opportunities for women were at least alluded to, if obliquely, in this reference: "And a good many comment on the sad truth that in architecture as in every other field women are paid considerably less than their male counterparts."[16] Otherwise all is "sweetness and light": "As for the women who, though trained in architecture, are not practicing, the vast majority are busy raising little architects."[17]

The Cambridge School

Perhaps that is the way most male architects—then as now—perceive women architects to be, but there was at least one strong-minded dissenter, Henry Atherton Frost, who was responsible for the success of the Cambridge School of Architecture and Landscape Architecture during its 25 years of operation from 1917 to 1942. Associated with Frost in the school's history was Eleanor Raymond, one of our country's most distinguished women architects. In her book, *From Tipi to Skyscraper: A History of Women in Architecture,* Doris Cole quotes a revealing comment by Henry Atherton Frost: "We had no training that helped us to understand that (when founding the Cambridge School) we had quite by chance been caught up in a small eddy of a greater movement in which women were beginning to demand equal educational rights with their brothers."[18] These educational rights were also demands made by the Cambridge School students to acquire sufficient architectural skills during their training there "to ensure that they could actively practice their profession upon graduation."[19] Frost and his staff of teachers carried out their mandate. "As of 1930, 83 percent of the graduates were active in professional work, making a very high ratio of more than five-to-one."[20]

The curriculum of the Cambridge School of Architecture and Landscape Architecture was similar to that of other professional schools of the period, except that both disciplines were closely integrated: "not only were landscape students given training in architecture, but architectural students were given training in landscaping. . . . Only much later, in the 1940s, after the Cambridge School closed and women were admitted to the Harvard Graduate School of Design, did Harvard stress the relationship between architecture and landscape architecture."[21] What the Cambridge School had initiated in its curriculum of the 1930s was the coming discipline of environmental design.

Despite its success—and the successful practices of its graduates—the Cambridge School was forced to shut down in 1941, and interestingly enough it was a women's educational institution that pulled the plug. Smith College had appropriated the Cambridge School in 1938 when university association became a requirement for accreditation for all architectural schools. Henry Atherton Frost had been in contact with Smith's President, William Allen Neilson, since 1928 and found his aspirations to expand the college into a women's university sympathetic to the programs and aims of the Cambridge School, which by the thirties had become mainly a graduate school for women in architecture. Accordingly, the affiliation of the two institutions seemed to suit both their needs. Unfortunately, however, President Neilson retired in 1939 and was followed by a new president and board of trustees with far more limited goals and the determination to cut costs and programs. The deficit that the Cambridge School had accumulated over the years provided the necessary grounds for terminating its activities in 1941.

The financial risk might not have been the only qualm that the Smith College administration had about the Cambridge School. From the perspective of the 1970s, its women graduates seem to have developed a consciousness of themselves as architects—and as women—that is quite contemporary. For example, they can be credited as a group with breaking the long-established precedent that a woman must choose between marriage and a career. Their successful life histories dispelled that notion, showing that far from being natural to women, it was just another of society's taboos that kept women in the home. Once that barrier had been overturned, husband and wife partnerships began to spring up in many areas of the country. Victorine DuPont Homsey was one of the first alumnae of the Cambridge School to join in partnership with her husband, and Sarah Pillsbury Harkness one of the last.

Above: *Victorine and Samuel Homsey,
dining area, Garden Tours Pavilion,
Henry Francis DuPont Winterthur
Museum, Wilmington, Delaware, 1960.
Photograph by Robert M. Damora.*

Top: *Elizabeth Scheu Close and Winston
Close, beach cabin, Osceola, Wisconsin,
1941. Photograph by Hedrich-Blessing.*

Husbands and Wives

The difference in scale between the offices they established, in each case within a year or so after marrying, is more telling of the times than of the women. After successfully completing her architectural training in the mid-twenties, Victorine Homsey "started her career as a draftsman in the office of Allen and Collens, Boston, Mass."[22] From there she could have chosen to practice privately, in what Doris Cole has so aptly termed "the domestic domain," or elect to join through a marriage partnership a group practice where the work would be more varied. Electing the latter course, Victorine Homsey married and established a joint practice in 1929 with her husband, Samuel Homsey. Locating their office in Delaware, they accumulated a wide range of successful building projects to their credit. Besides private residences, these include "schools, a library, a health center, a hospital, and an art center,"[23] as well as an embassy apartment building, a block of townhouses, a church, and work for the Winterthur Museum.

Another successful husband and wife partnership was established in 1938 by Elizabeth Scheu and Winston Close in Minneapolis. Like the Homseys, they married and formed their partnership in the same year, but developed a practice that was primarily residential in character and Midwestern in location. This specialization was due, most likely, to limiting their practice "to those who sought them out."[24] Since the Twin Cities area had only "four or five contemporary houses (all but one by Frank Lloyd Wright) when the Closes completed their first residence in 1939,"[25] they were necessarily drawing upon a limited clientele. However, their reputation soon brought them enough jobs to make a dent on the landscape, and as in the case of Victorine and Samuel Homsey, to win them professional recognition in the journals and the honor of being made Fellows of the AIA.

Hardly had the precedent of the husband and wife partnership become established, however, before it was disrupted, along with many traditions of American life, by the Second World War. One aspect of architectural practice that changed was the dramatic escalation of scale in organizational structures. Swept away with the "mom and pop" store was the one- or two-person office, with its roster of carefully spelled distinguished names. In its place emerged the corporate office with simple initials: IBM or TAC.

Jean Bodman Fletcher and Sarah Pillsbury Harkness

For Sarah Pillsbury Harkness, graduate of the Smith College Graduate School of Architecture (alias the Cambridge School of Architecture and Landscape Architecture) in 1940, becoming a founding member of TAC (The Architects Collaborative) in 1945 was an entirely logical decision. The same situation applied to her talented colleague, Jean Bodman Fletcher, who graduated from the Harvard Graduate School of Design in 1943. Both women married architect-husbands, and both teams competed and won Second and First Prize, respectively, in the Smith College Dormitory Competition of 1945. Although the project never went ahead, that competition, according to Norman Fletcher, now senior partner of TAC, was the impetus for organizing the firm that year.

Times were favorable for such an

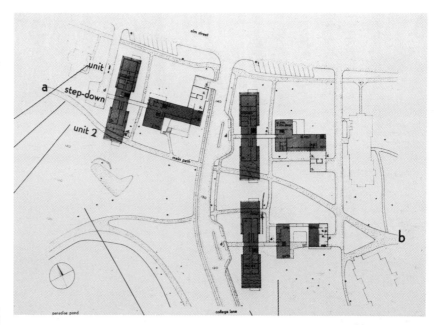

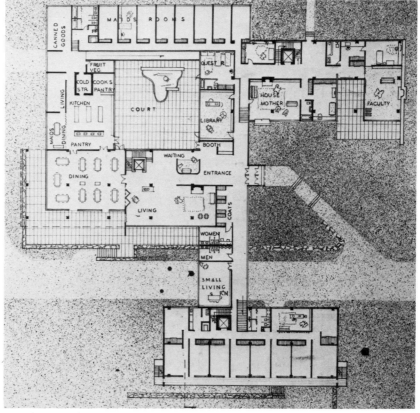

Sarah Pillsbury Harkness, 1973. Courtesy The Architects Collaborative.

Above: *Sarah Pillsbury and John C. Harkness, second level plan, second prize, Smith College Dormitory Competition of 1945. Courtesy The Architects Collaborative.*

Top: *Jean Bodman, Norman Fletcher, and Benjamin Thompson, general plan, first prize, Smith College Dormitory Competition of 1945. Courtesy The Architects Collaborative.*

event. Walter Gropius was then the head of Harvard's Graduate School of Design and the leading architectural educator both here and abroad. His presence had turned Cambridge, Massachusetts, into a mecca for young and talented architects of the post-war era. Moreover, Jean Bodman Fletcher had studied under Walter Gropius at Harvard and, in Norman Fletcher's words, "was influenced by him."[26] However, she, like her husband, had also been introduced to the practice of architecture through an apprenticeship (after graduating from architectural school and marrying) in the Saarinen office in Bloomfield Hills, Michigan.

The expansion of The Architects Collaborative from a small Cambridge-based firm into a multinational corporation went at a slow but steady pace during its first decade under the stewardship of Walter Gropius. Applying the principles of the Bauhaus to the internal organization of the office, he set the tradition of collaborative decision making that resulted in all the partners participating in a weekly review of all projects on the drawing boards. The immediate effect produced by each one looking over the other's shoulders and sharing design experience, expertise, and responsibility on each job was a higher and more consistent design quality in the firm's work, as well as considerable savings in time and costs as the efficiencies and improvements in details could be passed directly from one job to another. These procedures, along with commissions to do a number of public schools during the fifties, served to advance what was initially a design philosophy into a methodology. Instead of buildings, the firm began developing prototypes.

However, the success of these innovations led eventually to the dismantling of the original open office and its replacement by TAC's present tightly organized corporate structure. According to Norman Fletcher, Jean was "one of the prime movers in getting the office incorporated,"[27] which shows that the specialization of skills and responsibilities that often shunted women architects to office cubbyholes and backseats did not appear threaten-

Opposite page: *The Architects Collaborative, principals in charge: Sarah P. Harkness, John C. Harkness, and Herbert K. Gallagher, Fox Lane Middle School, Bedford, New York, 1966. Photograph by Ezra Stoller Associates © ESTO.*

Below: *The Architects Collaborative, principals in charge: Sarah P. Harkness and H. Morse Payne, Jr., interior view and stage configurations, Anita Tuvin Schlechter Auditorium, Dickinson College, Carlisle, Pennsylvania, 1971. Photograph by Julius Shulman.*

PROSCENIUM STAGE

ARENA STAGE

THRUST STAGE

ing to her, perhaps because of her established reputation and leading position in the firm.

The dramatic differences between TAC now and then came out in a 1976 interview with Sarah Pillsbury Harkness, who was reflecting back on the early years. "We followed our noses, took things as they came."[28] Household help was a major problem, but the two women partners in the firm worked out a routine where each worked half a day, Fletcher in the morning and Harkness in the afternoon, while sharing the same babysitter. Since each combined motherhood with architectural practice, Fletcher with six and Harkness with seven children, domestic commitments had to take priority. However, the "permissive attitude of the office in its first decade"[29] favored such flexible arrangements. Today at TAC, as in other architectural firms of its size and structure, only an insignificant number of women architects are members of the firm, and those that are of the younger generation have not had children. Typical also is the way TAC meets its affirmative action quota by hiring a high

percentage of women in subsidiary departments, like graphics and interiors. Aware of this situation, Sarah Pillsbury Harkness would like to see office routine become more adaptable to domestic commitments so that women architects are not again faced with making the choice between marriage with children and a professional career.

After a quarter century of successfully integrating her two vocations, Sarah Pillsbury Harkness has not only worked out a way of life for herself but perceived its much broader implications. "Work in an office is all part-time jobs, since once a person has gained a position of responsibility he or she takes on more than one project at any one time."[30] The difference between the division in her work day and that of her male colleagues at TAC is principally one of location. Custom accepts diversity in work assignments—in fact, it is associated with one's rank in the pecking order—as long as the divisions occur *inside* rather than *outside* the office environment. To Sarah Pillsbury Harkness and Jean Bodman Fletcher such formalities did not matter.

California Women Architects

Although collaboration was flourishing in Harvard Square, it was not in vogue in other regions of the United States during the forties and fifties. With the exception of Elizabeth Coit, whose professional association was always with public housing authorities, the women singled out by the *Architectural Record* in 1948 were either individual practitioners or partners with architect-husbands and, excluding Eleanor Raymond's Solar House in Belmont, Massachusetts, built in 1931, their work also shows few departures from the conventional and conservative building tradition. For example, Lucille B. Raport, AIA, designed many houses in Southern California during the forties and fifties that conform to the stylistic trends set by her male peers. Edla Muir's house for "Mr. Robert Taylor and Miss Barbara Stanwyck" is indistinguishable from (though it shows more modesty than most like it) the estates designed for newly rich and celebrated Americans.

Today this cautious attitude on the part of women architects of that time

Above: *Edla Muir, house for "Mr. Robert Taylor and Miss Barbara Stanwyck"; from "A Thousand Women in Architecture,"* Architectural Record, *March 1948. Courtesy* Architectural Record.

Top: *Lucille B. Raport, ski cabin for John Lockheed, Lake Arrowhead, California, 1948. Photograph by Julius Shulman.*

Opposite page: *Lutah Maria Riggs, Temple for Vedanta Society, Santa Barbara, California, 1956. Photograph by Robert C. Cleveland.*

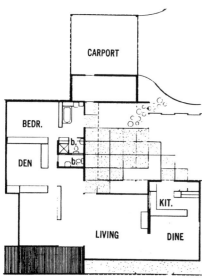

Above: *Greta Grossman, floor plan, cantilevered house, Beverly Hills, California, 1950s; from* The Los Angeles Times Home Magazine, *Aug. 11, 1957.*

Top: *G. Grossman, cantilevered house; from* The Los Angeles Times Home Magazine, *Aug. 11, 1957.*

signifies their cultural conditioning as well as their status in the architectural profession. Not in secure enough positions to be risk-takers with their few commissions, they express an understandable reserve in their work. Lutah Maria Riggs, however, points to the might-have-beens of the period. Not a native Californian, she moved west during the war to work as a stage designer in Hollywood and remained in Santa Barbara afterwards. Out of these connections came her commission to design the Vedanta Temple. What her example suggests is that American women architects then as now when given the opportunity were glad to escape from "the domestic domain."

Experimentation with new materials and structural systems—the use of cantilevering, for example, in steel and reinforced concrete—is seen only in the work of European-trained women architects. Greta Grossman's "dramatic cantilevered house"[31] in Beverly Hills demonstrates an architectural competence, in her case acquired at the Swedish Royal Institute of Technology and the Art Industrial School in Stockholm, that is

shared by Elsa Gidoni, educated at the Petrograd Academy of Art and Berlin Technical University, and Marie Frommer, who won her Doctor of Engineering degree at the I.T. Dresden with a thesis on town planning. Both the education of these women and the buildings they designed make them stand out from their less sophisticated American sisters when examples of their respective work are shown in articles like the *Architectural Record's* "A Thousand Women in Architecture." The comparison is especially evident in the work of West Coast women architects that was published as a series in *Home* magazine by the *Los Angeles Sunday Times* between 1956 and 1958.

Rather than showing a lack of talent on the part of American women architects, the comparison underscores the educational and professional obstacles in their path that have been described throughout this chapter. Even as late as the 1950s few American women received the same exposure—cultural and technical—in their professional training as their male peers. Although this may not have been official university policy, women candidates had at least two strikes against them in competition for place in professional schools of the first rank. One, endemic to women's schooling in general, was poor technical and scientific preparation during the critical high school and undergraduate years, particularly at all-women institutions that, on the one hand, lacked the proper facilities and, on the other, were by tradition inclined to the liberal arts. Second, and also culturally conditioned, was the assumption that because women students were likely to marry within a few years after graduation, they would not use their professional training to the same advantage as their male peers. This tilt in favor of the male was noted by the Association of Women in Architecture in one of their 1958 memos: "Mr. Pickens, Pres. Accredited Arch. Schools Assoc. said at our Founders' Day luncheon that he judged there were about 16,000 students of which about 2 percent were girls."[32]

Top, right: *Olive Chadeayne, kitchen, W. T. Theis House, 1950s; from* The Los Angeles Times Home Magazine, *Jan. 23, 1955.*

Bottom, right: *Cover,* The Los Angeles Times Home Magazine, *Aug. 11, 1957. "Four Houses Designed by Women"; project shown is Russell Law House, Malibu, California, by Edla Muir.*

Olive Chadeayne's

Kitchen With Everything

WHILE woman's place in the scheme of things has changed materially in 30 years, she still has a background of generations of housewives whose main objective was to maintain comfortable homes and happy families. Many have entered professions and the business world and some the field of architecture. With their natural background, women have an instinctive understanding of the needs of the home.

This natural instinct, combined with professional training, gives women architects many advantages when it comes to the design of kitchens. Especially workable plans with the newest equipment placed to save steps in preparing meals and cleaning up are always featured.

A pleasant atmosphere is important, too, as many homemakers spend a large percentage of their time in the kitchen. The many new surfacing materials for walls, work surfaces and floors give complete freedom as far as decorative schemes are concerned and are kept clean with a minimum of effort.

Another trend seems to be that of cubbyholes located near the range and work surfaces for the storage of much-used items such as coffee, tea, cereals, etc. The large kitchen would seem to be a thing of the past and these efficient and accessible storage units add materially to the workability of the smaller kitchen area.

In many cases laundry equipment is included as part of the kitchen, with a partial cabinet wall to separate the two areas. This is practical both from the standpoint of the related work to be done in the two and the fact that having the plumbing connections more or less centered is an economy in construction.

HOME

AUGUST 11, 1957

4

houses

designed

by women

Corporate Careers

Looking back at the work of women architects in the forties and fifties, one cannot avoid perceiving it as imitative—following yesterday's avant-garde. This observation shows the stamp of their minority position. The imperatives of our technology tend to separate the few who have been sufficiently trained to use its hardware—and in architecture this includes industrialized procedures and computer systems—to be plugged into high-echelon jobs and the rest who, lacking the prerequisites, are left to scramble for the lower paid and lower status jobs that "trickle down" from above.

The career of Natalie de Blois during this period is an appropriate example. Graduated from the Columbia School of Architecture in 1944 and awarded a Fulbright Fellowship to the École des Beaux-Arts in 1951, she rose in the firm of Skidmore, Owings, & Merrill from draftsperson to participating associate over a 30-year work span. Like Sarah Pillsbury Harkness and Jean Bodman Fletcher, she combined marriage and children with a demanding architectural career. What the life histories of these women demonstrate is that with the proper credentials, women can rise to the top of the profession as easily as men.

Cloethiel Woodard Smith also fits into this perspective. Founding her own firm in Washington, Smith has been engaged in work of the same scale as Natalie de Blois. Neither woman tried to change the system but simply to join it, and by playing by its rules made it to the top. For male and female architect alike the ambition of a typical young architect of the 1920–1960 period was to be hired by a known master. Natalie de Blois, in referring to the Pepsi Cola Headquarters building in New York City, wrote: "I worked directly with Gordon Bunshaft as the Senior Designer."[33] To be singled out as gifted was all the carrot that was needed to turn architects, first as students and later as practitioners, into dutiful followers, the trait serving them well in their climb up office ladders. The stick was felt in either situation when one rocked the boat.

Elizabeth Coit: Low-Income Housing

Fortunately there were at least two women, Elizabeth Coit and Catherine Bauer, an architect and a planner, respectively, who chose "the road not taken." They both devoted their professional careers to the public sector and to housing in particular. They shared the same concern over what the architectural and planning professions *were not doing* for the great number of American families, who from lack of means became the unwanted tenants of equally unwanted housing projects.

Catherine Bauer's exposure to public housing projects in Europe in 1930 at the age of 25 and her later association with Lewis Mumford led her to take positions on housing in America that make her stand out from her peers and her time. Her efforts in the thirties to help unions undertake low-income housing projects on the model of the Carl Mackley Houses in Philadelphia, backed by the American Federation of Hosiery Workers, are an indication of the pioneering work that she was doing while her colleagues continued what could be called their "dogmatic slumber." (For a thorough discussion of Bauer, see Chapter 9.)

Elizabeth Coit's professional career gives the same profile. Although to

Elizabeth Coit; from Architectural Record, *April 1931. Courtesy* Architectural Record.

many in the profession she may have been lumped with what was termed in those days "N.Y. housers," her life history dispels all categories. After receiving her professional training at MIT, Coit worked on her classic report on public housing from 1938–1940 under a Langley Fellowship from the AIA. Her findings were first published in *The Octagon,* the AIA professional journal, in October 1941 and were presented in revised form in "Housing from the Tenant's Viewpoint," published by *Architectural Record* in 1942. This research led her to a lifetime of work for public housing authorities, including the Federal Public Housing Authority from 1942 to 1947 and as Principal Project Planner for the New York City Housing Authority from 1948 to 1962. Perhaps her greatest contribution to women architects of the present and future is that she pointed the way toward turning an ordinary job into a creative process.

What she did in her investigation of the public housing projects of the late thirties was to tell in simple and accurate detail what it was like to live in them. Since few procedures—and even fewer social attitudes—have changed in the 35 years since she worked on her report, Elizabeth Coit's observations continue to apply. She did not report as an outsider but projected herself directly into the daily existence of the tenants and consequently asked many pertinent questions. She had no vested interest in the established approach to public housing and so was free to make any number of criticisms and innovative recommendations.

In one section of her "Notes on Design and Construction of the Dwelling Units for the Lower-Income Family," Elizabeth Coit makes the suggestion "that the architect and his family should live in the project he designed (preferably in the least desirable unit) as a source of information on what the 'housing consumer of the lower-income strata' needs in housing."[34] She recognized that the "workingman's home and the lower middle class home are designed as a somewhat abbreviated edition of the large scale home."[35] Instead of adhering to "the standard of the more articulate part of yesterday's people: namely, the well-to-do and the upper part of the middle class, where solutions of teeir shelter problem have long been recorded in books and journals . . . solutions already on their way to obsolescence as the record was being made,'' Elizabeth Coit correctly noted that housing for the vast majority of the population should aim at being ''serviceable today and half a century hence.''[36]

Elizabeth Coit was subtly but firmly advocating in 1941 that our society should be directing its experimental advances to housing for the many rather than the few. She also can be distinguished from her contemporaries of either sex and on both shores of the Atlantic by the way she went about her research. No detail of design or fabrication, from toilet to building system, escaped her attention, and no issue or barrier, no matter whether of technical or social derivation, was assumed by her to be a permanent condition. And she was by no means ignorant of the parameters governing her study: ''I have tried to learn what the low-income client thinks he needs or would like to have, and what architects and other experts in the more architectural aspects of homemaking think he ought to have, or can have, and how this or that solution works out in practice . . . but keeping in mind always the necessity of reconciling as far as possible expressed desires with the present-day procedure as to cost, design, construction.''[37] She also made this prophetic observation: ''Good housing for some two-thirds of the nation has apparently not been regarded as a good investment for some time past; nor, in general, can it be so regarded at the present time.''[38]

Elizabeth Coit's recommendations were equally perceptive. Concerned with underused, if not useless living space, she speculated at the end of her report on how a ''new nomenclature, combined with changes in plan and detail, neither radical nor costly, would restore to use these areas, increasing the efficiency of the shelter, and at the same time embellishing the small-scale family scene.''[39] Changing the name—as well as the concept of bedroom—''would help turn the

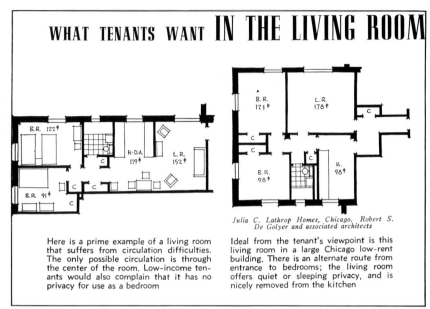

WHAT TENANTS WANT IN THE LIVING ROOM

Julia C. Lathrop Homes, Chicago. Robert S. De Golyer and associated architects

Here is a prime example of a living room that suffers from circulation difficulties. The only possible circulation is through the center of the room. Low-income tenants would also complain that it has no privacy for use as a bedroom

Ideal from the tenant's viewpoint is this living room in a large Chicago low-rent building. There is an alternate route from entrance to bedrooms; the living room offers quiet or sleeping privacy, and is nicely removed from the kitchen

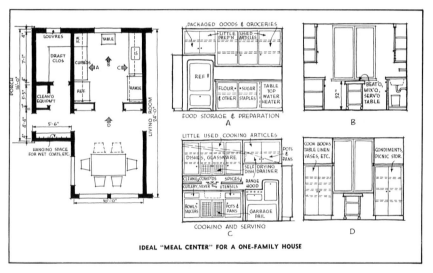

IDEAL "MEAL CENTER" FOR A ONE-FAMILY HOUSE

Above: *E. Coit, "Ideal 'Meal Center' for a One-Family House''; from* Architectural Record, *March 1948. Courtesy* Architectural Record.

Top: *E. Coit, "What Tenants Want in the Living Room''; from* Architectural Record, *March 1948. Courtesy* Architectural Record.

space into the daytime use to which it is entitled in modern heated dwellings, and thus relieve pressure in the general living quarters."[40]

Adaptability and flexibility were her priorities because she had seen so clearly how oppressive most environments turn out to be once they have been handed down from their original owners. Since the poor are the usual recipients of this cast-off housing, Elizabeth Coit's proposals stress that housing units should be provided at the time of their construction with the basic environmental amenities and spaces that can be used and reused in a variety of ways. "The object of housing, I take to be shelter from excess heat, cold, and noise, so combined with adequate provision of light, air, space, privacy and convenience as to be acceptable, and consequently useful, to those for whose service it is intended."[41]

Had her recommendations been implemented by the housing authorities for whom she worked during her productive years, 1940–1962, which also happened to overlap the post-war housing boom, public housing in America might have turned out very differently. Although her competence was recognized by the profession that made her a Fellow of the AIA and by the New York Chapter that honored her with their Pioneer in Architecture award in 1969, Elizabeth Coit's influence on policy making in public housing did not spread far beyond the professional circle, most likely because she was upholding a position on housing that has never been popular with the middle and privileged classes, and after all, she was a woman.

Few architects, male or female, have as yet developed much contact with, and consequently have not been able to serve well, the majority of Americans, the unknown residents of housing projects and the forgotten users of office buildings and industrial plants. This ignorance is all too plain in the 1948 report, "Better Housing for the Family," prepared by the Women's City Club of New York. Patronizing throughout toward families in need of public housing, the do-gooding women found exactly what they were looking for from the 458 families they interviewed: "Sincere appreciation for the vast improvements in their living conditions made possible only through government assistance was expressed by a large number of families, who hoped that their experience would be of value in the planning of other projects."[42]

Obviously those participating in the Women's City Club study had not come into contact with Elizabeth Coit, even though she was working at the time for the New York City Housing Authority. Nor had they profited from her comprehensive report. The oversight is easily explained, however, by the general climate of opinion towards public housing and public housing tenants until the 1960s when tenants began to organize and speak for themselves. Elizabeth Coit came as close as possible in her time to making them heard in her landmark study.

If very few of her contemporaries were likely to have singled her report out at the time of its publication in 1941, this reflects on the profession rather than on Elizabeth Coit (as was evident from the directness with which she answered questions in a recent telephone interview). Neither that sense of purpose that guided her into public housing in the first place, nor her adherence to the truths she discovered nearly forty years ago by being utterly honest with herself and her clients, has wavered. Both are parts of the record she leaves to her successors. At 84 this record allies her to the recent UN study that drafted a "housing bill of rights,"[43] whose content and concerns are exactly those outlined by Elizabeth Coit. Therefore it seems entirely becoming to this time as well as to the 1920–1960 period to have selected from the files of the Archive of Women in Architecture her document as the most significant work by a woman architect.

7. Some Professional Roles: 1920–1960

The professional roles fulfilled by the architects in this chapter are as diverse as the scope and style of their work. Although this diversity can be attributed to the variance in their personal choices and career opportunities, the difference is nonetheless indicative of the latitude of roles that women architects could and did assume during this period. Whether by preference or circumstance, all three had an interest and expertise in a single field: Eleanor Raymond primarily designed residences; Lilian Rice devoted most of her practice to building one community; Natalie de Blois worked on the design of office buildings for most of her career.

Their roles by no means cover the entire spectrum. These architects are primarily *designers,* and only occasionally did they engage in other activities in the architectural profession. Their historic and geographical circumstances qualify their roles more precisely:

Eleanor Raymond exemplifies a generation of American architects who needed to break away from traditional Beaux-Arts training in order to forge a contemporary identity. Her answer to a new architectural appropriateness was daring technical experimentation and use of a modern vocabulary regulated by classic method and vernacular inspiration.

Lilian Rice is a successful example of the architect integrated as a professional and social being within a community, sharing with its members their aspirations, life-style, and esthetic preferences.

Natalie de Blois reflects the personal and professional dilemmas of a more recent position for women, that of working in huge hierarchical corporate structures. In this context, and until very recently, a high degree of responsibility and complete dedication have not always earned for women the rewards of visibility and recognition as they have for men.

Eleanor Raymond
By Doris Cole

In 1917 Eleanor Raymond enrolled in the Cambridge School of Architecture and Landscape Architecture for women. Thus began an active and productive career in architecture that has spanned over fifty years. In 1919 she opened an office in partnership with Henry Atherton Frost, and in 1928 she began her own office in Boston, Massachusetts. These offices produced a domestic architecture that was noteworthy at that time and is even more relevant to the concerns of architecture today.

Though Raymond certainly was not typical of all early 20th-century women, she was similar to those other American women who strove to establish meaningful occupations beyond the boundaries of motherhood and home. For these women Jane Addams was the model, and teaching or social work were the accepted female occupations outside the home. Raymond shared this admiration for Jane Addams, but decided that a similar profession was not suited to her own inclinations. When discussing this decision, Raymond remembers herself as an independent young woman, with a preference for individual creative work rather than supervision of others, a growing interest in gardens and building, and little desire for marriage and family.

After graduating from Wellesley College in 1909, Raymond traveled in Europe, visiting historic and contemporary sites in France, England, Germany, and Italy. Inspired by her Wellesley landscape course and her travels in Europe, the young woman wished to continue her studies of landscape architecture. After some searching, she found Fletcher Steele, who was giving such courses for Boston ladies. Raymond remembers that these classes were primarily oriented toward young debutantes, but the information was there to be learned and Steele was a well-qualified teacher and practitioner. Soon these courses were not enough to satisfy Raymond's growing interest, and she asked Steele if she might work in his office without pay to learn more. Though her office tasks were perhaps minor, she

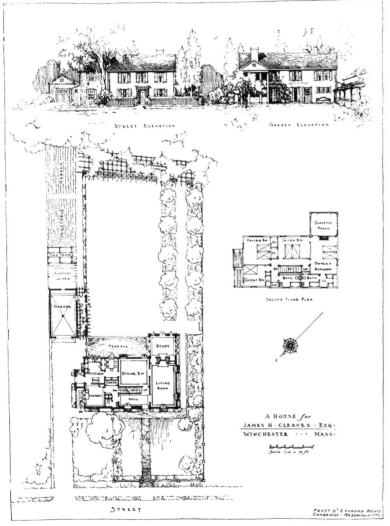

Above: *Eleanor Raymond, elevation and plans, James H. Cleaves Residence, Winchester, Massachusetts, 1919. Courtesy Eleanor Raymond, architect.*

Top: *E. Raymond, garden elevation, James H. Cleaves Residence, Winchester, Massachusetts, 1919. Courtesy Eleanor Raymond, architect.*

learned through watching and listening and was encouraged to continue her quest.

It was with this in mind, that Raymond entered the new, small Cambridge School of Architecture and Landscape Architecture for women in 1917. In those days landscape architecture was strongly linked to horticulture, and since she was no horticulturist, though interested in gardens and plants, she found herself drawn more and more to architecture. Her original interest in gardens never ceased and her projects are testimony to this, but the esthetic, technical, and functional challenges of architecture became a major part of her education, culminating in a Master of Architecture degree from the Cambridge School of Smith College.

The training that Eleanor Raymond received from the Cambridge School was based upon the Beaux-Arts style with its concentration on the classic orders. Vignola's handbook was the guide; capital and column, cornice and frieze were the order of the day. With this background it is quite remarkable that Raymond, and many of her contemporaries, changed and developed her own style of architecture through the years. Even her first commission, Cleaves House in 1919, which did employ the classic order, had a straightforward simplicity. Though her work soon transcended the rules of the schoolroom, an appreciation for the basic principles of proportion and form stayed with her.

Raymond's attitude towards historic and contemporary architecture is best described in her book, *Early Domestic Architecture of Pennsylvania,* first published in 1931 and reprinted in 1973. It was the relationship between the historic and contemporary and the investigation of timeless design principles and their application to future work that motivated her. In the Foreword she wrote, "I have not been actuated by historic or archaeological interests."[1] It was with the active practitioner's eye that she examined these structures in Pennsylvania and historical architecture in general.

It was the design principles of simplicity and harmony of form that Eleanor Raymond selected to illus-

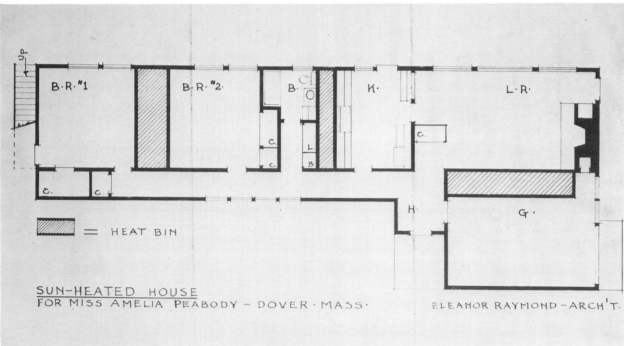

Above: *E. Raymond, plan of solar house, for Miss Amelia Peabody, Dover, Massachusetts, 1948. Courtesy Eleanor Raymond, architect.*

Top: *E. Raymond, solar house. Eleanor Raymond (right) and Dr. Maria Telkes (left), solar energy expert. Courtesy Eleanor Raymond, architect.*

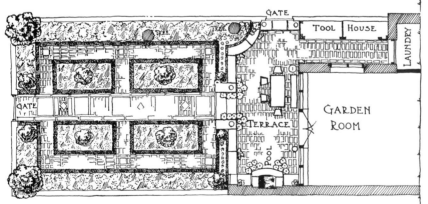

Above: *E. Raymond, plan of garden, 112 Charles Street, Boston, Massachusetts, 1923. Courtesy Eleanor Raymond, architect.*

Top: *E. Raymond, garden view, 112 Charles Street, Boston, Massachusetts, 1923. Courtesy Eleanor Raymond, architect.*

trate in her book and that she carefully studied and applied to her own work. Whether one looks at the renovation of the old Smith House and barn in 1926, the startling modern Raymond House of 1931, or the technically innovative Solar House of 1948, one sees a consistency of design, a progression from and a relationship to our early American architecture.

Raymond's concern for the integration of architecture and landscape architecture is reflected in all her projects whether located in the country or in the city. In each location her treatment varies with the demands of country or city living, climatic conditions, and the surrounding terrain. "I believe that the architect who designs a house must also plan the landscape and interior treatment as an integral part of the house. . . . I always think in terms of these three fields while planning a house."[2] The garden at 112 Charles Street of 1923 and the garden for Mrs. Potter in 1930 in Boston are two examples of her design of city gardens. At High Spruces in 1929 Raymond collaborated with the landscape architect Mary Cunningham to create gardens near the house that helped to make the visual transition from the building to the rolling meadows beyond. In fact, a Raymond house is so integrated with its landscaping that it is difficult to imagine or consider one without the other.

The extensive remodeling of the Barnes House in Haverhill, Massachusetts, in 1944, the Rachel Raymond House in Belmont, Massachusetts, in 1931, and the Sculptor's Studio in Dover, Massachusetts, in 1933 are three examples of Eleanor Raymond's ability to adapt and translate foreign architectural forms to the New England setting, to assimilate and understand their principles without ever becoming a mere copyist of the European styles. An appreciation for American design enriched by foreign influences, as expressed by Raymond designs, is yet relevant for architecture today.

Another difficult and intriguing architectural problem that Eleanor Raymond addressed was the utilization of new materials and technology. With an architectural practice spanning from 1917 through the present, Raymond witnessed tremendous changes not only in our living patterns but in construction materials and methods. She used this new technology in her buildings, often experimenting with the available resources. One such project was the home for Mr. and Mrs. Gordon Parker in 1941, in which she used many of the plywoods, panels, and experimental products manufactured by their company. Three other technically innovative projects—Plywood House of 1940, Masonite House of 1944, and Sun House of 1948—were all done for the same client, Amelia Peabody. In each house technology did not dominate or override the client's needs or her esthetic standards. Accordingly, Eleanor Raymond was able to incorporate this knowledge into the continuum of American architecture.

Though historical circumstance might have influenced the commissions she received, Raymond's interest in domestic architecture went far beyond mere necessity for professional survival. Speaking of "The Most Fascinating Job in the World—Building Houses," Raymond said:

Everybody is interested in houses because everybody has to live in one, and also because the house that children are brought up in means so much to them all their lives. If it has a good play area . . . if the outdoors offers space allocated to swing and sand box, the child will remember that house and that childhood with pleasure all his life. Furthermore, parents will do the same if frictions related to living together are removed as far as possible.[3]

For these reasons and others, Eleanor Raymond feels strongly that the importance of practicing domestic architecture must not be downgraded by young women architects today. As Raymond notes, and history demonstrates, women's traditions lie with the domestic in the broadest sense, and their activities are directed toward how people live and the effect of the physical environment upon those habits. Though the tradition cannot be denied, it is yet to be seen if young women will incorporate this tradition into their professional concerns.

Above: *E. Raymond, front and back facades, sculptor's studio, Dover, Massachusetts, 1933. Courtesy Eleanor Raymond, architect.*

Top: *E. Raymond, plywood house, Dover, Massachusetts, 1940. Courtesy Eleanor Raymond, architect.*

Lilian Rice
By Judith Paine

Posing as demurely as a Gibson Girl for the University of California's *Blue and Gold Yearbook* of 1910, Lilian Rice is the very model of serious young womanhood fulfilling the promise of education and professional status so long denied her sex. Underneath that exterior, however, was a lively spirit that fully participated in student life with the same enthusiasm and talent she brought to her career in architecture.[4]

When Rice entered Berkeley in 1906, she came at an auspicious moment. A new campus was taking shape under the direction of John Galen Howard, who had left a flourishing architectural practice in 1901 in New York to come to Berkeley both as Supervising Architect and as the head of the School of Architecture established three years later. In those exciting days, Rice could see firsthand the design process from plan through construction as new buildings were completed on campus. She also had the advantage of learning from a cadre of gifted young architects, such as Warren Perry and William Hayes whom Howard recruited for the architecture department and who enthusiastically taught the philosophy of the Beaux-Arts in Paris, where they had received

Lilian Rice, student yearbook photograph, Berkeley, 1910. Courtesy The Bancroft Library, University of California at Berkeley.

their training. When she graduated in 1910, she was among the first of many women who received their architectural degrees from Berkeley, creating a precedent as important to generations of women on the West Coast as the Massachusetts Institute of Technology was to their Eastern sisters.

Lilian Rice was born in 1888 in National City, California, a small town on the Mexican border between San Diego and Tijuana, the daughter of Julius Rice, an educator, and his wife, whose artistic talent expressed itself in small oil paintings. After graduating from Berkeley, she returned to Southern California, preferring to develop a professional career in her hometown area where she had friends and family, rather than migrating to a city to join a large or prestigious architectural firm. She was lucky to find a mentor in Hazel Waterman, who had studied art at Berkeley in the 1880s, worked with the noted architect Irving Gill at the turn of the century, and then, at his urging, became an architect in her own right. Rice divided her days between caring for her invalid mother and working in Waterman's office on various architectural projects, such as the Wednesday Club of 1913 in San Diego. An avid student, she learned about the properties of reinforced concrete and became familiar with the geometric forms and plain wall surfaces that Waterman like Gill employed. Thus she added a knowledge of this innovative material as well as some understanding of a modern esthetic to an architectural vocabulary already informed by her Beaux-Arts studies and experience with the Bay Area wooden shingle style.

In 1915, the Panama Pacific Exposition celebrating the opening of the Panama Canal took place in San Diego. It was dominated by the exuberant Spanish baroque designs of Bertram Goodhue of New York. There is no evidence that Rice worked on the grandiose buildings themselves, but she could not have ignored their presence. During World War I, she supplemented her income by teaching architecture and mechanical drawing at local schools, including San Diego State Teachers College,

now California State University at San Diego. Meanwhile, she began working for the firm of Requa & Jackson, whose traditional approach to design was neither as flamboyant as Goodhue's nor as original as Gill's. With that firm, she was given her greatest opportunity: to plan and directly supervise the development of a 14-mile tract of land northeast of San Diego owned by the Santa Fe Railroad.

In 1906 the railroad had bought the land to cultivate eucalyptus trees for use as railroad ties. The experiment failed, but the area became a huge orchard of 3 million aromatic, leafy trees. In 1922, hoping to recoup some of its losses, Santa Fe officials decided to divide the land into "gentleman ranchos" and to plan a garden city-type community named Rancho Santa Fe. Lilian Rice was put in charge of the project and established her own office at Rancho Santa Fe. So successful were her efforts that 5 years later, over 80 percent of the land had been sold. Although the area was in the middle of nowhere, Rice carefully created a sense of urban space by clustering commercial, school, and residential areas along a wide main street with a central strip planted with green grass and flowers. Sidewalks, white-walled townhouses with entrance gates leading to gardens, and arcaded walks created a sophisticated ambiance. Besides being responsible for its overall plan, Rice designed many of the buildings in the town. For example, she created the Rancho Santa Fe Inn, the library, a school, and various stores. Using adobe wall construction reinforced with concrete lintels, she recalled the days of the Spanish Missions and created a visual harmony that remains striking today. As an independent architect, she also designed many residences there. The Fairchild House, for example, is a gracious arrangement of rooms surrounding a large patio.

Lilian Rice was able to realize her talent in many ways at Rancho Santa Fe. As she recalled, "Working out the architectural development of Rancho Santa Fe has been a task of tremendous personal interest and satisfaction. With the thought . . . that

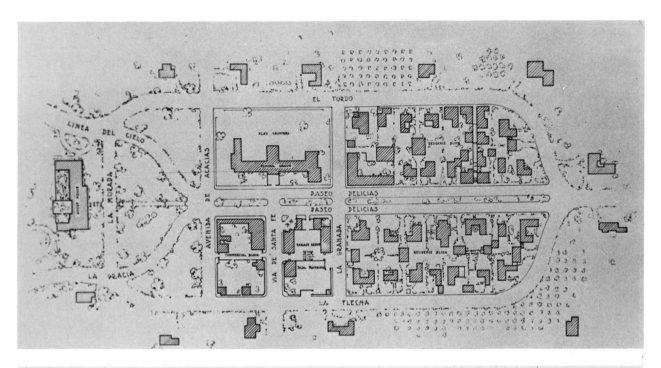

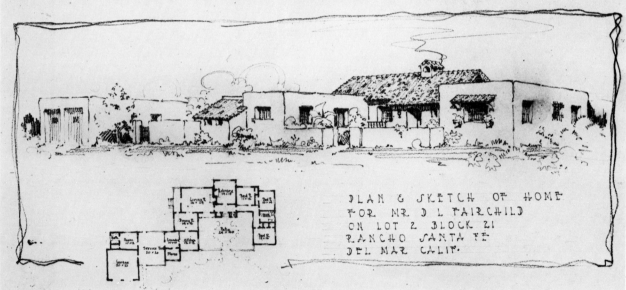

Above: *L. Rice, plan and sketch, D. L. Fairchild Home, Rancho Santa Fe. Courtesy San Diego Historical Society Library.*

Top: *L. Rice, plot plan of civic center, Rancho Santa Fe. Courtesy Rancho Santa Fe Association.*

L. Rice, Marguerite M. Robinson Residence, La Jolla, California. Courtesy San Diego Historical Society Library.

true beauty lies in simplicity rather than ornateness, I found real joy at Rancho Santa Fe. Every environment calls for simplicity and beauty. . . . No one with a sense of fitness . . . could violate these natural factors by creating anything that lacked simplicity in line and form and color.''[6]

She also worked in nearby towns. Some consider, for example, the Robinson House of 1929 in La Jolla the highpoint of her career. Built entirely of wood and stone, it perches on the top of a steep slope overlooking the Pacific at the end of a private lane that ensures a maximum of privacy. The flow of multileveled wood-paneled rooms creates a dusky, romantic feeling enhanced by its dramatic view. Inside and outside, intricate wood details catch light and shadow.

Rice also worked in the shingle style of the San Francisco Bay region. In 1932, she designed an exposed wood and beam clubhouse for the women's ZLAC Rowing Club.[7] Membership had grown so large that the headquarters was moved from San Diego to a site on Mission Bay, where Rice planned a simple wooden structure containing both a boathouse and quarters for members that is re-

miniscent of Julia Morgan's St. John's Presbyterian Church of 1917 in Berkeley. Typical of her sense of whimsy, Rice added a gate made of oars as an entrance to the club. (Because she was so active a member, a "Lilian Rice Trophy" was donated in her memory after her death in 1938.) In 1933, the San Diego chapter of the American Institute of Architects cited the clubhouse for an award of merit.

Rice was well known for her personal warmth, humor, and pleasant working relationships with clients. She followed the example of Hazel Waterman and Julia Morgan by employing young women recently graduated from architecture school in her office as well as men. She died at Rancho Santa Fe after a sudden operation. Sam Hamill, who worked as a junior draftsperson for her in the twenties, recalls, ''What I remember most . . . was the wholesome, sympathetic, and sensitive understanding she brought to student, employee, or client. Her residential designs . . . seemed to reflect the personality and life-style of the client. . . . As a result of this empathy between architect and client, I would venture that the summation of clients paralleled the equal summation of permanent friendships.''[7]

Left: *L. Rice, entrance gate made of oars, the women's ZLAC Rowing Club, Mission Bay, California, 1932. Courtesy San Diego Historical Society Library.*

Below: *L. Rice, interior, clubhouse for ZLAC Rowing Club. Courtesy San Diego Historical Society Library.*

Above: *Natalie de Blois. Photograph by William A. Niemic.*

Top: *SOM, Natalie de Blois, member of the design team, Pepsi-Cola Building (now owned by Olivetti), New York, 1959. The title "member of the design team" for de Blois is as provided by SOM. For all the buildings illustrated here de Blois exercised the function and responsibility of a senior designer. Photograph by Ezra Stoller © ESTO.*

Right: *SOM, N. de Blois, member of the design team, Union Carbide Building, New York, 1960. Photograph by Ezra Stoller © ESTO.*

Opposite page: *SOM, N. de Blois, member of the design team, Emhart Manufacturing Company (now owned by Connecticut General Life Insurance Co.), Bloomfield, Connecticut, 1962. Courtesy Emhart Corporation.*

Natalie de Blois
By Judith Paine

The Union Carbide Building, Pepsi-Cola, the Connecticut General Life Insurance Headquarters, Emhart Manufacturing Company, Boots Head Offices—the names themselves recall not only some of the most distinctive contributions made to modern architecture since World War II, but the firm responsible for them: Skidmore, Owings, & Merrill (SOM). Beginning in the early 1950s, such buildings earned SOM a reputation for tastefully innovative design, decisively disproving the myth that a large architectural office with a corporate clientele must be inherently conservative. Instead, by its sophisticated use of the steelframed glass curtain wall idiom, the firm became internationally famous for office buildings that were as esthetically elegant as they were commercially efficient. More than anyone else, SOM defined the style for corporate headquarters that was widely publicized but poorly imitated. Today it's as difficult to imagine an American city without its mediocre glass boxes as it is a major highway without the vista of McDonald's golden arches.

Yet how many people are aware that for 30 years a woman, Natalie de Blois, was responsible for much of that creative design for which the firm is noted? Or that right from the start she worked on the design team of SOM's chief stars—Louis Skidmore himself, William Brown, and most of all, Gordon Bunshaft? Nathaniel Owings, who founded the firm with Skidmore in 1936, was one person who recognized her real value, and in a remarkable passage from his autobiography, he describes how her anonymity was accepted. "The 'People' chart [of design associates] with seventy-five rings, included just one woman: Natalie de Blois. Long, lean, quizzical, she seemed fit to handle all comers. Handsome, her dark straight eyes invited no nonsense. *Her mind and hands worked marvels in design —and only she and God would ever know just how many great solutions, with the imprimatur of one of the male heroes of SOM, owed much more to her than was attributed by either SOM or the client*''[8] (italics added).

In several important ways, de Blois' career brings into sharp focus the handicaps women architects encounter in the profession. Her exceptional talent and determination matched that of her male associates, but certain crucial opportunities that would challenge her potential to its greatest expression were not available to her. Not that she didn't try. With a canny instinct for being in the right place at the right time, she joined SOM's fledgling New York office in 1944, the year she graduated from architectural school. After a few years, she won a Fulbright Fellowship to study at the École des Beaux-Arts in Paris. Returning to SOM after her study abroad, she worked directly with Gordon Bunshaft as a senior designer from the time she was 25. Wouldn't Bunshaft, 12 years her senior, have been a perfect mentor, grooming her for a partnership role at SOM that she was obviously qualified for? But this lone woman designer became no one's protegé. De Blois worked for over twenty years as a senior designer before SOM promoted her to the level of associate in the firm. She never became a partner, of whom there are now 26. And outside the professional architectural community, she is virtually unknown.

De Blois was born on April 2, 1921, the daughter of a civil engineer, who always encouraged her to study architecture. When the Depression upset her plans to attend the Massachusetts Institute of Technology, with its tradition of educating women architects, she applied for and won a scholarship to Columbia University's School of Architecture. In 1940, she was one of five women in the freshman class of eighteen; by 1944, her wartime graduating class of six students had twice as many women as men—all of whom have continued their design careers. After a brief stint as a draftsperson with the office of Ketchum, Gina, & Sharpe, she joined SOM to work on designing bathhouses at Jones Beach on Long Island.

SOM at that time was less than ten years old, with a reputation for competence rather than originality. Its distinction lay in its dedication to creating a large office organization with branches in several American cities that was as familiar with building investment and real estate values as it was with modern design technology. Such a departure from the usual small, highly individual architectural firms depended upon the anonymous input of specialized workers in various fields, which was then coordinated by higher-ups. This "plan-factory" approach to architecture encouraged the efficiency necessary to finish major projects on schedule, but discouraged personal recognition even among the most highly visible group, the designers themselves. Thus, as a result of SOM's failure to promote her to a more public position, as well as the assembly-line structure of the firm itself, de Blois' talents were so effectively blended into the whole that her work became nearly invisible.

But what work it was! She became basic design coordinator for the Terrace Plaza Hotel of 1948 in Cincinnati, working directly with Louis Skidmore and William Brown, and for Lever House of 1952 in New York, working with Gordon Bunshaft.[9] When she was 30, she, her husband, and child went to Paris for a year where she trained at the Atelier Mardeof, as a third-year architectural student at the École des Beaux-Arts. Since she was already in Europe, SOM asked her to become a senior designer on the important Consular-Amerikahaus program, which consisted of building consulates in several German cities under Bunshaft's supervision. De Blois continued to work as senior designer, or in SOM terminology "senior architect," with Bunshaft all the years she was associated with the New York office.

For each major project, SOM would assign a manager and a designer in charge, each of whom had a senior person working with him, who would in turn have many assistants, draftspersons, modelmakers, and so forth. As senior designer, de Blois was responsible for all phases of the job—programming, design, presentation, working drawings, and interior layout, as well as for dealing extensively with members of the structural and mechanical trades. She played an indispensable and crucial role on a variety of important projects. Among those she worked on, for example, was the spectacular Connecticut General Life Insurance Company Building in Bloomfield, Connecticut in 1957, which Henry-Russell Hitchcock, the noted historian, calls ". . . quite as significant as Lever House"[10]; the Pepsi-Cola Building of 1959 on Park Avenue in New York (now owned by Olivetti Corporation), an aluminum gem covering a reinforced concrete

Above: *SOM, N. de Blois, member of the design team, Boots Pure Drug Co., Nottingham, England, 1968. Photograph by Ezra Stoller © ESTO.*

Top: *SOM, N. de Blois, member of the design team, Connecticut Life Insurance Company, Bloomfield, Connecticut, 1957. Photograph by H. B. Farguhar.*

frame; the Union Carbide Building of 1960, the glass and steel skyscraper that straddles the underground New York Central railroad tracks; and the Emhart Manufacturing Company Building of 1962 also in Bloomfield, Connecticut, which was SOM's first big building of exposed, poured-in-place concrete, whose low horizontal spread was a radical departure from the shiny rectangular urban shafts.

De Blois continued working despite the arrival of three more children and an eventual divorce. In 1965, after 5 years of raising four boys single-handedly, she transferred to SOM's Chicago office so that the children could be near their father. She was finally made a design associate in the firm and worked first with Bruce Graham on the Boots Head Offices in Nottingham, England, in 1968 and the Equitable Life Insurance Building of 1960 in Chicago and later with Myron Goldsmith on Equibank in Pittsburgh completed in 1976.

By 1974, she had worked for SOM for 30 years as the senior designer on its most distinguished buildings. Although there were always women in the offices as draftspersons, landscape architects, and consultants, no other woman had worked in design at her level.

All during the fifties and sixties, when the "feminine mystique" was at high tide, de Blois never questioned her subordinate role on the design team. After all, she was already an anomaly by being a professional working mother. However, by the seventies, she had become increasingly aware of women's issues. Although she could easily have been a "token" woman, remaining aloof from feminist concerns, such an attitude would have been inconsistent with her open, questioning nature. She became an active member of the American Institute of Architects' Task Force on Women and helped write a landmark report detailing the prejudices faced by women architects. In 1974, she left SOM to spend a year writing and teaching. A year later she joined the Houston, Texas, firm of Neuhaus & Taylor as Senior Project Designer. After years of working in others' shadows, de Blois is finally in a position to claim her own work.

By Jane McGroarty and Susana Torre

8. New Professional Identities: Four Women in the Sixties

Certain periods, like the decade of the sixties, are pivotal in the history of a country. The combination of social, political, and cultural events directed against established institutions generated a consciousness of and a desire for change. Change was seen as a liberating force that could affect the whole of society as well as the individual. The four women discussed in this chapter—Denise Scott Brown, Chloethiel Woodard Smith, Mary Otis Stevens, Anne Griswold Tyng—cannot be considered products of the sixties in the sense that Joan Baez and Angela Davis were, but their work and ideas parallel some of the concerns that emerged during that decade.

Urban neighborhoods and new towns, the relationship between social change and design, the architecture and structure of collective form, the street and the strip, advocacy planning and architectural symbolism were dominant themes of this period. The work of these four women is very much a part of the ebullient discourse of these years. It is for this reason that we have chosen to discuss their work and ideas in conjunction with mainstream events, rather than through their personal careers as was done in preceding chapters. Other projects, also designed by women, are used to amplify particular themes, but the emphasis is placed on the segment of the four women's *oeuvre* that corresponds to this decade.

Chloethiel Woodard Smith was born in Peoria, Illinois, in 1910. She earned a Bachelor of Architecture from the University of Oregon in 1932 and a Master of Architecture in City Planning from Washington University in 1933. She has been a principal in several architectural firms since 1946, including Chloethiel Woodard Smith & Associated Architects founded in 1963. Smith has been responsible for a number of planning and urban design studies; among them the master plan for the Southwest Urban Renewal Area and Waterfront in Washington, D.C.; the plan for the new town, Marshall Hall, in Charles County, Maryland; and the plan for Intown, in central Rochester, New York. Smith has also designed many multifamily housing complexes, both urban and suburban, including La Clede Town in St. Louis, Missouri; the Waterview townhouses in Reston, Virginia; and Harbour Square in Washington, D.C. Smith became a member of the American Institute of Architects in 1946 and was elected to the College of Fellows of the American Institute of Architects in 1960.

Mary Otis Stevens was born in New York City in 1928. She received a Bachelor of Philosophy from Smith College in 1949. Her 1956 M.Arch. thesis at MIT was an urban study of Boston's waterfront, a project that replaced her initial thesis proposal for the design of a prison. Upon graduation, she worked at The Architects Collaborative for a few months, later joining an office of young architects founded by Thomas McNulty, whom she married in 1958. With McNulty she has designed a number of projects since then, including the Gallatin House in Kittery Point, Maine, in 1958, a proposed chapel for the Boston Archdiocese of 1958, and their own house in Lincoln, Massachusetts, of 1964–1965. They spent part of 1961 and 1962 in Ravello, southern Italy, working on their book, World of Variation, *which was published in 1969. After joining the New City project group of the Cambridge Institute, Otis Stevens continued to collaborate with Thomas McNulty in a series of studies and proposals for Boston inner-city neighborhoods, housing in Boston's South End, and Massachusetts prisons. The last study resulted in the creation of a Pre-release Center on the grounds of Boston State Hospital in 1972. In 1968 she designed a 100-foot long light mural for the architectural Triennale Exhibit in Milan, which was visually evocative of ideas developed with McNulty on urban movements and city rhythms. In 1969 she founded i press and published a book series on the human environment. As an author and critic, her articles have been published in* Espaces and Societies *and* Architecture Plus, *among other magazines. She has taught at the Boston Architectural Center since 1973, and founded the Design Guild in 1974, an office of architects and builders working in Boston's South and East areas. Her most recent project, sponsored by the National Endowment for the Arts, is a major historical survey of urban American settlements and their vernacular tradition.*

Anne Griswold Tyng was born in 1920 in Kuling Kiangsi, China, to American missionary parents. She received an A.B. degree from Radcliffe College in 1942. During her last two years at Radcliffe she studied design at the Smith College Graduate School of Architecture and Landscape Architecture, formerly the Cambridge School. Tyng then enrolled in Harvard's Graduate School of Design and received a Master of Architecture in 1944. In 1945 she entered the firm of Stonorov & Kahn (later the office of Louis I. Kahn) in Philadelphia where she remained until 1973. In the early fifties Tyng was an active member of a young planners and architects group in Philadelphia. She served as a consultant architect to the Philadelphia City Planning Commission and the Philadelphia Redevelopment Authority during that time. In Kahn's office she participated in a number of projects, including the Mill Creek Redevelopment Plan, the Erdman Dormitory at Bryn Mawr, the Trenton Community Bath Houses, and the Yale University Art Gallery. She collaborated with Kahn on the proposed City Tower, exhibited at The Museum of Modern Art in 1960. She has also been responsible for several projects of her own. In 1969 Tyng published "Geometric Extensions of Consciousness" in Zodiac 19. *Her doctoral thesis, "Simultaneous Randomness and Order: the Fibonacci-Divine Proportion as a Universal Forming Principle," was completed in 1975. She has been a lecturer at the Department of Architecture at the University of Pennsylvania since 1968 as well as a visiting critic and lecturer at many architectural schools in the U.S. and abroad. She became a member of the American Institute of Architects in 1949 and was elected to the College of Fellows of the American Institute of Architects in 1975.*

Denise Scott Brown was born in 'Nkane (now Kitwe), North Rhodesia (now Zambia), in 1931. She received an A.A. Diploma and a Certificate in Tropical Architecture from the Architectural Association in London in 1955. Having come to the United States for graduate study, she earned a Master of City Planning and a Master of Architecture from the University of Pennsylvania in 1960 and 1965 respectively. She joined the faculty of the School of Fine Arts at Penn in 1960 and remained there as an assistant professor until 1965. From 1965 to 1968 Scott Brown was an associate professor in the School of Architecture and Urban Planning at the University of California at Los Angeles and taught as a visiting professor at the School of Environmental Design, University of California at Berkeley. In 1967 Denise Scott Brown married Robert Venturi, a Philadelphia architect. She was a visiting professor in Urban Design at Yale University until 1970 as well as a visiting critic at several other architectural schools. In 1972 Scott Brown was offered the deanship of the School of Art and Architecture at Yale University, a position that she declined in order to continue her work and practice with the firm of Venturi & Rauch where she is a partner. Denise Scott Brown has authored numerous articles alone and in collaboration with Robert Venturi. Their major collaborative work, Learning from Las Vegas, *written with Steven Izenour, was published in 1972 by MIT Press. Scott Brown and Venturi together have developed a theoretical position toward design and planning that is presented in their writings, teaching, and design work. Scott Brown has been responsible for many projects in the firm of Venturi & Rauch, including the Philadelphia Crosstown Community (South Street) in 1968, the plan and urban design for California City of 1970, and the planning survey and recommendations for the Schuylkill River Corridor of 1974. Scott Brown is an associate of the Royal Institute of British Architects.*

Public, Private, and the Crisis of Architecture

The existing institutions were perceived by the young as inimical to the free, public expression of individuals and by minorities as inimical to their rights and social revindications. The sixties was a time when the concepts of public place and private realm were challenged and redefined. The public sphere is traditionally controlled both ideologically and physically by institutions that are presumed to act *pro bono publico*. During this period attempts to reoccupy the public sphere and return it "to the people" had an unprecedented and widespread upsurge. Protesters appropriated the streets of Chicago during the 1968 Democratic Convention and turned the "public" political arena of the convention hall into a besieged private place. In the same year the Poor People's Campaign marched to Washington, D.C., and built Resurrection City on public grounds, thereby moving the political forum out of the halls of Congress where "private" interests were served. Conversely, the private single family suburban home and the nuclear family became the symbol to many young people of narrow and oppressive values.

A great deal of internal and external pressure was applied to architecture as the discipline responsible for the form and spatial organization of the public and private domains. The crisis of architecture, however, has its roots in the legacy of the previous decade. Two pieces of legislation after World War II, the Housing Act of 1949 and the Highway Trust Act of 1956, had an overwhelming impact on the American landscape. Spurred by the efforts of early reformers in the prewar housing movement, Congress promised in 1949 a "decent house and suitable living environment for every American family."[1] The Title I section of the law allowed for the exercise of eminent domain by the state; that is, the state could appropriate private property for public *benefit*. Local governments were delegated responsibility for slum clearance, relocation of dwellers, planning, and rebuilding. The Highway Trust Act, billed as a "necessary defense measure"[2] and a needed boost to the economy, provided a 90 percent federal subsidy to state and local governments to build an interstate highway system.

Anxious to receive this generous infusion of funds, cities began ripping apart urban areas for road construction. In the name of "public benefit," hundreds of thousands of urban poor were displaced from their homes and frequently relocated to worse slums. Once their empty dwellings had been razed, the land was turned over to private developers who built housing, occasionally with architectural merit, for the middle and upper classes.[3]

Throughout the sixties tenants' unions, neighborhood organizations, and advocacy planners organized to fight the legacy of the fifties by challenging the political and social institutions that directed slum clearance, urban renewal, and highway construction. Many groups enmeshed themselves in the bureaucratic process to legally block repugnant schemes.[4] The Committee to Save the West Village, organized by Jane Jacobs in the early sixties, successfully blocked an urban renewal proposal for New York's Greenwich Village.[5] Militant groups organized rent strikes and squatter takeovers. In Boston tenants threatened with relocation were aided by MIT architecture students when they occupied a parking lot in an urban renewal area where they built "Tent City." The squatters' action brought the relocation to a halt, and a neighborhood committee was elected to oversee the urban renewal plan.[6]

Low-Rise, Low-Density Housing

The inequities of urban renewal and the failure of the tower-in-the-park model provoked many within the architectural profession to reevaluate social goals as well as formal solutions. There were a few examples of urban renewal projects that were considered substantial improvements. These projects' familiar low scale, intimate open space, and clustered layout were clearly influenced by similar features in American "new towns" of the fifties and early sixties. Both differ from the suburban model in that their initial plan provides a town center, designed to imply a sense of a communal place.

La Clede Town, a racially and economically integrated community on a 30-acre site, is one such project. This 680-unit "town" of two and three story wood frame houses in St. Louis, Missouri, was designed by Chloethiel Woodard Smith & Associates. In an article on new towns of 1966, Smith identifies a major problem in designing instant settlements: "They [architects] need to find out how to design and build hundreds and hundreds of structures at one time and come out with more than just a town that is new. . . . For it is the architect who must create the place man seeks."[7]

The Federal Housing Administration (FHA) initially objected to her design for La Clede Town on the basis that the proposal was too much like what had been torn down. Their assessment was not altogether mistaken. "I think of re-olding, not re-newing" stated Jerome Berger, the president of the La Clede Town Company.[8] The architect succeeded in pleasing the client not only by creating a Main Street look-alike, but also by giving careful consideration to the design of public and commercial space where organized and spontaneous interaction could take place. The popularity of La Clede Town has been attributed to the inclusion of a remarkable number of commercial and community facilities, which in 1968 included an English-style pub, deli, laundromats, hairdresser, clothing store, dry cleaner, art gallery, pool, take-out food facility, newspaper office, coffeehouse, saloon, church, and school.[9] A generous amount of open space, walkways, courtyards, play areas may have made it an attractive community for families with children.

La Clede Town has been the object of a polemical debate over its architectural symbology. Some critics saw this project as the banal embodiment of a *kitsch* sensibility, while others praised it for being "a backdrop where a reasonably satisfying life can go on."[10] In *New Directions in American Architecture* Robert Stern takes sides with the former view, characterizing Chloethiel Smith's architecture as "wildly eclec-

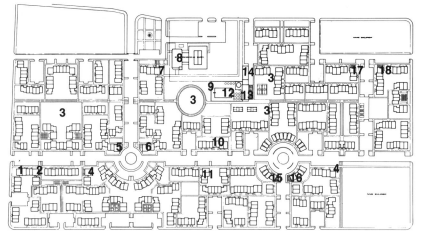

Above: *C. W. Smith & Associated Architects, site plan of La Clede Town, St. Louis, Missouri, 1967. Courtesy C. W. Smith & Associated Architects. (1) office; (2) delicatessen; (3) play areas; (4) laundromats; (5) pub; (6) take-out food shop; (7) dry cleaner; (8) church; (9) park; (10) newspaper office; (11) art galleries; (12) wading and swimming pools; (13) bath house; (14) maintenance; (15) school; (16) confectionery; (17) hairdresser; (18) ladies clothing.*

Top: *C. W. Smith & Associated Architects, English-style pub, La Clede Town, St. Louis, Missouri, 1967. Photograph by Larry Block.*

tic and often overly cute,"[11] but he is compelled to commend the appropriateness of scale and urban design in her projects. Smith's office has also been responsible for a large number of urban renewal and other new town residential communities, such as the Capital Park Apartments and the Harbour Square townhouses in the Southwest Urban Renewal area of Washington, D.C.

A clue to Smith's attitude toward architecture may be found in the emphasis given to process and building in her firm's public relations brochure.[12] Unlike most firms' promotional material, the finished product is shown as a result of decisions and compromises between client and architect at each stage of development.

Another urban renewal project reportedly as successful as Smith's La Clede Town is the Acorn Project in Oakland, California, designed by Burger & Coplans, an architectural firm in which Patricia Avril Coplans is a partner. The development achieves an urban density of 28 units to the acre while having three-quarters of the dwellings open directly on private open space at grade. Acorn's site plan separates vehicular and pedestrian movement, and the larger public spaces emphasize vistas focusing on the community buildings that are very different in form and scale from the housing. In contrast with La Clede Town, the design makes allusion to the clean, sparse vocabulary of the early Modern Movement.[13]

Social Change and Utopian Cities

Outside the planning and research agencies other models of settlement were explored and at times implemented. These models were utopian blueprints for the establishment of a new social order. They found their precedent and inspiration in a plurality of sources, ranging from Buckminster Fuller to Che Guevara, and from Fourier and the garden cities movement to the American utopian socialists.

The New City and Drop City are opposite interpretations of the sixties' ideal of communal life. The New City project was initiated by fellows and members of the Cambridge Institute in 1969 and involved several dozen participants over a period of 3 years.[14] Mary Otis Stevens, a member of the group, later summarized the group's political process, idealistic intentions, and final outcome of the project: "alternatives cannot be a substitute for reality."[15] The envisioned model community was based on cooperative ownership of property, a nonhierarchical political order, decentralized institutions, and planning by its own citizens. It was expected to draw an eventual population of 100,000 over a 10- to 20-year period, a population target deemed necessary to "achieve a cultural diversity and richness that would be truly urban in character."[16]

Otis Stevens surveyed a series of sites for the establishment of the New City, which was envisioned as having a distinct physical identity and as being beyond commuting distance from Boston. Suitable sites could only be found in economically depressed areas, where industrial and farming opportunities were closing down and job opportunities were diminishing. Fear of the technocracy by experts and consultants within and without the group, an ignorance and ultimate lack of concern with the prospects that the New City could offer to a blue-collar constituency, and the lack of a realistic strategy to raise funds and to create an economic self-sufficiency were some of the practical and pivotal issues to be solved before the project's actual implementation.[17] It was in the face of these issues that the internal contradictions and idealistic ideology of the group's planning process resulted in a series of crises and the eventual demise of the New City project. In her evaluation of this process Mary Otis Stevens writes: "These models outside our society were provoking reappraisal of tactics and long-term objectives, specifically how to relate actions taken by a few to the concerns of many."[18]

Otis Stevens' participation in the New City was a natural extension of projects and ideas elaborated in *World of Variation*, a book she wrote in collaboration with Thomas McNulty.[19] These projects were designed in re-

Above: *C. W. Smith & Associated Architects, model, Harbour Square, Southwest Urban Renewal Area, Washington, D.C., 1966. Photograph by Ezra Stoller © ESTO.*

Top: *C. W. Smith & Associated Architects, La Clede Town townhouses, St. Louis, Missouri, 1967. Photograph by Larry Block.*

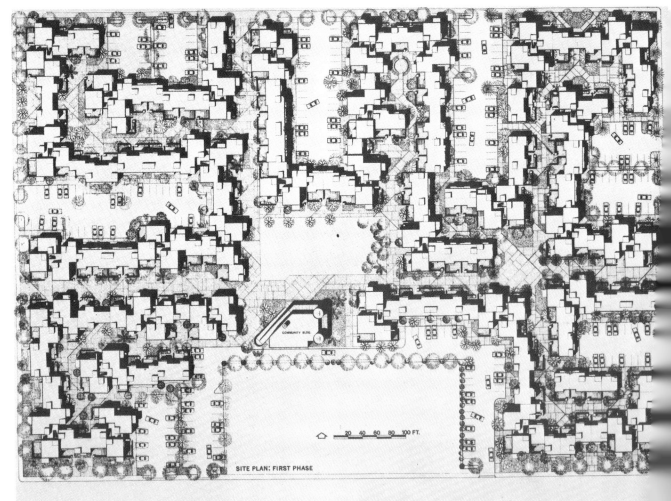

COMMUNITY BLDG.

20 40 60 80 100 FT.

SITE PLAN: FIRST PHASE

sponse to the urban crisis in American cities. Urban renewal, in her view, erased evidences of the cultural past of cities, while propagating forms associated with values and social uses no longer considered relevant. She considered the problem of historical continuity reflected in the built environment as crucial for the rest of the century, especially for the Third World countries, and suggested that a distinction be made between building for ongoing requirements and for temporary demands of a society. This would ensure the proper connection between past and future in countries creating their own cultural and economic identity through revolutionary change.[20] The following two projects were the design formulation of these ideas.

The Forum was intended to be for American cities while the Linear Society corresponded to the industrial and urban demands of developing countries. The American Forum project is conceptually related to the idea of public interaction as a democratic procedure and to the idea of "free" space in a city, differentiated in both setting and formal character from its surroundings. The visual image for the Forum was intended as an analogy of the earth; the ground level is a garden with openings letting the sunlight into the "darker and more intricate" spaces in the levels below. The lower levels were planned for public use, with facilities such as reading rooms, exhibition galleries, theaters, concert and lecture halls, music and practice rooms, studios for work in the arts and crafts, and other unspecified activity and retreat spaces. Facilities for large gatherings would be located around the circumference, leaving the center for individual activities that she sees as the main focus of the Forum. The Forum would play a dominant urban role, not by its size or monumentality, but through its social significance. The "building" would occupy excavated space, returning the surface to nature.[21]

The principles of the Forum are also reflected in another project, which makes use of the street as a "belt of civic activities."[22] The circular configuration is retained, but whereas the Forum was physically

and culturally a center, the raised street circumscribed and framed the urban fabric below. The circular belt was thought to symbolize and introduce a communal scale into the aggregate environment of the city and to function as a visual and social unifier of the disparate urban landscape. From the vantage points provided, historical monuments and anonymous street scenes could be viewed. The belt's dimensions would change in accordance with the context, widening to feature views along a waterfront or contracting to provide pedestrian and vehicular accesses to shopping centers in a commercial district. The function of the belt was one of leisure for an industrial society, including activities that would contrast with the work and home environments.[23]

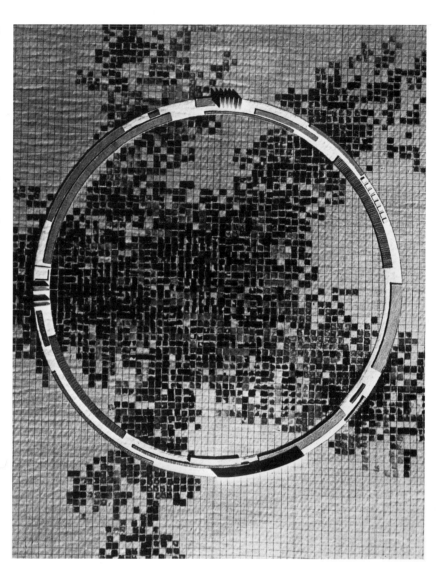

Mary Otis Stevens and Thomas McNulty, diagram for belt of civic activities, 1962–1963. Courtesy M. O. Stevens.

Opposite page: *Burger & Coplans Inc., Patricia Coplans, partner, townhouses and site plan, Acorn Project, Oakland, California, 1968–1970. Courtesy Burger & Coplans Inc.*

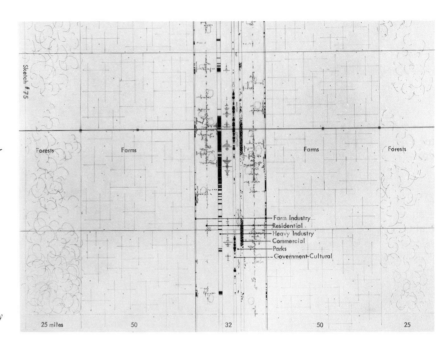

*M. O. Stevens and T. McNulty, plan of
the Linear Society, 1962–1963. Courtesy
M. O. Stevens.*

The Linear Society project is based on the concept of "growth lines,"[24] transportation routes as well as housing and industry belts articulating changes of activity, scale, and topography and connecting dispersed populations and settlements. In the prototypical plan, the functions of government, education, commerce, and industry are subdivided into parallel growth lines. Parks and different types of residential developments are the interim strips between these major lines. High-rise, high-density housing is located between the industry and government/cultural belts, while low-rise, low-density housing and isolated dwellings are related respectively to commercial and light industry and to farming and forest tracts. The total cross section of this prototype was 200 miles, but the width of each belt would vary according to particular topologies, population size, and social and industrial resources.[25] In a further elaboration of this plan the growth lines are interrupted by circular spaces that are concentrations of governmental, educational, and cultural installations visually distinguishable from their understated surroundings.[26]

The Linear Society prototype is strongly influenced by N. A. Miliutin's scheme for Magnitogorsk of the 1920s[27] and by Le Corbusier's later elaboration of Miliutin's idea, the Cité Lineare Industrielle of

1942–1943.[28] The Linear Society differs from these sources in two important aspects. While in Miliutin's city the housing is placed in the central belt and separated from the outer agricultural and industrial activities by a park belt, the Linear Society prototype places the governmental/cultural/educational functions in the central belt and the housing adjacent to the industry, commerce, and agriculture. Corbusier's linear plan assumes the existence of governmental and commercial exchange functions in radio-concentric cities linked by the linear industrial cities; conversely, the Linear Society prototype proposes a decentralization of the government functions located in a belt parallel to the productive functions at neighborhood-like intervals. Although inspired by the needs of developing countries, the Linear Society project assumes an ideal industrialized economy, the achievement of a "high level of technical inventiveness,"[29] and a socialist political structure. In this sense, the proposal does not take into account the limited resources, economic dependency, low level of industrialization and education that characterize the actual conditions of the Third World.

Otis Stevens' work in the seventies indicates a reevaluation of the more idealistic approach to design shared with the New City group. Her proposals for communal use of residual spaces in Boston's inner city and for the rehabilitation of local prisons, presented with Thomas McNulty between 1969 and 1971, took into account the political compromises implicit in the social decision-making process. The construction and furnishing of a Pre-Release Center on the grounds of Boston State Hospital were carried out using the prison industries as resources. The inmates' acquisition of construction skills was seen as a positive step toward eventual economic opportunities after their release.[30]

In 1976 Otis Stevens founded the Design Guild, a group of architect-builders working in the Boston area. The guild's most recent project is a proposal for a "Rachel Carson Center," an ecological and alternative energy research and museum facility for one of Boston's harbor islands. The relationship of the cities to their natural surroundings and resources, specifically in the case of Boston's waterfront, had been the theme of Otis Stevens' master of architecture thesis 20 years earlier.[31]

Dome Communes and Collective Form

Although large-scale endeavors proposing a radically new social structure failed to materialize, less ambitious communal goals, of the young in particular, provoked a multitude of experiments and a proliferation of rural and urban communes. The geodesic dome was the ubiquitous and infectious form preferred by the majority of these communal dwellers. The domes were widely used not only because they were cheap and relatively easy to erect or because their sophisticated yet elemental technology appealed to the American "do-it-yourself" spirit, but, above all, because their circular enclosure itself became the symbol of the "new cosmic consciousness."[32] The undisputed source of inspiration was Buckminster Fuller. His discovery of geodesic geometry in the 1940s demonstrated the structural irrationality and instability of the cube, spurring a wave of structural experimentation in architecture and of studies in

geometry as a method for organizing space. Using Fuller as a point of departure, Anne Griswold Tyng developed a theory of space based on geometry as an extension of human consciousness.[33] Her work includes abstract studies as well as actual construction.

One of her early projects, an addition to a farmhouse for her parents designed in 1953, uses an octahedron-tetrahedron truss influenced by Fuller's "octect" truss. However, this is possibly the first time that living space is within the truss itself. Tyng extends the truss to form dormer windows, sunshades, and trellises asymmetrically placed, which are reminiscent of the existing house and local barns.[34] Her geometric investigations have resulted in innovative and complex structural systems, as in her proposed Fair Building of 1963, where the tent forms of the pavilions are based on the tetrakaidecahedron (with eight hexagonal and six square faces). This system afforded a homogeneous partitioning of equal cells with a considerable economy of surface in relation to volume.[35]

Her proposed dormitory for Bryn Mawr College also of 1963 is conceived as a molecular plan of squares and octagons. The floor plan alternates on each level. The vertical shift from square to octagon is accomplished by a tetrahedron capital on the columns. This project shows a remarkable synthesis of structural complexity and functional requirements. The octagon-shaped dormitory rooms were dimensioned by bed lengths and door and window sizes; the square spaces are used for closets and utilities. The large communal spaces are formed by the corbeling of three levels of the octagon-square units.[36] This hierarchical ordering of spaces is an elaboration of Louis Kahn's ideas.

The small third story addition to her own townhouse, designed in 1967, is an ingenious structural solution to the tight constraints of the local building code. The additional height and increased volume of the space were achieved by using square box beams that rest on beams at the maximum height permitted.[37] The third story is camouflaged as a mansard roof—a plausible if unlikely

"hat" for this house.

This formal understatement is characteristic of Tyng's work. aas a designer she has successfully avoided an indulgence in structural expressionism. Tyng's work in architecture has been guided by her theories on the structuring of space rather than by an interest in structural technology. She has devised a conceptual model for the human consciousness of space. Spatial awareness, according to Tyng, occurs as "a repeating cycle in which man's perception and understanding have been stretched asymmetrically in different shapes of tension between the individual and the collective and between consciousness and unconsciousness."[38]

The cycle begins with the perception of "axial or bilateral space" related to the symmetry of the human body. It then proceeds to an awareness of "rotational space," which is that space around the rotating human body. The succeeding notion of "helical space" implies a recognition of the vertical dimension, not only in a physical, but also in a metaphysical sense, as a tension between past and future and the conscious and unconscious mind. Finally, the idea of "spiral space" may have occurred to humans by observing the hierarchical organization of social life.[39] Tyng differentiates between the awareness of space and the design of spatial form, identifying geometry as the instrument used by humans to consciously organize space.[40] But it is proportion, specifically the Divine Proportion, that provides an objective basis for design as "a fundamental subdivision of space."[41]

The design of collective form—Tyng's major focus—cannot be achieved by the mere summation of a single module, because the resulting aggregate structure would fail to reflect the true complexity of the whole. Thus collective form must be hierarchical, a term used by Tyng in the scientific sense.[42] She has explored the implementation of hierarchical principles in architectural scale and complexity in her proposal for an urban hierarchy of 1967 as well as in the earlier City Tower proposal done in collaboration with Louis Kahn. In the tower, the form of the building is

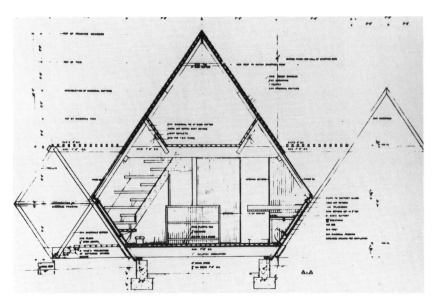

A. Tyng, synchronistic diagram. Courtesy A. Tyng. This diagram illustrates (counterclockwise from top left) the cycle from the geometry of inorganic evolution to the geometry of biological-organic evolution ("geometry of consciousness") to the visual-perceptual evolution and the discovery of archetypal space ("consciousness of geometry") to the pscyhic-conceptual evolution and the creative use of geometric-forming principles ("consciousness of creativity") leading to the creation of living geometric form.

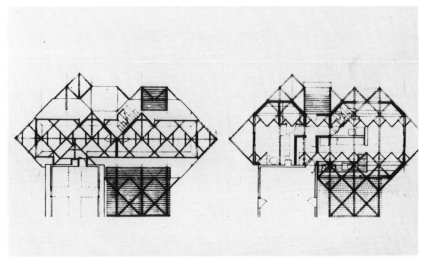

Anne Griswold Tyng, section and plan, farmhouse addition for Reverend and Mrs. Walworth Tyng, Cambridge, Maryland, 1953. Courtesy A. Tyng.

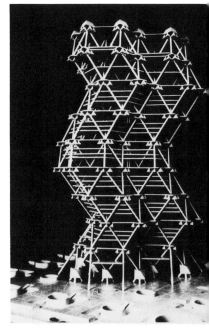

Above: *A. Tyng and Louis Kahn, proposed city tower, 1952–1957. Courtesy A. Tyng.*

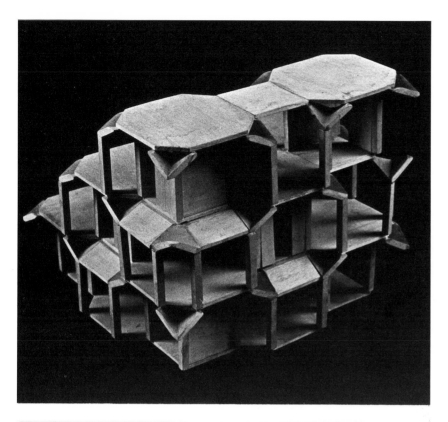

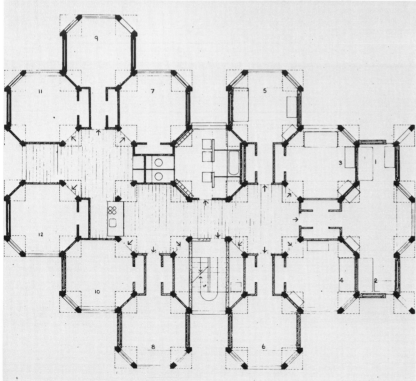

*A. Tyng, model and typical floor plan,
proposed college dormitory, 1963. Courtesy A. Tyng.*

perceived *both* as a whole and in increments due to a shift every six floors.[43] According to Tyng, the hierarchical principles of collective form can provide for degrees of "randomness and order" and for a reaffirmation of individual creativity and expression within the collective order.[44]

Anne Tyng's theoretical work, in correlating data from perceptual psychology, molecular biology, physics, philosophy, and other disciplines to understand form making in architecture, differentiates her concern with collective form from the concern with additive modular aggregation seen in the work of the Metabolists and other designers of megastructures.[45]

The Street as a Place of Social Interaction

The social and political momentum reached by the tension between public and private in the mid-sixties is echoed in the attention paid to new cities and the urban street by individual architects and planning agencies alike.

The street, being historically the communal place—the place "where the action is," to use a sixties' expression—became the focus of a wide variety of projects and architectural intentions, illustrated here by Mary Hommann's Caravan Plan for midtown Manhattan of 1965–1969, Mary Otis Stevens and Thomas McNulty's Living Environment in Lincoln, Massachusetts, of 1968, and Denise Scott Brown's projects with the firm of Venturi and Rauch for South Street of 1968 and the Bicentennial International Exposition Proposal of 1972, both in Philadelphia.

Mary Hommann's Caravan Plan was considered representative of a planning trend "to convert existing city streets for greater use by people and for more effective public transit."[46] Cars are eliminated and the street's right-of-way is reduced to a service corridor for cabs and emergency vehicles, while silent, electric transit "caravans" move along a fixed rail separating the wide pedestrian plaza on one side and the service corridor on the other. The proposal included cross-avenue buildings to create visual enclosures for the extended sidewalk, reserved for strolling, observing, and eating at sidewalk cafes. This redistribution of street uses and traffic priorities would result in the allotment of over 50 percent of the street surface for pedestrian-related uses and amenities,[47] reminiscent of European cities' promenades and the pedestrian use of their historic centers.

The Street as Living Environment

The residential environment in Lincoln, a suburb of Boston, built in 1968 by Mary Otis Stevens and Thomas McNulty, uses the street as a metaphor to the extent that they see architecture as "being essentially the design of human movement."[48] This idea bears some resemblance to the Corbusian principle of organizing spaces strung along a route, as in the Carpenter Center in Cambridge, Massachusetts. In the Lincoln house "the permanent and temporary living patterns"[49] branch off a stream of circulation where the curved walls function to close up sight lines or open up vistas as a person moves through the space. The house was designed as a supportive space for fluid and unconventional relationships between family members, closer in character to those between individuals in a communal situation than to the hierarchies and functional segregation of the traditional nuclear family. The house's open-ended, streetlike spatial organization is counterpointed by the sculptural, "basement construction" concrete walls, signifying the contrast between the changing flux of human requirements and the permanence of architectural forms and materials.[50]

Mary Hommann, Caravan Plan for midtown Manhattan, 1965–1969. Drawing by J. Parsons. Courtesy M. Hommann.

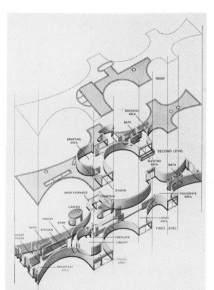

M. O. Stevens and T. McNulty, axonometric drawing, house at Lincoln, Massachusetts, 1964–1965. Courtesy M. O. Stevens.

Opposite page: *A. Tyng, Tyng townhouse addition, Philadelphia, Pennsylvania, 1967. Courtesy A. Tyng.*

Below: *M. O. Stevens and T. McNulty, exterior view, house at Lincoln, Massachusetts, 1964–1965. Courtesy M. O. Stevens.*

The Strip: Where
Social Concern Meets
the Architectural Symbol

The street was viewed in the sixties not only as the civic *res publica* for mass civil rights marches and for people strolling arm in arm or sipping espresso in sidewalk cafes, but also as the domain of the car. A visual romance with the highway—with the expansive movement that need not lead anywhere, or need not imply the commuting distance between domestic bliss and corporate servitude—was very much a part of the pop sensibility of the sixties.

The highway and the strip became the glorified habitat of "easy-riders" and "kandy-kolored-tangerine-flake-streamlined-babies."[51] A mental landscape dotted by soft melting objects, billboard sign imagery, comic strips, and Campbell soup cans is desiccated and frozen in the visual images of this period, as the pop artists and writers hold their ironic mirror to the face of American society. For some, these images were the material evidence of the American wasteland,[52] but others recognized in their "messy vitality"[53] the actual rather than imagined context within which most Americans dwell both in body and in spirit.

Denise Scott Brown, Robert Venturi, and their associates were among those steered to the *kitsch* of American cities and the commercial strip by the pop artists. Beginning in 1967 with her tenure as a professor at the University of California at Los Angeles and culminating in "Signs of Life: Symbols in the American City," a bicentennial exhibit at the Renwick Gallery in Washington, D.C.,[54] the *strip* and its private counterpart, Levittown, have been identified by Scott Brown not only as legitimate sources for architectural form making but also as the social context that architects should be concerned with today. "If the strip is not 'beautiful' in the accepted sense," she has written, "it is certainly vital, an organized chaos perhaps, and probably more fun to be in than some carefully designed urban plazas that no one visits. Artists may love the strip and preservationists may loathe it, but urban

planners and designers have to understand how the strip works if they are to make sensible prescriptions for suburbia."[55]

Other architects such as Kahn, Smithson, and Moore became interested in the public qualities of the California freeways as well as Disneyland during the mid-sixties, but Scott Brown was suspicious of their vision of the freeway *as monument,* indicating in a review article in 1967 that "the freeways should be *a framework* for a new monumentality, hopefully to be found in communal buildings and spaces and streets held in its web"[56] (italics added). The notion of *context as a framework* rather than as a wholly designed artifact appears consistently in the work of the Venturi & Rauch firm (where Scott Brown is a partner).

Denise Scott Brown, with Robert Venturi and others, offered a series of design studios at Yale between 1967 and 1970 where they encouraged students to see context as a framework and not to "try to make architecture"[57] (architecture almost becoming synonymous with "white-ish walls" in Venturi's reference). The programs for these studios written by Scott Brown included the analyses and design of a commercial strip, a subway station in New York, and a suburban Levittown development.[58] Documentation on the subway ("the people's freeway") studio stressed the design treatment of the program as a "three-communication system: direction, safety, and persuasion,"[59] as well as the importance of popular symbols, classified as *physignomic* (the hamburger-shaped hamburger stand), *locational* (the "corner store"), and *heraldic* (billboards, traffic signs).[60]

Scott Brown's remark—"Life is too complex for a one-medium approach to architecture"[61]—epitomizes the approach she took in the organization of this and other studios. In addition, the unorthodox nature of the problem given and the introducion of methods used in urban design and city planning, as well as emphasis on research and group work, represented a considerable departure from the traditional architectural studio. The research work in-

itiated in the studio on the commercial strip led eventually to the publication of *Learning from Las Vegas: A Significance for A & P Parking Lots,* authored by Robert Venturi, Denise Scott Brown, and Stephen Izenour.[62] The ideas discussed in this well-known book were judged controversial because of their indictment of accepted design doctrine and what was deemed an unwarrantable celebration of the prosaic. "Ugly and ordinary" were, in fact, the terms used by Scott Brown and Venturi to characterize their own projects, thereby inviting a polemic on the formal validity of the commercial vernacular.

However when one considers the entire scope of her work, Scott Brown can be regarded as a social advocate as well as a formal iconoclast. The South Street Project of 1968, which she directed, mandated considerable political involvement, since the architects were hired as advocates for particular constituency. The client—citizens' committee intent on preventing the construction of an expressway through their neighborhood—had succeeded in bringing the project to halt by picketing city hall. The final segment of the proposed expressway, if built, would have cut through Philadelphia's inner-city black community, replacing its existing main street, South Street. This expressway, like similar urban highways, was initiated in the early fifties and designed to form a ring around the central business district. When the government fear of political urban unrest had subsided, the Chamber of Commerce began to lobby for completion of the expressway. The citizens' committee hired Venturi & Rauch to present their case to the government and public at large.

Scott Brown's plan proposed a radical alternative: the community would control local planning and receive income and profits from any land development. The plan called for the refurbishing of South Street as a commercial "strip center," the rehabilitation of existing buildings for low-income ownership and rental housing and the improvement of streets, sidewalks, and parking.[63] Consistent with the position stated in *Learning from Las Vegas,* Scott Brown's only

ormal concession was applied ar-
hitectural symbolism and the use of
igns. With a modest expenditure
hese elements would give a distinct
lentity to the place, not unlike that
reated by street fair installations. Be-
ore the final defeat of the express-
vay, the Chamber of Commerce and
he State Highway Department made
counterproposal that included all the
acilities in Scott Brown's plan but set
hem on a megastructural cover over
he highway. When Scott Brown
keptically observed that this would
ever be built, and if built, would not
e for the poor residents of South
treet, the reply from a "self-styled
ity father" (whom she is fond of
uoting) was: "Where is your faith in
merica, Mrs. Venturi? Philadel-
hia will do it! Remember the
lauhaus!"[64]

The ideas and themes in Scott
lrown's proposal for South Street
vere later developed and continued in
hree other Venturi & Rauch projects,
vith her participation. However, in
hese projects—California City Signs
f 1970, the International Exposition
or the Bicentennial, and the Benja-
nin Franklin Parkway Celebration for
976, both in Philadelphia and both
esigned in 1972—the advocate func-
on, not being required by the cir-
umstances, is replaced by an em-
hasis on the formal and architec-
onic value of signs and on the
street/strip" notion as a place with a
ariety of cultural and commercial
unctions. In the California City pro-
ct Scott Brown's plan accepted as a
iven the existing land subdivision of
he 100,000-acre development in the
Mojave Desert. A reassessment of
he road system was accompanied by
cological recommendations and the
esign of image-making elements.

The "theme-image-role-playing"
otif of California City's signs had
een previously discerned by Venturi
c Rauch as one of the main attrac-
ons in the Las Vegas strip; in this
roject the signs were proposed to
ighlight the driving experience along
he highway connecting California
lity's downtown with Galileo Hill's
otels and recreational facilities, as
vell as serving as a selling device for
he developer. The signs' flower
nage (with its "high reader" outline

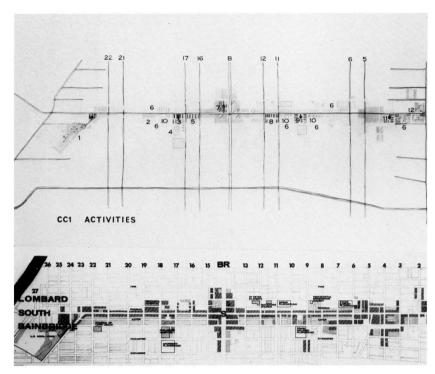

CC1 ACTIVITIES

for visibility and its "low reader" for
detailed information) was chosen for
its direct appeal, as flowers are conventionally associated with the idea of
beauty.[65]

In the Bicentennial International
Exposition proposal the relationship
between street and sign is restated,
but whereas the California City signs
functioned as spatial hiatuses in the
highway, the exposition signs span
the street, defining spaces and creating a rhythm along the road. The
main element, the street itself, is
flanked by pavilions, restaurants,
souvenir kiosks, and services. Wide
entrance ways cut perpendicularly,
leading toward theme and international buildings and creating open or
mazelike spaces in the intersections.
The "little buildings," or pavilions,
would reflect individualistic and
idiosyncratic esthetic expressions,
adding to the variety of the different
zones, while the signs would architecturally organize the space at the urban
scale.[66] The emblematic simultaneity
of past fairs' symbols—the ball and
spire of the 1964 New York World's
Fair, the Crystal Palace, the Eiffel
Tower—is replaced by an emblematic
narrative of signs displayed sequen-
tially. In the Benjamin Franklin
Parkway Celebration project, the
urban landscape is itself turned into a

*Venturi & Rauch, architects and
planners, Denise Scott Brown, partner-
in-charge (with the assistance of Steven
Izenour and David Manker), activity plan
and ground floor land use plan, the
Philadelphia Crosstown Community
(South Street), 1968. Courtesy Venturi &
Rauch. Top, Activities: (1) reuse of Naval
Home; (2) Amalgamated Clothiers' Housing; (3) Neighborhood Services Center;
(4) Children's Hospital; (5) Center City
Library; single-person turnkey housing;
(6) Leased-Housing Program; (7) Museum
for Negro Culture and History; (8) Diag-
nostic Relocation Center; (9) Neighborhood Services Center; (10) 221H Home
Ownership Program; (11) Neighborhood
Services Center; (12) intensive renewal
area. Bottom: The land use map is a device that attempts to suggest the atomistic
quality of the land use in a diverse vital
area and the dynamics of proposed developments. This strategy devised for the
study of Las Vegas, is a departure from
traditional land use mapping.*

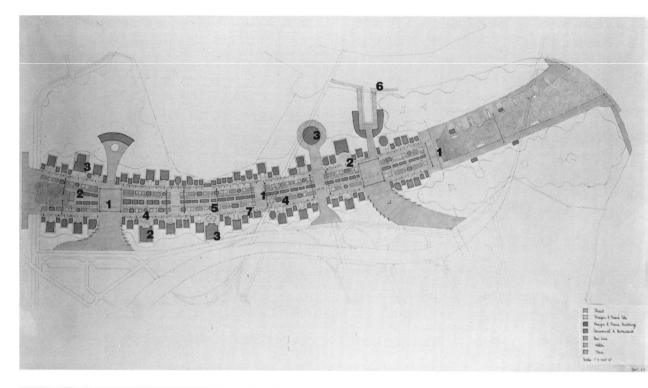

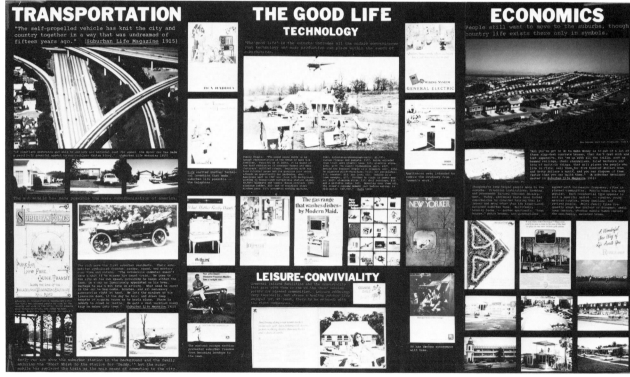

Above: *Venturi & Rauch, architects and planners, D. S. Brown, partner in charge of research and text, with Missy Maxwell and Elizabeth Izenour. Detail of ''Themes and Ideals of the Suburban Landscape,'' panel from the home section of ''Signs of Life: Symbols in the American City,'' a 1976 exhibition at the Renwick Gallery, Washington, D.C.*

Top: *Venturi & Rauch, architects and planners, master plan, International Exposition for the Bicentennial, Philadelphia, Pennsylvania, 1972. Courtesy Venturi & Rauch. (1) Street; (2) foreign and theme site; (3) foreign and theme building; (4) commercial and restaurant; (5) bus line; (6) water; (7) trees.*

sign at night by the use of powerful light streams shooting into the sky, creating archways for the boulevard and theatrically highlighting the monuments.[67]

The lively and often enraged polemics over Scott Brown's ideas center around the issues raised during her unrelenting attempt to articulate the problematic relationship between social concern and esthetic concern in architecture and urbanism, as she considers that "neither should be ignored for the sake of the other."[68] A brilliant polemicist, she has taken issue with socially concerned planners and form-conscious architects alike, reproaching the former for their lack of understanding of form as the embodiment of social meaning and castigating the latter's presumed contempt of social issues and their relevance in architecture.[69] However, as in all prescriptive "theories" of architecture, her well-known critical arguments are addressed less to the theoretical clarification of the relationship between social function and esthetic form in our culture than to the justification of the position represented by the work of Venturi & Rauch. Scott Brown and Venturi's argument courageously straddles the yet unreconciled domains of the social and the esthetic. However, their attempt to face squarely this favorite *bête noire* of both architects and planners remains unresolved as their defense of Levittown and Las Vegas has yet to include a critical assessment of the reasons that may explain the American middle class's craving for applied architectural symbols derived from a disparity of sources— where early American colonial meets Art Deco and the federal style joins the Renaissance—all scrambled up within the ultimate ersatz environment

Beyond Traditional Roles

The four traditional roles historically performed by women in architecture have been identified by Gwendolyn Wright as the "exceptional woman," the "adjunct," the "anonymous designer," and the "woman outside."[70] Although fragments of these roles may apply to the careers of Chloethiel Woodard Smith, Anne Griswold Tyng, Mary Otis Stevens, and Denise Scott Brown, the scope and significance of their work transcend these categories and point to new directions for women in architecture.

It may not be accidental that this period in their careers coincides with the beginning of women's public visibility, although their attitudes toward and participation in "women's issues" are as diverse as their personal and professional pursuits and accomplishments.[71] Chloethiel Smith's competent deliverance of a traditionally conceived architectural product; Anne Tyng's formal understatement through the use of contextual analogy juxtaposed to a complex structuring of space; Mary Otis Stevens' interest in the tension between the permanence of form and the impermanence of human existence; and Denise Scott Brown's reaffirmation of devalued popular symbology and social concern define a context of professional competence, creativity, and intellectual commitment where the idea of *woman as architect* begins to find cultural recognition.

CLIENT AND ARCHITECT.

BY MRS. SCHUYLER VAN RENSSELAER.

FANCY a painter unable to make pictures except when some one says to him : Paint now, paint this or that, and paint it thus and so ; or a poet or musician forced to wait for similar behests, and getting them, very often, in the shape of uncongenial themes and narrow limitations. Imagine this and you will realize the architect's actual position, and the contrast between his life and that of other artists. Of course, the difference is neither accidental nor designed, but inevitable. It is the natural result of the fact that architecture is not an art pure and simple. It has a practical side. Its products are not mere objects of beauty. They are useful objects made beautiful, and they cannot be spun out of the artist's brain, but must cost a great deal of money. When useful, costly things which take up a great deal of space are in question, demand must precede supply. The poet or the painter caters to the public's taste ; the architect serves the public's express wishes.

These facts mean two things. They mean that the architect must be something more than an artist, and that the client has a part to play which is only less important—which from one point of view is even more important—than the architect's own. As neither perfectly fulfils his duty in America to-day, it may be worth while to define in brief what that duty is. Let us begin with the client.

I.

The client—whether a unit or that multiple of units called a committee—should remember that architecture is not practical only, but that its æsthetic side is as inevitable and important as its utilitarian, should realize that he who meddles with artistic things owes a duty to others as well as to himself, and know that this is especially the case when the result is to stand conspicuous-

Women
As Critics

Mariana Griswold van Rensselaer [Mrs. Schuyler van Rensselaer] (1851–1935) was the most prominent pioneer woman critic in the U.S. Her study of Henry Hobson Richardson's work was the first full-fledged monograph on the work of an architect to be written in America. Her architectural criticism, which was copious, appeared frequently in the Century *magazine and was mainly directed to the lay public. This is the opening page of her article "Client and Architect,"* The North American Reivew, *September 1890, pp. 319–328. Photograph by Sarah Cedar.*

Perhaps because architectural criticism as a profession has never been institutionalized to the same degree as the practice of architecture, women as critics were able to achieve a stature, influence, and recognition incomparably larger than that of women designers. The work of the four critics discussed in this section influenced architectural thought beyond professional and academic circles, affecting the consciousness of decision-makers and the public at large on environmental, architectural, and planning issues.

Rejecting the view that good buildings can be designed in a historical vacuum, they felt compelled to explore and reveal by their writings the principles that relate the form of a building to the social, economic, political, and esthetic conditions presiding over its inception. Eschewing the architectural historian's fear that value judgments are in some way inimical to true scholarship, these critics had the courage to challenge complacency and self-satisfaction in the design professions. Their critical contribution was made in the service of intellectual and public causes, going beyond prevalent fashions, personal preference, and accepted beliefs. To a greater extent than most of their male colleagues, their convictions prompted them to accept the role of activists and public figures as part of their professional commitment: Catherine Bauer working in connection with labor unions and housing authorities; Jane

Jacobs picketing in defense of a neighborhood's autonomy; Sybil Moholy-Nagy lecturing, teaching, and engaging in polemical debate everywhere; Ada Louise Huxtable writing for a daily paper rather than professional journals.

Women have proverbially played modest albeit instrumental roles in the preservation and improvement of their communities' environments. However, the work and ideas of the critics discussed here set examples of method, discipline, perseverance, and knowledge that appropriately underscore the importance of the critic's role in influencing the evolving form of our built landscape.

By Suzanne Stephens

9. Voices of Consequence: Four Architectural Critics

With America's enthusiastic embrace of modern architectural and planning principles from the 1930s to the 1960s, four architectural critics emerged as important forces in an ongoing appraisal of its consequences. The four—Catherine Bauer, Jane Jacobs, Sibyl Moholy-Nagy, and Ada Louise Huxtable—share certain characteristics: besides being female, all have wielded an impressive amount of influence in the formulation of housing, planning, and architectural policies through writing and related activities. Many of their articles have appeared in professional architectural journals; some almost exclusively so. Although none of these women was trained as an architect, each was able to postulate and communicate trenchant and prophetic insights on architectural issues both to the profession and to the general public. Their discourse was to influence the decisions that gave shape to the evolving physical landscape.

On a specific level their differences are dramatic: they diverge in attitudes, focus, methods, and the particular nature of their contributions. Still, each critic was able to successfully galvanize public and professional interest in housing, urbanism, preservation, and architecture. They may not have been the first to come forward with a certain diagnosis or prognosis, but in the tremendously optimistic period of American growth following World War II, all four showed a willingness to slice through thickets of self-satisfaction, complacency, obstinacy, and protectionism in the various design professions. It took courage, an ability to communicate to public and professionals, and a belief in the power of written language to alter the built environment. They were able to grasp the prevailing zeitgeist, analyze its flaws, and synthesize its solutions. Through their writing, the values, beliefs, and ideals of succeeding years would be revealed. Because of the compressed nature of this chapter only a limited number of examples of published writing by the four critics could be cited. See the Selected Bibliography for a more extensive listing.

Catherine Bauer

In 1946 *Architectural Forum* declared, "The name of Catherine Bauer is synonomous with public housing in America."[1] From the beginning her role was that of a housing reformer and activist. First, she helped introduce the socially minded goals of the early modern European architects to the United States with her seminal book, *Modern Housing*, published in 1934. Then, seizing upon the European notion of labor union sponsorship of low-rent housing, she actively promoted it here. She helped formulate the legislation that led to the revolutionary U.S. Housing Act of 1937. With this bill the American government confronted the fact that housing the poor was not a private affair: it decided to implement a federal loan and subsidy policy to promote the construction of decent low-income housing. Bauer also advanced the design of public low-income housing as an abiding concern to an architectural profession predominantly characterized by its white-gloved involvement in creating Tudor villas for the affluent.

Graduated from Vassar College in 1926, with a year in between spent studying architecture at Cornell University (1924–1925), Bauer first went to Paris to live. She came back to New York to become head of Butterick Patterns promotion department

Catherine Bauer, early 1940s. Photograph by Roger Sturtevant.

and then an advertising manager for publisher Harcourt Brace. She was not particularly successful in either position, but had met Lewis Mumford and through him her interest in the architectural field was rekindled.

A trip to Europe in 1930, when she was 25, formed the cornerstone of Catherine Bauer's housing expertise when she toured many of the newest housing projects there. As she later commented about her trip, "What I saw in Europe was so exciting it transformed me from an aesthete to a housing reformer."[2]

Upon her return she approached *Fortune* magazine with a photographic essay on housing in Frankfurt. They suggested she submit an article to an essay contest, "Art and Industry," sponsored by Edgar Kaufmann of the Kaufmann Department Store in Pittsburgh (and the eventual client of Frank Lloyd Wright for whom "Fallingwater" was designed). Bauer won the contest, was published in *Fortune* in May 1931, and became an "instant housing expert." Circuitously, *Fortune* decided to ask Mumford to write a series of articles on housing; he in turn asked Bauer to collaborate as a researcher. Although only several of the series were printed, Bauer took another trip to Europe where she compiled enough research to write her own book in 1934.

Most of the important leading architectural work she came in contact with in Europe was low-income housing, including Walter Gropius' Siemensstadt housing of 1930 for Berlin and J.J.P. Oud's Workers' Housing at the Hook of Holland of 1926. Exposure to the principles of *existenz minimum* — the goals of decent, safe, sanitary housing for all being promulgated in Europe — were to affect her subsequent work back in the States. In terms of architecture she urged in *Modern Housing* that a new functionalist vernacular replace chaotic and eclectic housing being built in the U.S. Even the new International style, she argued, was being accepted only on stylistic terms in this country, not for the housing and planning ideas implicit in its forms.

However, Bauer did not eschew style. In fact in a review she wrote on the 1932 International style exhibit at the Museum of Modern Art,[3] Bauer argued that style implied a common acceptance of a basic norm of design. This insures that architecture will be a social art since it is the expression of those forces that keep people together. Nevertheless, the show's attention to the single-family house bothered her: "Any house however . . . cunningly planned is somewhat outside the most important practice of modern architecture." Instead she stressed, building is "seven-eighths planning."[3]

Through the thirties Bauer continued to maintain that architectural attention be given to public housing. During this period she also avidly promoted housing sponsored by labor unions to compensate for the lack of interest from the private sector in building low-income housing. When Bauer's book first appeared, private home building was at a virtual standstill due to the Depression, and there was no public housing on the federal level. In 1933 the Public Works Administration's Housing Division formed a limited dividend program to encourage low-rental housing by non-profit sponsors. When the Carl Mackley Houses in Philadelphia, backed by the American Federation of Hosiery Workers and designed by Oscar Stonorov, were constructed—the first under the program—Bauer was hired by its sponsors to help other unions learn from this prototypical effort. From there she became involved with a group of housing reformers who were devising legislation that led to the passage of the landmark Housing Act of 1937. Under this legislation, the U.S. Housing Authority was created to lend money and give subsidies for low-income housing through local channels. By then Bauer, 32, had served as the Secretary of the American Federation of Labor Housing Conference to promote labor's involvement in housing and was in 1936 the first person to win a Guggenheim Fellowship in the area of architecture and planning. It is no surprise that she was hired as the Director of Research and Information of the newly created U.S. Housing Authority.

Bauer maintained that the underlying problem in housing the poor was the categorizing of land as a commodity, which forced prices up in high-density areas. Initially she advocated slum clearance and urban renewal procedures to provide low-cost housing and endorsed standardized construction along with "superblock" planning. The superblock was seen as a means of providing open spaces and play areas, while abolishing the overly constricting street grid. Through standardized housing, costs would be reduced.

Bauer later modified both these positions as the pitfalls of the monotonous tower-in-the-park solution became too clear in the fifties. She wrote in an article entitled "Dreary Deadlock in Public Housing" in 1957 that public housing had not garnered the support of citizens and leaders it should have: Only a small percentage of eligible people actually applied, and most represented the desperate sector of low-income households. Standardization had led to institutionalization; those superblocks had created large bland buildings that turned their backs on surrounding neighborhoods. The identification of a housing project with the lowest income group had thus become reinforced. As Bauer wrote, "We have embraced too much functional and collectivist theories and tended to ignore certain subtleties and esthetic values and basic social needs."[4] What was needed, she wrote, was more individual diversification in design, allowance for personal initiative, and inclusion of private space outdoors.

Catherine Bauer had early foreseen the danger of urban renewal as a form of "people removal" from existing slum neighborhoods. In her articles she urged a balanced clearance and relocation effort so that residents of poor neighborhoods would be able to live in the same community during the process and be guaranteed accommodations in the new housing. Furthermore, she proposed zoning to cluster different scales of housing and urged reduced property tax assessments to encourage the construction of low-scale community facilities and shops.

She proposed that public housing

agencies work with private investors to create an agglomerated housing market that would support the full range of community services for the new housing. As suburbanization became widespread following World War II, Bauer began calling attention to housing as a regional problem. With cities now having to face competition from the spacious outlying suburban districts for the tax dollar, regional land controls, housing policy, and transportation should be unified.

To the end of her life Catherine Bauer never forsook the early ideals of her youth for raising the standard of housing in this country. Shortly before her death, she observed that the poor in this country still didn't have a minimum standard of housing. She castigated the early modern architects for not continuing the experimentation of their youth: instead of investigating new problems in the continual development of a rational design, Bauer noted that they clung to the old principles and turned them into a "doctrinaire stylism" instead of "rationalism, . . . a technocratic symbolism."[5]

On November 21, 1964, Catherine Bauer was found on the California coast near Mount Tamalpais dead of a brain concussion and exposure, apparently having fallen while on a walk. She had been associate dean of the University of California at Berkeley's School of Environmental Design where her husband since 1940, William Wurster, was a retired dean.

Catherine Bauer's accomplishments over her thirty-odd year career in housing reform were prodigious. Her role was truly an historic one: not the sort that is later recognized as having prophesied our destinies, but the kind that formulates them. Perhaps because of the nature of that function or the shifting issues in the special area of public housing itself, she is not as well remembered today as her efforts would warrant.

Jane Jacobs

If Catherine Bauer's name was at one time synonymous with public housing in America, Jane Jacobs can claim the same sort of distinction with regard to current city planning theories. Her book, *Life and Death of Great American Cities* published in 1961, has forcefully redirected city planning thinking away from its obsession with giant urban renewal schemes and toward a respect for the small-scale buildings, close-knit neighborhoods, and street life. In large part because of her efforts, city neighborhoods are now viewed as cohesive social and physical matrices that should be retained. The full participation of community groups urged by Jacobs is now welcomed in the formulation of planning policy. Even the United Nations Conference on Human Settlements in 1976 endorsed these principles that Jacobs first advocated and that city planners in the U.S. have come to accept as their philosophy.

Jacobs' subsequent book, *The Economy of Cities* published in 1969, has not had the impact of the first— yet. However, following New York City's near default in 1975, Jason Epstein cited in the *New York Review of Books* Jacobs' economic argument as one of the basic reasons for the city's financial flounderings.[6] In that book, Jacobs took the diversification of neighborhoods a step further into

Jane Jacobs. Photograph by Peter Chr. Holt/Toronto Island Archives.

the economic realm. Calling for the "valuable inefficiencies and practicalities of cities," she pointed out that the new services are spawned by the presence of a quantity of different enterprises.[7] New York was characterized for a time—until the construction industry took over in the sixties, Epstein points out—by an abundance of small businesses that operated on a larger-than-craft scale, but smaller than a mass-production level. Therefore they could afford to thrive in this climate that both supported them (because large size did not mean high overhead) and encouraged the formation of related businesses.

Similarly, Jacobs inveighed against standardization of housing, instead recommending an infill approach where experimental construction techniques could be applied at a reasonable scale.

Jane Jacobs established herself in the field of architectural journalism and criticism primarily as an associate editor and then senior editor for *Architectural Forum*. Her blunt prose, hard-hitting comments, and liberal use of slang and hyperbole gave the articles she wrote for *Forum* during her stay there, 1952–1962, a distinct punch mixed with common sense.

Early in her career, Jacobs began assailing the shortcomings of the urban environment everyone acknowledged but few confronted. For example, in an article she wrote in *Forum* in 1956 on Washington, D.C., she accused its planners of giving the city over to parking lots, the Smithsonian of taking over the Mall, and architects of spreading "governmental monumental" style over the city. Human scale, Jacobs argued, is important in Washington: "It is not merely a matter of building size, although that helps. It is rather that all buildings insist on a consistent scale; they show it with stoops, railings . . . all indicators as familiar to us as the height of man."[8]

In an article on the "New York Office Boom" in 1957, Jacobs reveals her powers for observing the social nuance. Explaining why corporations want to concentrate in one area, despite electronic advances that make this agglomeration unnecessary for communication, Jacobs stated: ''The value in face-to-face confrontation is to be able to peek at figures, numbers not to be broadcast, the shared martini, the subtle sizing up, the chance to bring the full weight of the personality to bear.''[9]

Writing about the new office building architecture before New York's zoning revision in 1961, Jacobs summed, ''If you combine the New York zoning formula of 1917 with simple minded modern, this yields a cityscape that appears to have wall-papered over bumps.''[10]

Too presciently, Jacobs warned about the results of the 1961 tower-cum-plaza zoning resolution that was soon to come: ''No one building can stand as an isolated gem with a setting. If it is not regarded as a problem in town planning, coincidental plazas can total up to happenstance, and blobbed-together meanders. This kind of problem cannot be solved very well by municipal regulations. A deft application of government design rules is not an American characteristic.''[11]

Like Catharine Bauer, Jacobs also criticized the polarization of cities for the poor and suburbs for the wealthy, blaming the faulty relation between federal housing and local governmental policies. In a 1957 article she suggested changing city government to a series of federated units within a large metropolitan area ''with some sovereignty surrendered to a metropolitan government.''[12] Governmental workings have long been an interest of Jacobs', and her next book, which she is now writing, turns to this subject.

When Jacobs took a leave of absence from *Forum* between 1959 and 1961 to write *Death and Life* on a grant, its editors probably did not expect that she would be producing the most important city planning document to be published in the sixties. Suspicious of the grand plans of city planners, Jacobs wrote in *Death and Life,* ''To approach a city or even a city neighborhood as if it were a large architectural problem capable of being given order by converting it into a disciplined work of art is to make the mistake of substituting art for life.''[13]

Here again, Jacobs argued for scale, urging that controls were needed for not just *kinds* of uses, but *size* of uses. With regard to public housing, Jacobs pointed out that high-rise apartments sitting in open parks may provide the light, air, and modern living conditions so highly valued by housing experts, but pluck their occupants from the well-functioning matrix of social relations that kept crime down and bolstered community pride. The occupants of decaying tenements depended on the street as well as the stoop and easy accessibility afforded by low-scale buildings for this interaction and surveillance against intruders.

Jacobs did not rely solely on her writing to make her point. Like Catherine Bauer, she was an activist. But whereas Bauer worked within the political systems of government mechanisms, Jacobs assumed the role of an adversary on the local level. One of her best-known battles resulted in the defeat of an urban renewal plan for the western' portion of New York's Greenwich Village in 1962. When the city announced its plans for high-rise apartment buildings to be erected on a 14-block area of the low-scale 19th-century neighborhood, Jacobs jumped in. A resident of the Village, she succeeded in forcing the city not only to drop its plans but to agree to an alternate scheme for low-rise housing at the same scale as the rest of the community.

Although built of conventional construction without any wasted space for long corridors and expensive elevators, the project's costs have marred original renting intentions. Bureaucratic delays and inflation have more than quadrupled maintenance costs for the middle-income cooperative apartments, and in 1975 when it finally opened, the city changed it to a rental project, with partially subsidized rents.

Aside from these unforseen difficulties, most admit that the ideas for this kind of thinking about urban housing were sound. If executed in a short amount of time in the early sixties, the West Village Housing might have been economically successful. In the meantime at least the Village's identity and character have been preserved.

Jane Butzner Jacobs was born in 1916 in Scranton, Pennsylvania, the daughter of a physician. Instead of going straight to college upon graduation from high school, she took a job as a reporter for the *Scranton Tribune.* After a year Jacobs moved to New York where she worked in various secretarial jobs and began selling magazine articles. Along the way she took some courses at Columbia University, married architect Robert Hyde Jacobs in 1944, and had three children. Working for the Office of War Information, Jacobs began writing articles on American architecture for their overseas publications. She was 36 when she took a job with *Architectural Forum* and embarked on a catalytic career as an architectural critic and urbanist. When she moved to Toronto in 1968, New York lost one of its most creative architectural thinkers. She has set an example: totally inventive, not necessarily academic, always unorthodox, and ever willing to implement the policies she advocates.

Sibyl Moholy-Nagy

Sibyl Moholy-Nagy was 47 when she began writing regularly on architecture. In fact she didn't begin publishing frequently in this country until the death of her husband, designer Lazlo Moholy-Nagy, in 1946. Her immense grief and sense of loss over his death apparently spurred her to produce a book in 1950 on the famous Bauhaus designer's work and her life with him, *Experiments in Totality*. During the next 20 years until her death in 1971, architectural criticism poured forth with tremendous force. Not only did she write four more books, but she appeared in the architectural press almost once a month, sometimes more.

Her articles always generated vehement rebuttals, avid discussion, and considerable controversy. They usually centered on strictly architectural issues, but ones that were highly volatile. In many cases she was dead right—but she had a way of saying it and a time for saying it (too early to be acknowledged) that struck raw nerves. About the "Architecture U.S.A." exhibit at the Museum of Modern Art in 1952, she wrote, "The triumph of Modern Architecture is the triumph of (photographer) Ezra Stoller and his colleagues."[14] Regarding the show's accompanying book, *Built

Sibyl Moholy-Nagy, India, 1968. Photograph by Dileep Purohit. Courtesy Sibyl Moholy-Nagy Papers, Archives of American Art, Smithsonian Institution.

in U.S.A., she said it "drives home every negative aspect threatening the future development of the progressive architects: preciousness, academism, historical consciousness, lack of social consciousness."[15] In a period when the modern movement was getting off the ground in this country and its formulators could do no wrong, Sibyl Moholy-Nagy scored Mies van der Rohe's apartments of 1951 for their uniformity, lack of privacy, lightless, airless bathrooms and kitchens, impassable dining bays, and living quarters that faced each other.

In 1955 Sibyl Moholy-Nagy harshly criticized the University of Mexico for adopting the modern idiom for its new campus without any regard to local site and sunlight conditions, building techniques, or the vernacular architectural tradition.[16] Her remarks scraped against a protectionism of modern architectural efforts that was thickly layered. Architects from the States defended Mexico's courageous efforts (for a "relatively poor underdeveloped country") in a way that showed they neither understood their own fears, projections, condescensions, nor her too apt remarks.

Behind every comment, a strong, literate, articulate voice could be heard in the service of architectural values. In 1954—only two years after Lever House was built—as dozens of kudos could be found in architectural periodicals for the new glass skyscrapers, she would say: "The boredom of the skyscraper box, hardly relieved by aluminum, and the gaunt ugliness of the residential matchbox, still drive the emotionally unsatisfied masses to the applique facades of true Williamsburg-Baroque."[17] She particularly mistrusted the Bauhaus beliefs in modular (prefabricated) assembly. She felt that architectural values would die a "cheap, fast and totally uniform death" under the thinking pushed by Walter Gropius.[18]

Although she was too suspicious of technology and allied to a rather conservative stance, her commitment to architectural excellence was one that could stand as an example to the profession. Her criticism warned that an intense caution should be exercised for she quickly discerned that too

often in the fifties architects and the public enthusiastically embraced materials and technologies only because they were new.

Although knowledgeable about urban design and planning, her interest always focused on its relation to architecture. Thus she disagreed with Jane Jacobs in her book *Death and Life of Great American Cities* for implying that cities were not an architectural problem: "No journalistic sleight of hand can transform streets into primary causes unconditioned by the architectural volumes that define their vacuum."[19]

Where others ignored the issues of architectural quality, Sibyl Moholy-Nagy quickly reminded the public—and the profession—of its importance. Therefore she faulted Philadelphia in 1961 for having "not a single memorable architectural design created in the multimillion-dollar buildings of Penn Center and its new residential centers."[20]

Whereas architects were applauding the efforts of planner and architect Edmund Bacon there, Moholy-Nagy felt no compunction about violating here and elsewhere what she scorned as the "American taboo on criticism of current structures and architects."[21] This particular observation touches on a major problem of architectural writing in the post-World War II construction boom. The architectural magazines, justifiably interested in creating an appreciation for the new modern architecture and the innovative construction techniques, often hesitated to criticize the actual work. Journalism too frequently was purely descriptive; where criticism did appear, it seemed as if the critic were making a personal and singular attack on the architect. Sibyl Moholy-Nagy's critiques were no exception.

Her bias explained the essentially formalistic criteria underlying her criticism. Hers is a discussion of the way a building's various component parts visually relate, the kinesthetic experience of its internal and external spaces. During the last years of her life this concern was generally viewed as outmoded by a generation of architects interested in a socially relevant architecture that would accommodate society's immediate physical needs, for example, housing, and involve users in the design process. Architecture created as an art object or executed by a single architect was mistrusted.

Now attitudes have shifted a bit. There is a growing appreciation of buildings as embodiments of meaning, as a combination of elements that relate socially and culturally to the society and to its past. The visual and kinesthetic perception of architecture —the understanding of its expressive function, its content—reminds one of an observation Sibyl Moholy-Nagy made in 1952: "Man needs to relate to what he sees: to symbolic content in the past, to light, color and form in the present."[22]

Sibyl Moholy-Nagy was born Dorothea Maria Pauline Alice Sybylle Pietzsche in Dresden in 1903. Her father, architect Martin Pietzsche, was head of the Dresden Academy. After graduating from the Municipal Lyceum at Dresden-Neustadt, she attended the universities of Leipzig and Frankfurt. But before long she undertook an acting career in Breslau, Frankfurt, and Berlin, with roles ranging from Shakespearean plays to drawing room comedies. But the actress could also write and eventually took over as the scenario editor for Tobin Motion Picture Syndicate in Berlin. Here she met her future husband Lazlo Moholy-Nagy, and they collaborated on several art films such as "Black White and Grey," "Gypsies," and "Berlin Still Life." After they were married in 1932, Sibyl free-lanced stories, scenarios, and essays while helping her husband with his writings.

When the Moholy-Nagys emigrated to the States in 1937, she taught at the Institute of Chicago that Lazlo helped found. Academic life appealed to her. She continued teaching at Bradley University in Peoria, University of California at Berkeley, and Schaeffer School of Design in San Francisco before eventually settling down for 18 years as an architectural history professor at Pratt Institute in New York.

Sibyl also became a novelist of sorts. One of her earliest works published in the United States was *Children's Children,* written under the pseudonym S.D. Peech in 1945. (Peech was an old nickname for Sibyl.) The book's protagonist, not too surprisingly, is a high-spirited, very intelligent young girl who leaves school to become an actress on the Berlin stage. The vivid portrayal of Germany heading for Hitler adds a strong political dimension to the novel, as well as gives clues about the ideals—philosophical, artistic, and political—of the author herself.

Not until after 1950 and the publication of *Experiments in Totality* did the architectural critic and historian fully emerge. Although Sibyl had been married to one of the Bauhaus teachers for 14 years, she felt no obligation to defend what the Bauhaus represented or what it generated. As she wrote about its functionalist credo years later, "In 1933 Hitler shook the tree and America picked up the früit of German genius. In the best of Satanic traditions some of this fruit was poisoned. . . . The lethal harvest was functionalism and the Johnnies who spread the appleseed were the Bauhaus masters, Walter Gropius, Mies van der Rohe, and Marcel Breuer."[23] These were strong words for the man—Gropius—who wrote the introduction to *Experiments in Totality* and for former friends and colleagues of both her husband and herself. Nevertheless in the same article spicily entitled "Hitler's Revenge," Sibyl explained her antagonism: "Functionalism terminated the most important era in American public architecture . . . there (had) emerged a native delight in articulation, ornamental detail and terminating form born from steel and concrete. The Empire State, Rockefeller Center and Chicago's Palmolive Building stand as witnesses."[24]

In the 20-year span until she fell fatally ill in 1971, she made a name as an outstanding, though controversial, critic, historian, and teacher. Her intelligence, style, commitment, and courage made architects stop and think, and this was after all her goal.

Ada Louise Huxtable

Ada Louise Huxtable differs from the three writers previously discussed in the exact nature and scope of her work. Bauer, Jacobs, and Moholy-Nagy did not or have not relied on the printed work alone to communicate their insights and opinions on architectural issues: they were activists or teachers as well as critics. Huxtable, however, has devoted herself to writing, period. She deliberately eschews a public role, even avoiding speaking engagements. Yet the extent of her influence is extraordinary. As the first architectural critic appointed to a national newspaper—*The New York Times*—Ada Louise Huxtable has effectively shifted the public's appreciation of architecture from a dignified dilettantism to a major concern. Since her selection as the *Times'* architectural critic in 1963, more than a dozen papers have followed suit. The *Times* even hired an architectural critic, Paul Goldberger, for its daily paper when Huxtable was elevated to the Editorial Board in 1973. In this role she writes unsigned editorials for the editorial page, besides producing a column for the Sunday paper.

Although it is nearly impossible to estimate Huxtable's power in quantifiable terms, architects and clients

Ada Louise Huxtable. Photograph by Dorothy Alexander.

quickly acknowledge her influence in swaying decisions. Zoning laws have been passed, historic buildings have been saved from imminent demolition (though not all), architectural reputations endangered all because of her articles. Ada Louise Huxtable readily concedes that she tries principally to reach the people who do make decisions about the environment—the reason she prefers writing for a newspaper's general audience rather than only for professional journals. And she has a point: if her name is not a household word with the person on the street, it is with the people who decide what happens to that street— architects, planners, real estate developers, financial scions, and city officials.

Huxtable is also unique in her early efforts to stimulate a growing public interest in preserving America's often neglected and ever diminishing architectural heritage. Her endeavors have been directed to saving not only identifiable historic landmarks, but more ordinary chunks of the urban fabric that embody the nation's past ideals and values in physical form.

To communicate architectural principles to a public that generally has evidenced little interest or knowledge of the subject takes a special kind of talent. The question is not simply a matter of style, but of conceptual approach. Huxtable's critical stance is more broadly based than, say, Sibyl Moholy-Nagy's. Taking political, social, and economic issues into account, Huxtable is generally more pragmatic and less concerned with a purely formal explication of architecture—though standards of architectural quality constantly lurk in the background or foreground of any of her critiques.

This attitude clearly derives, consciously or unconsciously, from the sort of pragmatic philosophy propounded by William James. Like the Jamesian definition of truth, the Huxtable form of architectural judgment assumes that the "idea" is contained in the architect's intention or concept, the "reality" is within the built product and its context, and the "truth" is the relation of one to another as that reality is experienced by the critic and the users. The standards according to

which she analyzes the built environment clearly encompass this concept:

The architecture critic is dealing only tangentially with the production of beautiful buildings. What counts today are multiple ways any building serves a very complex and sophisticated set of environmental needs. What is it part of? How does it work? How does it relate to what is around it? How does it satisfy the needs of men and society as well as the needs of the client? What does it add to or subtract from, the quality of life?"[25]

More theoretically oriented architects sometimes criticize Huxtable for not standing behind one school of thought or entrenching herself in one internally consistent system of values. Instead, she adamantly adheres to the validity of multiple architectural approaches, arguing that no particular school of thought is necessarily right. None takes into account all the problems in a situation. Unplanned side effects may occur in any appealing new program, which the critic must point out, she reasons: "This is why criticism is essential."[26]

The pragmatic critic recognizes that this flexibility allows for the possibility of incremental change: as newer truths emerge and are recorded, the existing context or reality can be altered. As this changes, new truths emerge; as they are recorded, reality can be altered; and so on. Acknowledgment of the mutability of truth and reality meshes well with Huxtable's historical stance: "Everything should be seen as of its time," she has asserted. "The original strength of a movement at one period may eventually become its weakness during the next."[27]

In addition, because her value system is not entirely explicit, her critical comments can be unpredictable. Readers may expect a certain tack, but there remains that element of doubt and surprise—and therefore the readership. Huxtable's objectives are directed toward creating the cultural framework through which the internal workings of reality are revealed. That effort depends on the message being delivered with a particular kind of style to heighten the impact. You could call it the vent-the-spleen

school restrained by an elegant diction. The language is neither ethereal nor esoteric. Rather the images are concrete, the meanings neatly fastened down by her choice of words. For example, "The let-them-eat-travertine perfectionism of SOM superstar Gordon Bunshaft is seldom less belligerently antihuman these days"[28] (a criticism relating to New York's curved facade Solow building).

Because words are combined with rather emphatic literary devices such as alliteration, accentuated rhythms, and discordant juxtapositions the statements read precisely and powerfully. Phrases like "drop dead size," "doggedly popular-pretty posh," or "elephantine esthetic poverty" stick (these phrases were used to describe the Kennedy Center). Often an idea elaborately presented in a long sentence will be epigrammatically summarized by a short sentence that follows: "It is a sad commentary on our culture that so many people, in sheer gratitude for those desperately needed theaters can believe or argue that their design is unimportant. Spilt marble matters."[29] Although Huxtable has expressed a fear of too much alliteration or epigrammatic phrasing, the vivid expressions have gotten the message across.

Ada Louise Huxtable is a native New Yorker, born in 1921. After graduating magna cum laude from Hunter, she did graduate work in architectural history at the Institute of Fine Arts at New York University. From 1946–1950, she worked as an assistant curator in the Museum of Modern Art's Architecture and Design Department when Philip Johnson was the director. Then in 1950, Huxtable left for Milan on a Fulbright. When she returned 2 years later, she organized a circulating exhibit on Pier Luigi Nervi for the Modern and published her first piece, an article on Nervi in the June 1953 issue of *Progressive Architecture (P/A)*. During the next few years, articles began to appear by Huxtable in *Arts Digest, Craft Horizons, Interiors.* Then from 1956 to 1958, she initiated a series on "Progressive Architecture in America" for *P/A*—a technical discussion of historically significant

American buildings, seen from a structural as well as an architectural viewpoint. For these efforts, she was awarded a Guggenheim in 1958, and in 1960 she published a book, *Pier Luigi Nervi*.

By the early sixties she was contributing frequently to *Art in America, AIA Journal,* and *P/A* as well as to *The New York Times.* Her pieces in the Sunday magazine section in those years which she considers jejune today, prompted the *Times'* job offer.

The rest is well known, laden as it has been with honorary degrees, including the first Pulitzer Prize given for distinguished criticism in 1970. Interestingly enough the well-deserved acclaim owes not so much to one particular quality as to an interlocking set of attributes. Pragmatism without the sense of ethics would subvert the nature of the "truth"; the moral tone without a firm objective sensibility and strong factual basis would appear as inchoate outrage. And finally Huxtable's tone of objectivity and reliance on fact would mask the message without her persuasive prose.

A Critical Consciousness

Obviously this brief summary of the contributions of four writers risks emphasizing certain isolated aspects of their work and neglecting others, including their shortcomings. But such a method does allow the juxtaposition of contradictory and complementary viewpoints to be easily discerned.

Furthermore, in the enthusiasm of surveying the prodigious accomplishments of these four writers, one can too easily lose a certain perspective relating to the role of architectural criticism itself. Like other creative endeavors, architectural criticism cannot easily take place apart from architectural production. Without architects and planners as agents of environmental change, there would be little cause for appraisal—and little hope for improvement in the built environment. The work of a few talented architects has certainly affected the physical landscape more than that of any one critic. However, there are many factors that influence

the built form, some of which have little to do with the most talented architect's best intentions. These factors include not only political, economic, and social considerations, but often the weakness in the design concept itself, as Bauer, Jacobs, Moholy-Nagy, and Huxtable consistently made clear.

As women in a period that would have presented innumerable obstacles to their affecting architectural thought through actual practice (even if they had wanted to), the role of the critic permitted proper latitude. Because of the lack of a well-developed tradition in this country for architectural criticism and because of the inroads made by women in other forms of journalism, it would seem that this particular area was and still is accessible regardless of the extent of education, age, or sex. Fortunately, the measure of the critic has been not who you are, but what you do or say.

At a time when the modern movement was often promoted uncritically by their colleagues, these writers overcame the limitations of the journalist-as-proselytizer role. They could do so because they combined the necessary characteristics of conscience, courage, and common sense. They knew their audience; they knew how to communicate in a language and a conceptual framework their readers would understand. And they were outside the system of architectural patronage and buddyism of their architect-colleagues. The fear of losing a commission, deviating from one particular school of thought, or even making enemies has too often crippled design professionals in their own published work.

Because these four critics could bring their special attributes to this unique role, they were able to promote and keep alive a critical consciousness much needed in America's euphoric growth of the fifties and sixties. Their insights, recognitions, and sense of awareness advance the cause of architecture as a phenomenon worthy of serious attention.

Women in Design: the next decade, a conference for women who work with public visual and physical forms, Ma

Women in the Architectural Profession: A Contemporary Perspective

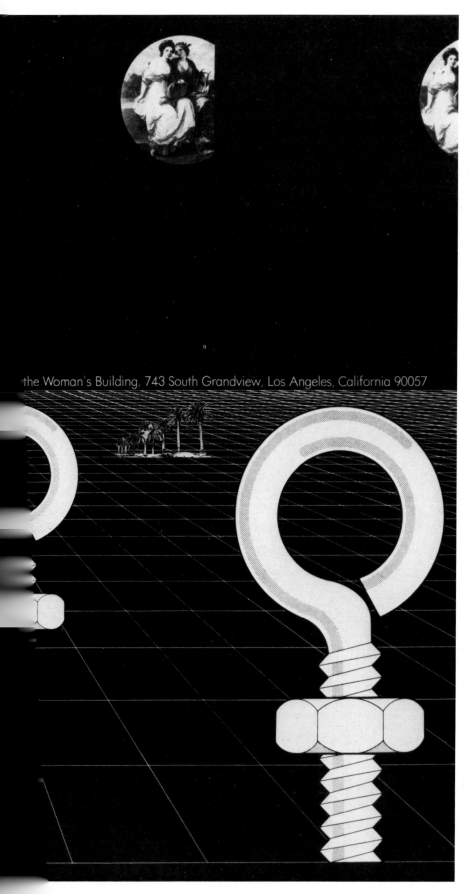

the Woman's Building, 743 South Grandview, Los Angeles, California 90057

Sheila Levrant deBretteville, poster for the Women in Design Conference at the Woman's Building in Los Angeles, 1975.

Architecture, like every other profession and activity, has not remained unaffected by the demands for equality posed by the Women's Movement. Women's professional organizations, forums, conferences, and alternative educational institutions have sprung up, inspired by the two-fold aim of improving the status of women in the design professions and reexamining from a feminist perspective some basic tenets of architectural practice.

The 1974 national Women in Architecture Conference at St. Louis (held in the same city chosen for the first convention of women architects 52 years earlier) initiated a wide public debate of issues that has continued since. These issues have now been expanded from the initial consciousness of job and salary discrimination to include a wider examination of women's relation to the design professions, individual achievement and the social power of the architect, conflicts between family and career, and the expression of women's experiences and aspirations in designed and built forms.

This section charts the process followed by contemporary groups and organizations and discusses the impact of their strategies and the efficacy of their methods. It also presents recent projects and current ideas that advance possibilities of change both within and without the established profession. These new directions proposed by some groups and individuals give evidence of a new sense of re-

sponsibility toward the specific needs of women as users of the environment, and have challenged prevalent design criteria and built form in their failure to embody and respond to woman's newly acquired consciousness of her prospective social and cultural role.

By Susana Torre

10. Women in Architecture and the New Feminism

If you have been told that you should be an interior designer, you should probably be an architect.
In *Architecture for Women: Some Notes* by Mimi Lobell, a pamphlet distributed during registration at Pratt Institute, Brooklyn, in 1975

In the U.S., a marked difference in "environmental competence" between girls and boys is noted by environmental reseachers Susan Saegert and Rogert Hart.[1] Girls are more restricted by their parents in their *movement* in the environment; girls are also more restrained in their *manipulation* of the environment. Girls build less frequently than boys; girls build also build less grandly— houses and rooms rather than cities and airports. Interestingly too, girls modify the spaces in imagination rather than actuality (a bush becomes a wall), whereas boys *build* walls, windows, roofs. Girls concentrate instead on the "detailed elaboration of the interior." Saegert and Hart do not wholly accept Erik Erikson's psychosexual explanation.[2] Instead, they point to the "powerful effects of socialization": boys are clearly being prepared for adult roles as creators and builders, girls for work within interior spaces.

This early socialization in its multiple forms has caused women to be perceived as being peripheral to a full professional and creative involvement in architecture. "The planning of houses is not architecture" stated an 1876 editorial, simultaneously ratifying and devaluing the marginal role assigned to women. From the same editorial: "a good many [women] . . . if they were ready to devote the necessary years to a difficult study, would prove valuable *coadjutors* to architects"[3] (italics added). Stereotypical attitudes toward women are well documented in professional journals since the turn of the century.[4] For example, an article appearing in the *Daily Chronicle* of August 1909 stated that a woman possesses by instinct and training certain knowledge in regard to residential building that a man, by reason of his mode of life, cannot have in the same degree.[5] This purportedly encouraging article was based on a hardly progressive assump-

tion, but nevertheless merited a rebuffing response in *The Architectural Review* of the following month:

The unknown contributor bases her claim on the hypothesis that women are fitted by domestic training to practice house building. Yet she admits that a long course of training in an office is necessary. How then can a girl whose life is spent in office work have any more intimate knowledge of such things than her brother in like case, the very personification of "male ignorance"? She makes no mention of the relatively small part that is played by design in the routine of an office, of the drudgery of specification-writing, tracing and similar mechanical work. And as she limits her remarks to domestic architecture there is happily no need for us to hazard similar surmises as to feminine suitability for any other class of building.[6]

Throughout the article, a fear is expressed that women were attempting to compete for the scarce jobs available, robbing men of their career and survival opportunities. After all, why wastefully open these opportunities to people who were likely to get married and stop their professional pursuits at some predictable time in their lives?

Joseph Hudnut, dean of the Graduate School of Design at Harvard, wrote an article in 1951 quaintly titled "The Architectress." After referring to women as "that uncertain, coy and useful branch of the human race," he states quite clearly but without citing sources: "Less than 5% of the women who earn professional degrees in architecture actually remain in the profession for more than 5 years; less than 2% become independent practitioners; and 95% are housewives."[7] Given this great university's view of itself as the training ground for future influential roles in professional, academic, and public domains, it is doubtful that the education of prospective housewives would be seen as a priority. And yet the Cambridge School of Architecture and Landscape Architecture, staffed with Harvard's best faculty, produced a remarkably high percentage of women practitioners: 80 percent of all the graduates and 60 percent of all the married graduates were professionally active in the 1930s.[8] When the Cambridge School closed in 1942, Harvard was pressed to admit women as candidates for degrees.[9] What took place between the war and Hudnut's statement was apparently a policy reversal. As one student recalls:

I well remember the angry buzzing about the lack of commitment to continue women at HGSD after the war was over, and no one was fooled for a minute about why Harvard had been willing to accept women for these degrees. We knew they needed us to replace the men being drafted.[10]

In spite of these views and obstacles, women *have* become architects and have learned their craft. And more women are now studying architecture. In 1972–1973 women were 8.4 percent of all graduates and undergraduates; four years earlier women were less than 6 percent.[11] However, architecture compares poorly with most other professions; the percentage of first-year women in medical schools went from 11 percent to 19.7 percent between 1970 and 1973.[12] The impact of this increase in numbers is already being felt.

It's in the professional schools— in the proliferation of conferences, courses, and research of interest to and about women.[13] It's in alternatives to the professional organizations. Finally, it's in the education directed outside the profession toward nonprofessionals. These directions of change are only the beginning of many efforts made by women in the design fields to communicate with one another, to understand their personal connections to the profession, and to define meaningful values and goals in their own terms.

Conferences

In their study on "Women and Architecture," Kay Standley, Ph.D., and Bradley Soule, M.D., provide some insights about the reasons why women in the architectural profession shun the political and personal involvement that have characterized the majority of women's groups in the past few years. Analyzing "sex-typing"[14] in the profession,

they state that architecture has a special status in that "it incorporates activities of both masculine and feminine cast. While the construction of a building is culturally viewed as a masculine activity, a preoccupation with design and esthetics is frequently seen on a popular level as more refined and ultimately more feminine."[15] Generally, the woman who decides to become an architect, according to this study, "aspires to outstanding intellectual achievements and to a position of high social status," thus "not merely supplementing, but to some degree rejecting traditional feminine roles." It is not strange, then, that this woman will attempt to survive in "a working world where the mannerisms and values are defined by men by identifying with its men" rather than with its women.[16] In spite of this identification, many more women are now coalescing around recognized common problems. More often than not, collective action will be accomplished around a profession-related goal.

To a large extent, articles in newspapers and journals on women in architecture can be credited with creating a context in which these organizational efforts have found support, encouragement, and recognition. The early women's organizations—such as Alpha Alpha Gamma and the Women's Architectural Drafting Club —which grew out of the need to end women's isolation within the profession, became progressively involved in diffuse and generalized local concerns. Their initial political impact withered away for lack of dialog with other groups, who were not known to each other, and for lack of a responsive context, where a consciousness of discrimination is more likely to emerge.

In the spring of 1972 the few women teachers and students of the architecture department at the University of Oregon in Eugene called a meeting to organize a group. Fewer than 10 women attended. The discussion focused on the discrimination they had encountered, but they found it difficult to be specific about how it had affected their careers.[17] This group reorganized during the fall of 1972, and the women understood that

Logo, Symposium on Women in Architecture held at Washington University's School of Architecture in St. Louis, Missouri, March 1974. Drawing by Fernand Léger.

Announcement, West Coast Women's Design Conference, University of Oregon, April 1974. Poster designed by Glenda Fravel Utsey.

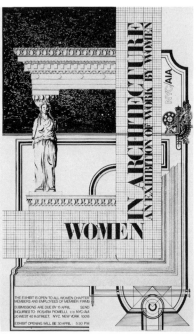

Above: *"Women in Architecture," exhibition sponsored by AIA, New York Chapter, Spring 1974. Poster designed by Woody Rainey with Karen Kalmer.*

Top: *Photograph from* What Can She Be? An Architect *by Gloria and Esther Goldreich. Photograph by Robert Ipcar.* © *Lothrop, Lee & Shepard Co., Inc., 1974. Courtesy Lothrop, Lee & Shepard Co., Inc.*

breaking the isolation pattern could only be achieved by creating communication networks with other women outside Eugene. So they proceeded to organize a regional conference. Simultaneously, a group of women as Washington University in St. Louis was organizing a national conference, which was finally held a month before the West Coast Women's Design Conference, at Eugene in April 1974.

These conferences, like many other events, were the result of a now identifiable process followed by most women's organizations in the seventies. First, there is a general period of getting to know one another and consciousness raising. Although every woman in the group generally feels the need to organize in order to support each other, divergent ideological positions are likely to emerge during this period: whether to focus on feminism or architecture or whether to take action on issues of discrimination or remain as a discussion group without projecting an assertive public image. The second stage invariably involves defining a specific project: for example, research on the lives and work of early women graduates,[18] participation in committees regarding hiring and admission policies,[19] presentations at professional conferences,[20] organization of lecture series and exhibits on the work of

women architects,[21] creation of courses in architecture and planning on women as users or practitioners,[22] implementation of educational projects to communicate alternative career images in grammar and high schools.[23]

Symptomatic of nonhierarchical modes of interaction developing among women during this process was the Oregon's group interest in a critique of the so-called star system in architecture. Early plans to invite a keynote speaker in order to attain official validation in the academic arena were abandoned. In fact, the projected keynote speaker, Denise Scott Brown, addressed the audience at the conference on the subject "Sexism: The Star System in Architecture." In this speech Scott Brown identified three main deterrents to women's progress in architecture. First, architecture in America has been an upper class profession, dominated by a social class that explicitly defines the differences between men's and women's roles. Second, males more than females tend to organize in "gangs," causing established professions to become much like men's clubs where women have been traditionally seen as intruders. Last, architecture is still influenced by the protégé system whereby a young man is trained personally by a professional, allowing him to learn special skills. Scott Brown feels men rarely choose women as protégées since they fear the presumed social embarrassment of having a woman follower.[24]

As expression of the need for continuity of thought and action, the proceedings of the Oregon conference contain both a reference to the plans for the creation of a women's summer school formulated at the earlier meeting and a memo from Sheila Levrant deBretteville to Dolores Hayden of MIT expressing the hope that a new conference to discuss "The Next Step" can be organized at the Woman's Building in Los Angeles a year hence.

The striking contrasts found in these first two conferences were described in a review of the St. Louis conference: "On one hand, a small energetic group of women students had accomplished the enormous task of organizing a national conference—a feat even for seasoned professionals who are paid to do such things. On the other hand, the event and its actors revealed poignantly the vast gulf which separates women in architecture from their rightful roles and full potential."[25] Still, it was a rewarding experience; being protagonists for once, the women began to discover and enjoy professional contacts and friendships.[26]

While the St. Louis conference featured a rather conventional program of activities and a keynote speaker,[27] the "Women in Design: The Next Decade" conference at the Woman's Building in Los Angeles on March 20–21, 1975, had a flexible program that allowed changes suggested by the participants. The organizers'[28] concern was to discuss professional issues from a feminist perspective. A number of questions were asked in the printed announcement that demanded a profound reexamination of personal and professional goals:

Does your identification as a woman enrich or endanger your viability as a professional?
What tensions exist between your personal and professional life?
Do you feel that physical and visual forms have the capacity to communicate values and attitudes?
How are your values and attitudes manifest in your work and life?
How do you deal with the narrow application of affirmative hiring which rigorously maintains male standards of acceptability?
What are your standards of acceptability?
What are your aspirations for yourself as a worker in the next decade?[29]

More important than the tentative or evasive answers was that these questions could be asked at all. The open and public discussion of these highly vulnerable issues had been inhibited previously by the academic settings of the two preceding conferences. These issues were later restated, at least in intention, in the following conference, "Women in Design and Planning," at the Boston Architectural

Center on November 8–9, 1975.[30] Much of the ground mapped at the other conferences had to be defined anew, as two competing attitudes reemerged: of women who considered themselves to be architects first or of architects who considered themselves to be women first. However, it is important to note that in the short span of one year women in architecture learned to develop and use communication networks and showed a willingness to engage in discussion of polemical issues. Whether future gatherings will shift more toward professional complacency than further critical examination seems to be crucial to the growth and vitality of these exchanges.

Exhibitions

Recognizing that in professional architectural circles the visibility of the work itself is the means to establish an architect's competence and ability, women architects have organized a number of exhibits of their work. These exhibits, nonjuried and local or regional in character, have been mostly addressed to professional and preprofessional audiences. In many instances, such as the New York exhibit[31] of April 30–May 28, 1974, and the Philadelphia exhibit, "Women in the Design of the Environment," of May 1974,[32] such exhibitions have been sponsored by local chapters of the American Institute of Architects. In these cases, the exhibitors were required to be members of the AIA or employees of members. In the introduction to the New York exhibit, Rosaria Piomelli, organizer of the show, observes that "the few dozen offices which are participating in this exhibit represent less than one-tenth of the AIA sustaining firms in New York City. How many firms are not represented? Is this because they have no women? Is the old sign '. . . the management reserves the right . . .' still hanging? Shall we rejoice or be saddened that (only) one office has forbidden a woman to exhibit her work?"[33]

The following data, as quoted in a review of this particular exhibit, re-

veal an interesting profile of the women working in the large, established firms, the major constituency of the AIA: "More than half the exhibitors were born abroad and a third were educated outside the U.S. The facts illustrate the greater acceptance of women in the field in places like Scandinavia, Greece, Israel and Eastern Europe. Only 16 of the women whose work is shown are registered, and a large proportion are not actually engaged in the central activities of architectural practice like planning and design, job coordination, or construction supervision, but rather in such vital but ancillary fields as interior design, delineation, information-systems planning, architectural journalism, furniture design, and environmental psychology. The women's ages range from the 20s to the 60s, and the handful who have achieved associate or partner status seem to have taken a very long time to do it, despite their generally high level of educational attainment. Very few women architects have their own practices; some are in partnerships with their husbands. There is a heavy concentration of residential work, but schools, hospitals, and public buildings are well represented, too."[34]

Although another reviewer noticed that in this exhibit (and possibly in many others) "the letterhead is solidly male,"[35] the importance of these shows cannot be underestimated. By presenting their work, not only do women architects acquire public exposure, but the public becomes aware of their accomplishments. More importantly, the work is judged by the women themselves and by others on its own merits; through this evaluation women raise their own demands about the quality of their work and finally validate their image as professionals for themselves.

Above: *Neski Associates, Architects, Barbara Neski, partner, Simon House, Long Island, New York, 1973. Photograph by Bill Maris. The plan of this weekend house is a 30-foot square angled on the site; it is divided into four squares that coil up and down about the central stair-well spine. The shifting levels of this pinwheel spatial organization are expressed in the windows and outside porches. The entry bridge and stair cylinder contrast with the cubic shape of the house.*

Right: *Warner, Burns, Toan & Lunde, Rosaria Piomelli, project designer, Brown University Science Library, Providence, Rhode Island, 1971. Photograph by Louis Reens. The esthetic image of this building emerges as a logical consequence of a rational use of modern building technology and materials. The slip-formed tower walls are self-supporting and enclose the mechanical shafts. There is a clear span of 54 feet between walls; the lighting is housed in the coffer formed by the T-beams. The ground level includes a terrace and a pool on either side of the entrance lobby.*

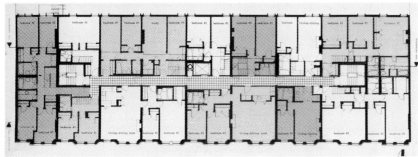

Fourth floor plan, Nine-G Cooperative.
Courtesy Edelman & Salzman.

Edelman & Salzman, Judith Edelman, partner-in-charge, Nine-G Cooperative Brownstones, New York, 1968. Photograph by George Cserna. Nine adjoining brownstones in New York's West Side Urban Renewal Area were rehabilitated to form a single apartment building, with each apartment custom designed for the owners-occupants. The redesign added a corridor connecting the nine buildings, an elevator in the center, and a new facade in the rear.

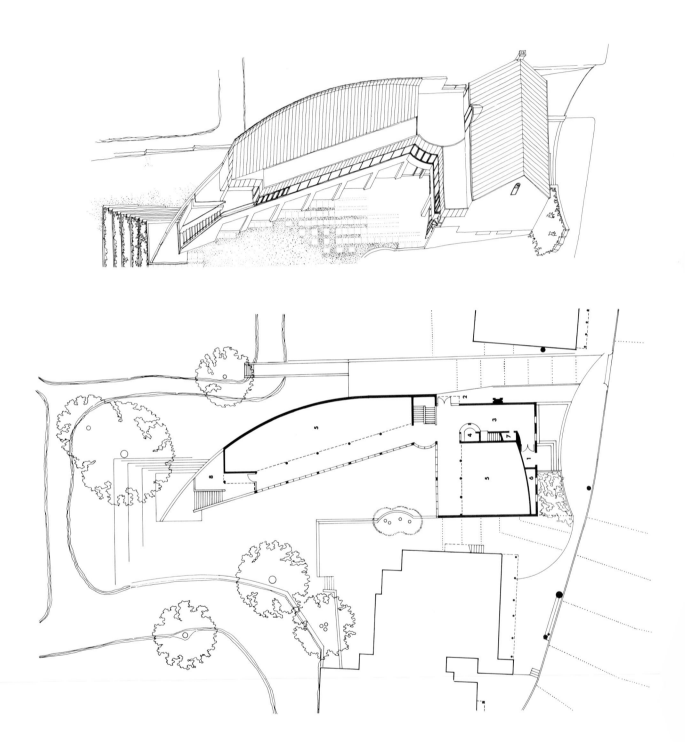

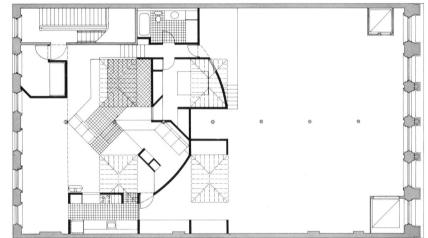

Above: *Etel Thea Kramer, interior, Friedberg/Searles Loft, New York, 1974. Courtesy E. Kramer. The space, located on the top floor of a cast iron warehouse, is 48 x 88 feet. It contains four large skylights and a central line of wooden posts. The volumes of the two bedroom "house" were designed using the existing skylights and columns as spatial references. In section, a series of seating and dining areas, interior garden and bedrooms are differentiated by two platform levels and two heights of lowered ceiling. Doors and windows to the large open studio increase the sense of house enclosure and "backyard" workspace.*

Right: *E. Kramer, floor plan, Friedberg/Searles Loft. Courtesy E. Kramer.*

Opposite page: *R. M. Kliment and Frances Halsband, Architects, axonometric and street level plan, museum extension and gallery renovation, Woodstock Artists Association, Woodstock, New York, 1974. Courtesy Frances Halsband. The project called for the renovation of an existing structure and design of new spaces for exhibitions, performances, art classes, and storage. The new wing and the sculpture garden were designed to make the new and the old appear and function as one coherent system.*

Lynda Simmons, vice-president and director of development, Phipps Houses, program for the Henry Phipps Plaza West (lower center in drawing), New York, completed 1976. Drawing by Ernest Burden. The program for this $43 million urban renewal housing specified an "outdoor living room" with trees, ivy, sitting places, and playgrounds connected with the ground floor laundries, a maximum apartments open to the sun, and cross-ventilation and buildings of various heights to avoid blocking sunlight and views. Two-thirds of the apartments have two exposures; there are no internal kitchens; and warm, friendly colors were specified throughout. Simmons' intention in formulating the program was to ensure the enhancement of individual and family life. The architects for Plaza West were Frost Associates.

Opposite page: Meeting announcement, Alliance of Women in Architecture, New York, February 1973. Courtesy Alliance of Women in Architecture.

Alternatives to Professional Organizations

In 1974, 12 professional women's organizations were listed in publications.[36] Since then, the number has grown considerably. Early in 1971, some two hundred women were asked to join in a Women's Architectural Review Movement. The questionnaire and exhibition proposal came from Regi Goldberg, a New York architectural designer. Of the small number replying, only a few wanted to show their work with other women.[37] In 1972, with the support and facilities of The Architectural League of New York, a meeting was called, and the Alliance of Women in Architecture (AWA) was founded. The programs established through the different workshops had a distinctive professional bias: an education workshop made plans to reach young women through the media, career counseling, and video presentations; a discrimination workshop took steps to gather precise data and advise women of appropriate recourse; a licensing workshop encouraged women to obtain their registration.

In contrast with AWA's work and policies on professional improvement, Women in Architecture, Landscape Architecture, and Planning (WALAP), a Cambridge-based organization, was particularly concerned about changing the very structure of the design professions. A group within this organization[38] discussed work schedules as they relate to women's lives and wrote an article, "The Case for Flexible Work Schedules,"[39] as a joint effort. Another group met regularly to discuss the advantages and disadvantages of creating an all-women's office based on two main principles: the office would be a nonhierarchical, cooperative venture, and it would attempt to subsidize through grants and its own profits those clients not able to afford professional fees. The Open Design Office (ODO) was created as a result of these discussions. Since its foundation ODO has completed a number of projects, collaborating with community organizations and feminist commercial concerns.[40]

The issue of various levels of discrimination was basic in the formation of these organizations. In a 1973 survey, 70 percent of the women interviewed acknowledged discrimination, and 95 percent of the men denied it.[41] A report prepared by the Task Force on Women in Architecture of the AIA with Judith Edelman at its head amply discussed and documented it.[42] Some of the statistical information assembled in this report indicates that women represent only 1.2 percent of all registered architects and 3.7 percent of the total U.S. "architectural population."[43] The most serious problems of sex discrimination were found in the area of employment, beginning at the start of the woman's architectural career and usually continuing. When hired, women are generally placed in "limited, stereotyped positions, regardless of their qualifications."[44] The lack of opportunity to come in contact with clients and assume responsibility for contract administration or site supervision further reinforces imagined or real prejudiced attitudes of contractors and construction workers. It was also found that the average income of male architects is 61.22 percent higher than that of female architects. Discrimination against married women and women with young children is not uncommon; the report notes the existence of a double standard regarding part-time work: "Men who take time off to teach are encouraged by their employers. Women who take time off to care for children risk losing their jobs."[45]

Setting standards for professional conduct, the American Institute of Architects might be expected to act on women's status, and has done so by endorsing studies and exhibitions. A resolution passed at its 1973 convention stated that the institute will take action to integrate women in the profession as "full participants," but a clause demanding elimination of sexist wording in all AIA documents was deleted. Three years later, at its 1976 convention, a resolution presented by the Sierra Valley, California, Chapter was adopted; it demanded from manufacturers of architectural products and their media agency representatives raising their level of excellence in the practical dissemination of relevant information by ceasing "the unnecessary and exploitative practice of using nude and scantily clad [female] models in advertisements, product literature and information."[46]

While this type of initiative is naturally worthy of praise, it will ultimately be in the approval and release of funding for further studies and affirmative action implementation that the AIA's commitment to women will have a real, rather than illusory, impact. Raising its 1 percent female membership, establishing special scholarships for women students, revising the status of women in its members' offices, changing promotional practices, and setting up programs designed to reach the public sector as well as the construction industry and the manufacturers are some areas where the AIA can play an influential role.

ALLIANCE OF WOMEN IN ARCHITECTURE

Coffee break at the Women in Design Conference, the Woman's Building (formerly the Chouinard Art School), Los Angeles, California. Photograph by Susan Roberta Mogul.

Alternatives to Educational Institutions

The Woman's Building. Outside the established educational system, new institutions have begun to take form. The Woman's Building in Los Angeles founded in 1973 (80 years after the first Woman's Building) is an alternate public center devoted to the exploration of women's culture. It was first located in the former Chouinard Art School, and presently it is in an industrial area contiguous to diverse racial and ethnic neighborhoods. It is a nonprofit collective, housing various research and art studio programs, offices, and gallery and performance spaces.

An example of the institution's concern with making women aware of how to modify the environment was the course "Redesigning in Support of Ourselves," created by Sheila Levrant deBretteville, a graphic designer, and Claire Forrest, an architect teaching at the University of Southern California. The students, mostly nonprofessional women, were asked to document their movement and activities in public and private spaces, to identify their specific needs as users, and to make maps and models that could visually communicate their experiences. These maps and charts signify a considerable departure from traditional user–need identification methods in that they formalize *qualitative* rather than *quantifiable* responses.

The Feminist Studio Workshop of the Woman's Building has also explored and devised feminist methods of supportive criticism while producing excellent and innovative graphic work incorporating women's experiences and concerns. In a poster announcing an exhibition of Eileen Gray at the building, deBretteville defines some of these concerns as found in the work of the Irish-born designer:

Her work, like that of other architect/designers of the modern movement focused on an abstraction of function, structure and materials, but was far from simply materialistic she was not concerned entirely with the formal manipulation of technology. Her respect for contradictory

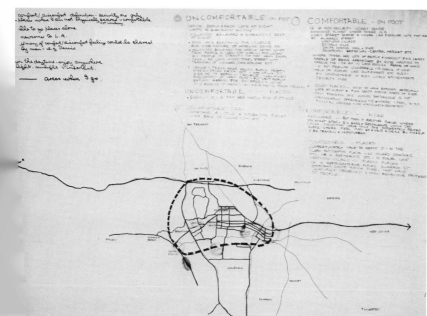

Eileen Gray, perforated metal double screen separating access from bathroom, Studio Apartment, Paris, 1930–1931. Courtesy Deborah Nevins.

Bobbie Wilson, cognitive mapping response in the course, "Redesigning in Support of Ourselves," at the Woman's Building, November 1973. Courtesy Sheila deBretteville.

Above: *"Cake Campus," group discussion, Women's School of Planning and Architecture. Courtesy Women's School of Planning and Architecture Archive.*

Top: *Participants, Women's School of Planning and Architecture, Biddeford, Maine, August 1975. Courtesy Women's School of Planning and Architecture Archive.*

spatial and personal requirements modified her use of the International Style open plan. Others were creating stark, spare, open interior spaces to correspond to the hard, smooth, floating planes of exterior form. Eileen Gray was developing threshold and interior space as well as furniture which were rich, sensual and complex. Her development of multiple use of spaces and objects arose from a desire to accommodate choice and articulate a response to the variety of ways a person moves and rests in a private environment. Eileen Gray broadened the nineteenth century concern with efficient use of space to include multiple use of space.[47]

The Women's School of Architecture and Planning. The first such school to be completely founded, financed, and run by women—The Women's School of Architecture and Planning (WSAP)—grew from the experience and convictions of seven women who first met through women's professional organizations and the conferences in Eugene and St. Louis.[48] The initial planning was accomplished largely by mail andpphone from the coordinators' homes in Detroit, New York, Cambridge, and San Francisco. Eight months later, in August 1975, the first two-week session was held at the campus of St. Francis College in Biddeford, Maine. The 52 adult participants ranged from 18 to 49 and came from a variety of backgrounds.[49]

A core curriculum of five courses permitted the participants to work intensively in small groups. However, several sessions of each course were open to the entire school, allowing for a breakdown of the isolation among small groups commonly found at traditional schools and conferences. "The Community Context of Town Development," taught by Ellen Perry Berkeley, had detailed discussions with local women, mostly nonprofessional, who are active in local planning and development. "Demystification of Tools in Relation to Design," taught by Katrin Adam, focused on carpentry construction as a way of understanding "how things go together" in design.

"Professionalism Redefined," taught by Marie Kennedy and Joan Forrester Sprague, investigated the changing role of the professional and the expanding participation of client and/or user in the design process.[50] "Urban Design: The Outside of Inside," taught by Bobbie Sue Hood, made a team study of the impending growth of St. Francis College and redesigned the campus to accommodate future plans for a medical school. "Women and the Built Environment," taught by Noel Phyllis Birkby and Leslie Kanes Weisman, utilized techniques of fantasy projection, brainstorming, and conceptual block-busting to redefine the present and future environment from the perspective of women as users. In an article about this process, they wrote:

If . . . women's needs are [to be] environmentally supported, then each woman must become her own architect, that is, she must become aware of the ability to exercise environmental judgment and make decisions about the nature of the spaces in which she lives and works.[51]

In organizing the school, the implementation of nonhierarchical and flexible structures was given careful consideration. Coordinator-instructors and students were considered *participants* on an equal basis. The "Prix de Biddeford" awarded at the end of classes consisted of toy wooden towers that came apart, so

that each participant "won" a part to take home. This gesture, however lighthearted, nevertheless challenged the symbolic ritual of official reward based on raising one outstanding individual above the rest.

A second session of WSAP[52] was held for two weeks in August 1976 on the campus of the University of California at Santa Cruz.[53] A number of students from the previous session became coordinators and/or instructors. Entirely new courses added to the original curriculum were "Politics and Ideology of the Urban Planning Process" and "Architectural Design."[54]

Both the Woman's Building and WSAP suggest new interactions between design professionals, as well as new attitudes toward "nonprofessionals." More importantly, they suggest an increased effort to make the general public aware of women's needs so that the built environment will not be so frustrating and demeaning for women in the future.

Although the sheer increase in numbers of women entering architecture may well contribute to its "democratization"—by changing its public image of being a "gentleman's profession"—the emerging attitudes discussed in this chapter may well advance badly needed changes in its practice.

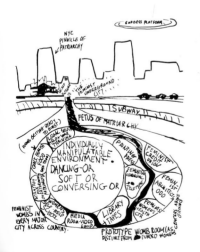 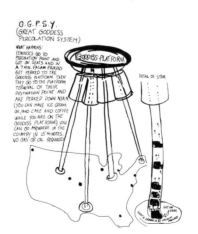

"Fetus of Matriarchy" and "Great Goddess Percolation System," anonymous drawings from the Birkby/Weisman Collection of Women's Environmental Fantasies.

By Susana Torre

11. A Current Portfolio of Projects and Ideas

The ideas discussed in this chapter are organized as threads woven within a matrix. This form is a metaphor for the conclusions to be reached as it establishes a cross-current between the essay's organization as an abstraction and its content, substance, and sources. The excerpts included are from texts about women and architecture written in the past 5 years. Their polemic quality is better conveyed by actual quotes rather than paraphrases. In addition, the projects illustrated here are organized in a nonhierarchical manner. They are in alphabetical order and are given equal space and visual treatment. This format illustrates yet another form/structure consciously used by women in the past few years to signify a temporary suspension of hierarchies—of rank, physical, or psychological authority —giving to each and all the members of a group the same opportunity for personal expression. Although it is true that this format often demands the temporary suspension of critical judgment, it also calls for a temporary suspension of disbelief, thus allowing proposals or achievements hitherto unacknowledged to claim legitimate attention.

The projects were selected only from those submitted to the Archive of Women in Architecture between 1973 and 1976, and therefore many projects of equal value may have been involuntarily excluded. These projects were all designed and/or built in the seventies by individual women or by partnerships where the woman had a major design responsibility. In this particular decoupage, most programs for the projects were generated by the designers themselves or formulated with a significant contribution on their part. This is obviously an anomaly since most architects design what clients order and haee little influence on what gets designed or built. In this case, the projects may be more representative of a particular individual or group's design statement in a limited situation than of the actual opportunities for designing that are available to women today. (Some illustrations of these possibilities can be found in the preceding chapter.)

In addition to traditional as well as recent project and building types represented (house, school, park, museum, mental health center, botanical garden, temple, monument, adaptive reuse of extant buildings), three broad categories provide the context for the particular intentions of the projects. First is living environments designed and built by and for the designers themselves where the form and organization is generally determined by technological experimentation, available resources of materials and labor, or esthetic idiosyncrasies. Second are projects that reflect an extensive program or design participation by others during the design process and projects that formalize the designer's intention to encourage public use and expressive participation after completion. Third are projects in which the designer challenges prevalent attitudes towards architectural form and architectural composition methods or proposes a different programmatic content or social ritual for a known building type.

Although the projects are not meant to literally illustrate the ideas discussed in the text, the range of correspondence and discrepancy between the two nevertheless epitomizes the particular position that architecture has always occupied within culture. Bertolt Brecht once said, "There is no new art [*or architecture*] without new objectives"—and, one could add: and without the means to achieve those objectives. Although architects may be able to recognize and embody new purposes and values in their work, the objectives have to be defined by society itself.

"Architecture Is for People"

A standard is established on some basis, not capriciously, but with the surety of something intentional and o a logic controlled by analysis and e periment.
All men have the same organisms, th same functions.
All men have the same needs (italic added).

Le Corbusier, *Towards a New Architecture.*

The idea of "standard as a virtue" was introduced in the ideology of modern architecture by Herman Muthesius in his 1911 keynote speech to the Werkbund's Congress.[1] Ultimately destined to facilitate the implementation of Germany's military requirements in the ensuing war, the idea of a standard was later adopted as the basis for design throughout the world under the influence of the Bauhaus.[2]

Although the most obvious and superficial effect of a standard can be found in its technological and military applications, its origins are anthropomorphic. A standard, especially a spatial standard, has to be based on some unit of measure. That unit is the male human body. Le Corbusier fully acknowledged the "humanistic" implications of the standard in his creation of the Modulor. Thereby he married the idea of a human scale based on the male body with the rational inevitability of technology. His objective system acted as no less than a "guiding light in so-cial, economic and spiritual life," as indicated in the Girsberger edition of Le Corbusier's work.[3] Through its widespread application, the Modulor replaced that earlier ideal inhabitant of architecture—Leonardo da Vinci's man within a circle.

It has been noted that in ergonomics (the science that studies human measurement and proportions in their interface with objects and machinery) most human-factors design data continue to be based on

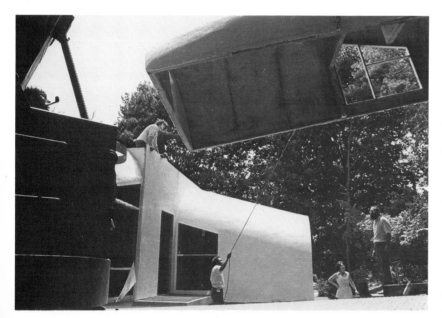

Valerie Batorewicz, assemblage of an "Environ A," an isocyanurate and fiberglass house, an energy-saving housing system invented (patented), designed, and manufactured by the architect, New Haven, Connecticut, 1972. Courtesy V. Batorewicz. This house is one of the prototypes for a patented housing system. The house bridges a gap between conventional building ideas and new plastics materials and technology. It is assembled on the building site. Fiberglass cloth is stretched from a central core to end walls; then everything is sprayed with isocyanurate foam to create a homogeneous building. The prototype shown consists of five "satellite" rooms and a central core containing bathrooms, kitchen, structural supports, and the heating, cooling, electrical, and plumbing systems.

V. Batorewicz, "Environ A" house. Courtesy V. Batorewicz.

white males between the ages of 18 and 25. "As the few books . . . that deal with ergonomics show, the data has been gathered almost entirely from draftees inducted into the army (McCormick), Navy personnel (Tufts University), or Dutch Air Force personnel (Butterworth). Aside from some interesting charts in Henry Dreyfuss' *Designing for People, there simply exist no data concerning really vital measurements and statistics of women, children, the elderly, babies,*

the deformed, etc." [4]

The ideologues of standardization seem to have been guided by an exclusive preoccupation with the male as physical and spiritual protagonist of unrestricted environmental settings. To be sure, this view has been under attack for some time as the widespread application of standardized principles in housing, for example, has failed to respond to the demands, desires, and physical requirements of the majority of the population. For an

environment that fails to embody the *specific* as well as generalized and impersonal needs of a population cannot be said to be truly supportive and humane. It is too frequently forgotten that a society has first to create "the social and economic situation where people wish to be more equal and then think about the kind of physical environment they need to make a statement about wanting that equality, to make it possible for them to live with greater equality—given also that

Above: *Merle Lynn Easton, exhibit space: Science and Technology. Courtesy M. L. Easton. This project is designed to cut time and expense in school construction, to revitalize high density inner city neighborhoods and to provide a more complete and relevant education including the entire community in the processs. The school utilizes "found" spaces, such as streets and empty lots. Prefabricated classrooms and toilets, multimedia domed meeting rooms and retractable barrel vaults plug into a community and draw upon people, existing businesses, and institutions as educational resources.*

Right: *M. L. Easton, model, Street School Concept, Pennsylvania, 1970. Courtesy M. L. Easton.*

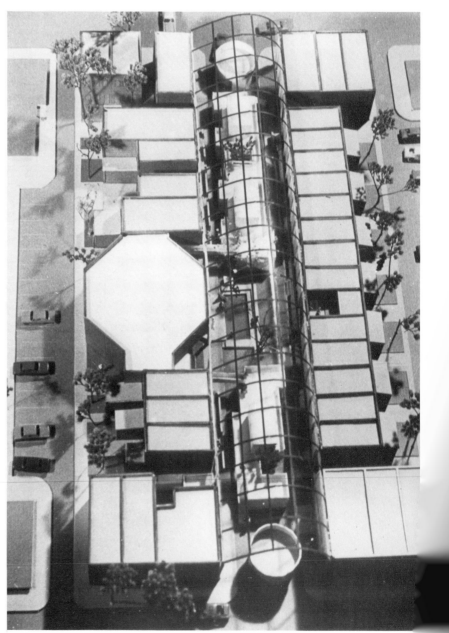

families are different, that individuals are different, that you probably don't want everyone in this society in an identical house because it would really be totalitarian.''[5]

The most important thing about architecture is the effect it has on the people who live in it, work in it, and use the outdoor spaces it creates. Debates on form versus meaning, or purity versus social comment, or classicism versus romanticism miss the point that little is known about these effects (ex-

cept upon the upper classes). . . .

Almost nothing is known about spatial perception and its interpretation into meaning. But it is now known, for instance, that visual sense data coming into the brain are modifed by input from the frontal (associative) cortex— i.e., previous experience—before it even registers as an image on the visual cortex. In other words, the interpretation of ''reality'' takes place prior to and determines perception.

Therefore it may be nonsense to talk about a building's or an environment's

or a form's effect on people, until we know who, what kind of people, with what kind of experience they are perceiving architecture. It *is* an economic class experience, and a race experience, and a sex-gender experience, and other kinds of experiences. And yet there *is* a basic universal human substratum, in the structure of the nervous system. So that there is sense in speaking of and striving for universal harmonies of proportion and form, of fundamental *order*. The interrelationship of these two aspects of the experience of

Top, left: *Anne Hersh, Solar House (under construction), Hornby, New York, 1974–1975. Photograph by Anne Hersh. The house, a 24-foot square A-frame, consists of a general purpose room, kitchen, and bedroom. A children's wing is planned for the future. A hot air solar heating system was chosen for ease of construction and economy of cost. Air passes over a black metal plate covered with two layers of glass. The heated air then enters a 15-ton rock pile under the house that stores the heat. The rock pile is also used as a preheat for the electric-forced air furnace. Construction is wood frame with corrugated aluminum siding.*

Left: *A. Hersh, diagram of heating system, Solar House. Courtesy A. Hersh.*

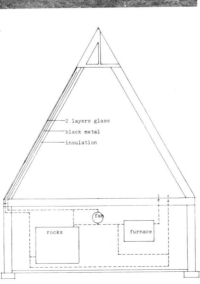

architecture is what is important to think about and to do. It is not one versus the other. That is the easy way out. One aspect without the other produces weak buildings and hostile environments, of which we have a great many at our time in history.

The most unified architecture in history has been built for the functions of social ritual (public architecture) and for the homes and leisure activities of the wealthy. Architects have always known more about and cared more for the universal harmonies in rich people,

simply because they are the ones with the money or in control of it to commission all kinds of buildings and environments. When I was job captain on my first large housing development, an associate of that office bragged that he has never had to do housing. He was a nice fellow, but he didn't have the stomach or the conviction to fight with the city bureaucracy or the contractors for the right of poor and moderate income people to the biological advantages of good aesthetics.

(Excerpted from Lynda Simmons,

"Thoughts of My Life in Architecture," 1973, Archive of Women in Architecture.)

"The Architecture of Sex Roles" [7]

"Architecture is, next to men, the most oppressive force in our society; obsolete architecture is one of the things that is holding us back," one female conscience, recently raised, proclaims.

How does residential architecture affect the woman tied to the home?

Right: *Carol R. Johnson and Associates, playground, North Common Project, Lowell, Massachusetts, 1972. Courtesy Carol R. Johnson & Associates, Inc. The North Common Project consists of the rehabilitation and redesign of an 11-acre common located in Lowell's model cities neighborhood known as the Acre. Extensive community participation was sought with the aid of the Acre Model Neighborhood Organization, a group elected from among the 10,000 Acre residents. A number of questionnaires allowed citizens to have a voice in the kinds of activities and improvements desired for the North Common.*

Bottom, right: *Questionnaire, North Common Project. Courtesy Carol R. Johnson & Associates, Inc.*

Does current architectural design have anything to do with Women's Liberation?

These are only a few questions asked to determine if architecture reflects significantly a system now censored for its contribution to the oppression of women, and whether it can be re-constructed in such a way to respond to women's changing self-concept. Sometimes the questions elicit anger; to many women, architecture is a lost cause.

When new feminists are asked how

architecture relates to them, they often answer that they cannot be concerned with its implicit esthetic function until the original architectural problem is resolved: to provide reasonable places to live in. "My kitchen is a windowless cage," says a Washington, D.C. housewife. "It is the center of my house because it is where I do the cooking, washing, telephoning and thinking. It is where I work and where I monitor the machines that work for me. And since I spend so much time here I think it should be a light tower or a

garden through which I can connect with the outside world; instead it is an isolated, surrealistic space that actually prevents me from knowing what is going on outside. I see no sunshine or shadows, feel no change in temperature, smell no blossoms in a new season. I don't hear real noises, just machines humming and telephones ringing and timers going off. These are sounds that have nothing to do with what is happening or what I am doing."

(Excerpted from Adele Chatfield-

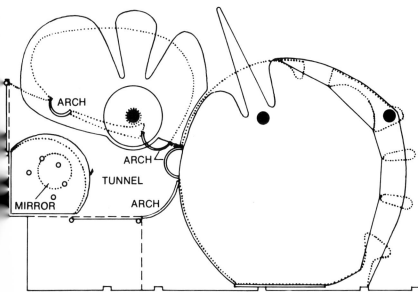

Left: *Aleksandra Kasuba, passageway and the exhibit hall as seen from the rotunda, Twentieth Century Environment, Carborundum Museum of Ceramics, Niagara Falls, New York, 1973. Photograph by Todd Watts. This stretch fabric environment encloses 5,400 square feet of exhibition spaces in the SOM-designed Carborundum Museum of Ceramics. The stretch panels are fastened to floor and ceiling with Velcro fabric fasteners; in some cases the reinforced fabric seams are pressed into split vinyl tubing that runs along the floor and ceiling. Although the floor plans of Kasuba's stretch fabric environments originate in programatic and circulation requirements, the ceiling plan (indicated by the solid line) expresses the sculptural quality of the spaces. In various similar environments, the shape of the continuous fabric wall can be rearranged by moving the concrete weights that anchor the fabric to the floor. Depending on the lighting, the fabric becomes translucent and dematerialized or solid and textural. These soft environments, formed by complex curved topologies, challenge the viewer's perceptual memory of rectilinear, cubic space and nurture a fresh relationship between observer and space.*

Bottom, left: *A. Kasuba, plan, Twentieth Century Environment. Courtesy A. Kasuba.*

Taylor, "Hitting Home: You Can't Make a Silk Purse out of Suburbia," *Architectural Forum,* March 1973.)

Of all the spaces defined by social use, the house is the most private. A "woman's place," as distinguished from a "man's castle," the house contains spaces that are further segregated by sex-related functions and rules. The *kitchen* and the *workshop* are such spaces; within them, each sex fulfills conventional tasks and exercises a territorial appropriation. Neither sex has been traditionally welcomed in the opposite sex's exclusive domain—at best, only tolerated. But although this paradigm of middle class life may be shifting toward a more flexible share of domestic space, the actual spaces, bearing on their surfaces and the objects they contain the stamp of their sex-specificity, reinforce inequality and perpetuate patterns of culturally sanctioned behavior. "We make our buildings and our buildings make us"; space is a social form that influences and shapes behavior.

Not all spatial segregation in the home is so obvious or well defined; a subtle evidence of territorial dominance can be found in the spacious or particularly comfortable chair in the living room or den that the husband reserves for his own use. There, his "rest after work" is given a special spatial designation. The cavalier out-of-place position in which these chairs

Right: *Vassia Kiaulenas, interior, Kiaulenas Studio-Museum, Farmingville, Long Island, 1959–1970. Photograph by V. and H. Laura Kiaulenas, architects-builders-owners. "A place to work and create, surrounded by my collection, my husband's paintings, in a setting he would have loved to work in and show his work—a living museum. But, at the same time, unconspicuous living quarters for the guardians of the place." The house was designed by Vassia Kiaulenas and built almost entirely by her and her daughter. It stands on what was formerly only sand; all trees on the site have been preserved.*

Below: *V. Kiaulenas, ground floor plan and section, Kiaulenas Studio-Museum. Courtesy V. and H. L. Kiaulenas, architects-builders-owners.*

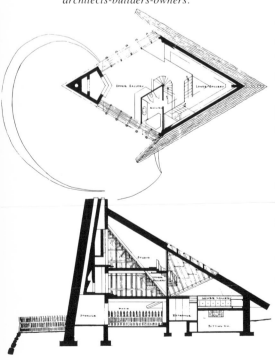

are usually found indicates "that the man in the household can effectively control the use of space and his mate's design of the interior of the house."[8]

The spatial specialization of the bourgeois household begins in the 18th century, later evolving elaborate examples of sexual segregation in the use and character of objects and rooms: the boudoir, draperies and frills, *confidantes,*[9] languorous couches and divans are the new

creations corresponding to an evolving idea of a feminine stereotype. Throughout the 18th and 19th centuries women are depicted in paintings as either nudes or fully clothed figures, half sitting and lying in suggestive and inviting poses surrounded by upholstered furniture, pillows, and draped fabrics.[10] What a difference from the setting of the medieval French house, which Phillipe Aries describes as a space where sleeping, writing, music making, eating,

cooking, lovemaking, and learning went on simultaneously as people of both sexes and all ages and social stations mingled freely![11]

"Letting go with color"; "Pure vanity in a room that is practical too"; "A bedroom the color of her lipstick"; "Spring-like colors make you feel you're in the garden even in the winter"; "In the wide world of to-day's sheets, you can find patterns that express your own needs and desires"—these random headings in

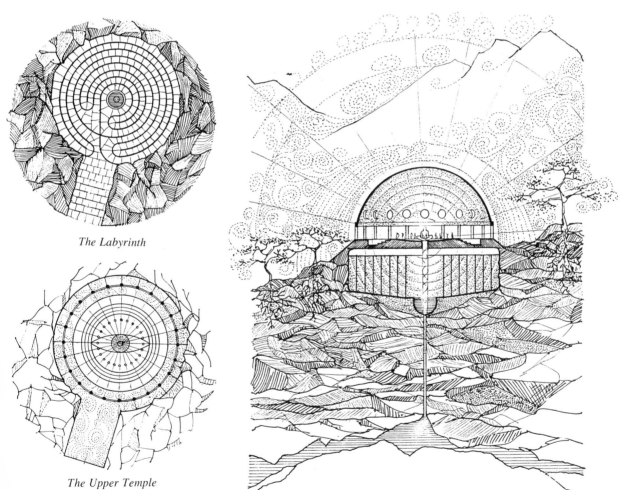

The Labyrinth

The Upper Temple

Above: *Mimi Lobell in collaboration with Jan Clayton, plans, the Labyrinth and the Upper Temple, the Goddess Temple, Aspen, Colorado, proposed 1975. Courtesy M. Lobell. The temple, a celebration of the feminine principle, is designed as a symbolic representation of the physical body of the Great Mother Goddess and the spiritual reunification of the visitor with his/her feminine nature. The lower temple*

is characterized by an entrance passage whose walls are covered with various fabrics and a sloping labyrinth that leads to the silver grail pool. Through this, one reverses the process of birth and individuation. Submergence in the pool reenacts a primal baptism and opens one to the feminine principle. A helical ladder leads from the dark, moist, physical feminine to the light of the spiritually transforming feminine in the upper temple. The raised

circular altar is inscribed with a mandorla representing the all-seeing enlightened wisdom of the Goddess. The temple is the feminine archetype, which lives eternally in the human psyche, materialized in architecture.

Above, right: *M. Lobell with J. Clayton, section, the Goddess Temple. Courtesy M. Lobell.*

today's interior decoration magazines speak of a continuing trend of sex-specificity in spaces and objects. One feels tempted to argue that the defeat of the "good design for the masses" crusade initiated by The Museum of Modern Art in the 1940s was ultimately caused by the androgynous formal qualities of well-designed objects. The success of *kitsch* can be seen in its appeal to conventional class and sexual stereotypes.

It seems unlikely that within these settings a woman can have the space and time to plan, think, and develop a sense of self on her own terms and free from the demands, intrusions, and expectations of others. This is not to deny that every human being's sense of self is indeed formed and, so to speak, "negotiated" through the contact with and the demands of a given context. But the privacy needed to establish a healthy psychological independence is more elusive for women than it is for men in the middle class household, and women seem to have more difficulty creating the necessary means to protect their psychological space without actual physical isolation.

Sociologist Nona Glazer-Malbin has hypothesized that the less distinctive a space is from surrounding spaces, and therefore the less gender connected it is, the more likely each sex is to do the work of the other. This is suggested by recent evidence on the sex-role behavior of camping, where men do women's work in a de-

Sandra Moore, executive director, and all Trenton Design Center participants, brochure, Trenton Design Center, Trenton, New Jersey, 1973. Courtesy S. Moore. The Trenton Design Center (TDC), developed by Sandra Moore with the aid of Art Symes and Bob Frew, was a program to expose inner-city young people to the professions of architecture and urban planning. The building that the Design Center occupied was remodeled, and furniture was designed and constructed by participating students. The TDC worked on many architectural and planning projects and gave young participants the opportunity to learn valuable skills and become involved in community planning and design issues. The center collected all available information on the 701 district, an area of East Trenton destined for urban renewal. It was responsible for the initial feasibility work on the Monument–Willow Housing Project in Trenton, as well as many other projects.

gree proportional to the natural, gender-free quality of the physical setting.[11] Glazer-Malbin has further argued that space segregation according to sex "functions to limit contact between the sexes, excludes each sex from a fuller understanding of the other, limits learning of a variety of skills, and reflects back on concepts of the self."[12]

These problems do not seem limited to the unrestricted use of domestic space. Sex-role differentiations in the use and symbolic perception of the environment have also prevented women from free and uninhibited enjoyment of so-called public spaces. First-class restaurants, bars, shopping areas in stores, restroom lounges, children's playgrounds, and even streets at night are some examples where spatial segregation by sex-roles is still predominant.

The woman alone, the suburban housewife, and the pram-pushing mother are generally seen as the most prominent agit-prop images of the Women's Movement. To be sure, these users of the built environment have far less idealized needs and desires than those attributed both to Modulor man and the woman whose bedroom is the color of her lipstick. Until the time comes when their environmental demands need no longer be the target of feminist-influenced political pressure, the following clever environmental strategies for pram-pushing mothers suggested by

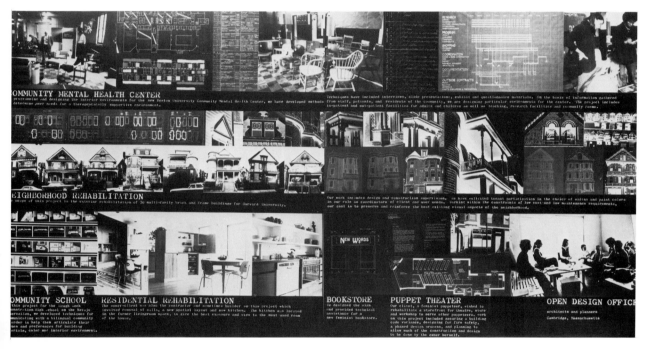

Open Design Office, Architects and Planners, Kathryn Allot, Magda Brosio, Marie Kennedy, Mary Murtagh, Lucille Roseman, Joan Forrester Sprague, members, exhibition documenting work in the spring of 1974 in the Boston area and in Arizona. Courtesy Open Design Office, Architects and Planners. This compendium of a range of projects and processes documents the first years of the Open Design Office. Process techniques to involve users and clients in design include exhibits of materials and furnishings as well as slide presentations, group discussions, and questionnaires. Other working tools include photography as the basis for contract documents in rehabilitation work. Projects include programs and interior environments for a Community Mental Health Center and a Community School Neighborhood. Rehabilitation of 30 residential buildings, rehabilitation of the interior of a builder's house, and specialized services for feminist enterprises—a bookstore and a puppet theater.

British architect Margaret Withers may prove effective: ''Remedies for planning idiocies such as the shoe-shop with women's shoes on first floor and children's in basement: leave pram (with occupant if applicable) in care of surprised young man who sells men's shoes on ground floor. For a bank with high windows and a revolving door, send a rude letter to the managing director of the big four bank and start a current account at the co-op. Tate Gallery (permission refused to take push-chair around after lugging it up all those steps): endeavour (though I don't hold much hope for success) to persuade attendant that small child is a disabled dwarf. Every woman who has been through all this gets a good idea of the obstacles facing the disabled in wheelchairs. It is, I am sure, no accident that recent legislation to help the disabled, including improved access to buildings was pushed through by determined pressure stuff by those much-maligned institutions, the women's organizations.''[13]

The life situation of women in the central cities is largely defined by their race and their class. It is of course also defined by sex. To be ghettoized and impoverished and a woman is different in some ways than to be ghettoized and impoverished and a man. As to which is worse, I am not sure. To struggle to make one's living as a janitor or day laborer is also different, in important ways, than to struggle to

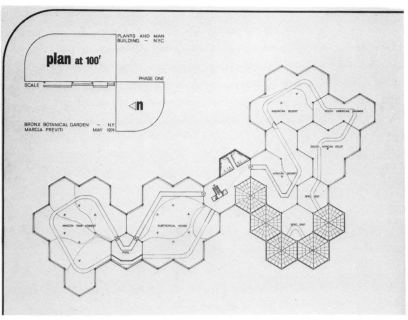

Top: *Marcia Seitz Previti, model, Botanical Garden, Bronx, New York, Bachelor of Architecture thesis, 1974. Courtesy M. S. Previti. The Botanical Garden is a "created outdoors." It is an attempt to simulate many climates in the "real outdoors." The differences in climatic conditions require that each climate be enclosed but not enclosed so that it becomes "indoors." To amplify the illusion of "outdoors," it is necessary to eliminate the sensation of walking into a sheltered place from the "real outdoors." This is done by leading the visitor through an "indoor" space into the "created outdoors" of the gardens. The ideas of growth and nature manifest themselves in the form and structure of the enclosure. The crystalline form of the individual module appears to grow out of the earth.*

Bottom: *M. S. Previti, plan, Botanical Garden. Courtesy M. S. Previti.*

make a home as the wife of that janitor or day laborer. Again, I am not sure which is worse. But the life of the matron in Scarsdale, thwarted and oppressed as we now understand it to be, is entirely different from the life of a welfare mother in Brownsville. I have no difficulty in deciding which is worse, and neither would either of them. In other words, when I say that the life situation of women is defined by race and by class, I mean that sex roles cannot be understood except in the context of race and class.

In these terms, there is a large disjunction between the women of the central city and the women of the Movement. I think it is for this reason that much of what the Movement has said about the situation of women, and much of what it has done, is irrelevant, in some cases even antagonistic, to the interests of women in the central city.

The class bias that limits the Movement as a whole also has limited the thinking and activity of women in planning on behalf of women. This is most

obvious in meetings of women professionals which, it seems to me, have been mainly concerned with the discrimination that women planners and associated professionals confront in planning agencies and schools dominated by men. As if sensing that demands regarding their own advanced education, hiring and upgrading do not reflect the most fundamental issues of social justice in the United States, women professionals often make the argument that if women were the planners, all the other women out there

Top: *Nancy Stout, reconstructed log house, Lowell, Ohio, reconstruction: 1974, addition: 1975. Photograph by George Cooper. Nancy Stout, a lecturer on crafts whose special interest is American domestic art and international indigenous architecture, dismantled a 19th-century log house and reconstructed it on her own property in 1974. Family and friends put the upper story in place during an afternoon house raising. Preservation was given careful attention as were siting and low energy usage. During the summer months Stout removes the mortar between the logs to increase ventilation. In 1975 a board and batten wing, wired for electricity, was added to the original structure.*

Bottom: *N. Stout, interior, showing the mortar removed between the logs to increase ventilation during the summer. Photograph by George Cooper.*

who are the presumed clients of planners would be better off. The argument is weak, of course. The mass of black people are not better off for having a few black officials to cooperate in their rule. Such arguments are better understood as an embarrassed acknowledgment of class differences than as an actual strategy for reform. . . .

Central city women do not, of course, only need money. They also need decent housing, clean and safe streets, parks, schools and shopping facilities. These are not unseemly demands; they are merely the minimum that Americans have been led to believe people ought to have. Planners often have some influence in the policies that determine who will get decent housing, and whose housing will be destroyed to make way for new projects; who will get the new schools that are being built; where the pleasant shopping malls that are being planned, or the vest pocket parks, will be located, and therefore who will benefit from them. All of these public policies involve group and class interests, and in each instance we ought to consider which groups will lose, which will benefit, and endorse the proposals that make life easier for those who have least.

(Excerpted from Frances Fox Piven, "Race and Class," *Design & Environment,* Spring 1974.)

Changes within and without the Profession

For some time, the architectural profession has been deemed by social

Above, left: *Sharon Egretta Sutton, model, outdoor play sculpture, the Children's Art Carnival, St. Nicholas Park, New York, 1974. Courtesy S. E. Sutton. A structural frame called "Dooit City" was used to create imaginary streets and urban environments. A simple post and lintel configuration employed a West African system of joinery. The concept was to introduce children to basic principles of architecture and urban planning and increase environmental awareness. With the neutral frame as a struc-* ture, *participating children could express their ideas and build their own mini-environment. Because it allowed the participation of children in the community, this project expanded upon the official Department of Parks definition of outdoor sculpture and had to be reclassified as playground equipment, for which approval is pending.*

Above, right: *S. E. Sutton, Children's Art Carnival Outdoor Construction Class. Photograph Robert A. King.*

critics to be incapable of understanding or coping qualitatively with individual and collective demands. As social issues have been hauled in the last decade to the dazzling heights of professionalism (every step of the way endlessly discussed and debated), the role of the architect is challenged in the face of increasingly complex social demands and of the political if not always economical validation of these demands.

The criticism is not new, and many steps in different directions have been already taken by individual architects, groups, and professional organizations to bridge the gap between exclusive professional concerns and broader public interests. The wane of the passionate—but not always efficient—advocacy in planning and architecture has convinced many that the architect should not attempt to replace the social scientist or the political pressure group in their specific areas of competence. Two evolving attitudes seem to point in opposite directions: some architects obsessively begin to claim the absolute autonomy of architecture from social concern, and others seek not only to understand how a plurality of social demands may be suitably translated into physical form, but to consciously accept a plurality of esthetic preferences, especially those outside the esthetic canon of the "architect's architecture." However, few will deny that architecture as a profession occupies in our

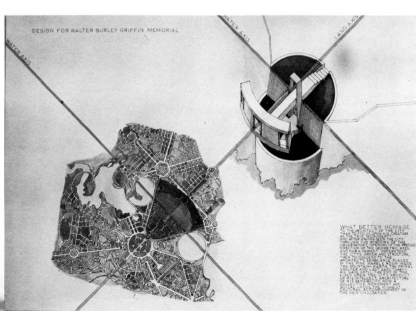

Top: *Susana Torre, site plans, project for a competition for a memorial to Walter Burley Griffin, designer of Canberra, Australia. Drawing by C. Scheerr. This memorial to Walter Burley Griffin, designer of Canberra and husband of Marion Mahony Griffin, can be considered an "antimonument" in that the building is not meant as a monument to a man, but rather as a means to focus the observer's attention on an idea conceptualized as a monument of culture. The visitor is led through a passage aligned with the city's land axis into the observatory's tridimensional facade where three windows open on the city's main axes and civic monuments. After seeing the city below from the conceptual perspective composed by the windows, the visitor descends to the lower level of the observatory. There, in a pink marble "room" dug into the mountain, whose entrance is on the level above, is Griffin's effigy. Water from the upper-level fountain cascades around the marble room into another fountain that surrounds the observation platform one level below. From this vantage point the city is again viewed, framed by the stairs, which are aligned with the city's diagonal axes. The spatial metaphors of water, earth (as primal shelter and last sanctuary), door, passage, and "house" are archetypally female in honor of the presence and influence of Marion Mahony, who was not chosen to be honored in this memorial by the organizers of the competition—although it was Mahony's exquisite presentation of Canberra's plan (as well as her design collaboration) that reputedly won the prize and opportunity to build Canberra for Griffin.*

Bottom: *S. Torre, conceptual drawing showing spatial relationships between the city and the monument, Memorial to Walter Burley Griffin competition. Courtesy Susana Torre.*

society a rather anomalous position, since it combines a relatively high status with relatively low power and is in an endemic state of crisis. Everett Hughes' classic remark—"Profession is a symbolic label for a desired status"—seems applicable to the architectural profession. The options are not many; they seem to lie between status professionalism and occupational professionalism.

In the U.S., especially since World War II, the main setting for practice is the large organization, which has gradually replaced small- or medium-sized offices. Consequently, most architect-employees are effectively insulated by the organization from what might be construed as a potentially threatening contact with the actual users. Moreover, professional progress depends almost entirely on reputation within the profession, and disassociation of professional advancement from user satisfaction is stoutly maintained, although seldom acknowledged. The professional ideal, it seems generally agreed, has three important aspects: the notion of service, an emphasis on professional judgment based on specialized knowledge, and a belief in professional freedom and autonomy in the work situation. Having passed their examinations and served the prescribed apprenticeship, professional architects are free to practice, immune from lay scrutiny.

In the context of this book, it is

Top: *Lauretta Vinciarelli, "Towards the Definition of a Spatial Fabric," 1975. Photograph by eeva inkeri. This project is part of a theoretical study on the compositional definition of a spatial fabric. The chart indicates (A) the catalog of spatial situations considered, from frames and boxes progressing to multiple enclosures and walls, (B) the generative transformation of the nonhomogeneous grid in the plan, obtained by triangulation, (C) the translation of the bi-dimensional grids into cubic modules that do not yet constitute a spatial fabric, and (D) the juxtaposition of the spatial situation considered in (A) with the spatial modules in (B)—which generates a series of rules for the compositional definition of the spatial fabric.*

The plan of the spatial fabric shows one of many possible spatial configurations obtainable by the compositional application of the transformational rules. The objective of this theoretical study is to challenge the simplistic geometric organization provided by homogeneous grids, which are still the basis of architectural composition. The project further proposes that spatial geometry not be considered in isolation from culturally defined architectural situations if the objective is to achieve a spatial/architectural fabric rather than a self-contained architectural object.

Bottom: *L. Vinciarelli, plan of the Spatial Fabric. Photograph by eeva inkeri.*

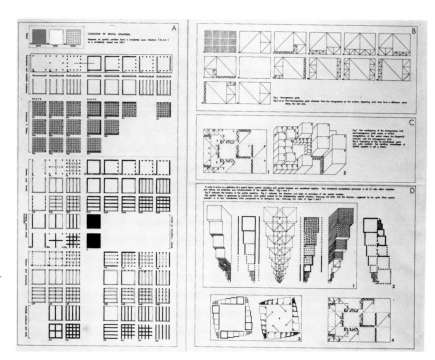

important to note that a critique of the profession *as a whole* has been a concern of women architects as important as their vested interest in denouncing their own discrimination within the profession. The current criticism voiced by women's groups is raised against specific aspects of the described professional ideal. They have claimed, for example, that if the professional is to act *pro bono publico,* the current competitive drive to get business has to be abandoned or drastically curtailed. In other words, they see social responsibility as being incompatible with the profit motive. The validity of professional judgment has also been under attack, although the general idea is being retained that there are design and technical decisions that the professional is best qualified to make. This critique specifically questions the principle that architects should claim all the decision-making power in those areas that contain indicators of social hierarchies and values, such as esthetic expression and the spatial organization of buildings.

Henry Atherton Frost, director of the Cambridge School for women, observed in 1941 that ''[the woman architect's] interest in her profession embraces its social and human implications.''[14] This interest has been rekindled today in the aims expressed by many women's ''design collectives'' and individual practitioners to identify with so-called nonprofession-

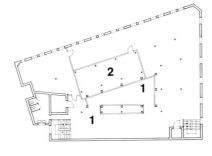

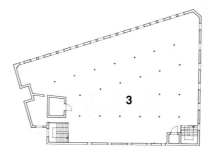

Left: *Lobby, the Woman's Building. Photograph by Maria Karras. The Woman's Building, a public center for woman's culture, Los Angeles, California. Design/construction coordinators: Sheila Levrant deBretteville, Cheryl Swanack (with 2,350 volunteers). Within 2 months, 30 years of warehouse grime were removed and new spaces created in an existing industrial building. The process involved hundreds of initially inexperienced people in the building of a place with a sense of optimism and possibility. The design emphasis was placed on open forms and circulation spaces as places of planned and chance meeting, conversation, protest, and celebration. By leaving an indoor street along the periphery, the natural light remained part of the shared public environment and an easy understanding of the whole container was maintained. Within this active field for personal, professional, and cultural interaction, a minimum of new walls creates a variety of smaller, more articulate, and private spaces, with only a few restricted to a single use. In contrast with the formidable facade, a softly colored, descriptive welcome invites the use of the bookstore, galleries, cafe, and graphics lab.*

Bottom, left: *Renovation, the Woman's Building. Photograph by Maria Karras.*

Bottom, right: *Second and third floor plans, the Woman's Building. Courtesy the Woman's Building. (1) gallery spaces, (2) screening room, (3) performance space and cafe.*

als (especially other women) and to educate them in the identification of their environmental needs and exercise of environmental judgment. Perhaps the most interesting aspect of this relationship is the attempt to devise mechanisms and channels for professional accountability to non-professionals at large. Some of the changes proposed by women, both within and without the established profession, have already been raised in the preceding chapter. In general these proposals have focused on the analysis and redefinition of architecture as a social phenomenon and architecture as an institution. Those advocates of change within the established profession have sought to identify various forms of discrimination, have proposed revisions of the office's work structure to incorporate flexible schedules as a standard practice, and have devised new approaches to the professional award system, based on evaluation provided by the actual users of a building after a certain period of use, instead of the evaluation of professional experts immediately after the building's completion.[15]

Those advocates of change outside the established profession have begun to form design collectives, now proliferating in various locations.[16] The organization of these collectives differs from that of the traditional office in several aspects, but especially in one: all the members of the collective participate equally in the decision-making process. Although the accomplishment of a consensus through this process often demands a considerably longer period of time, it also implies something closer to the real meaning of *efficiency* (*efficientia* was a Latin noun for "quality"). In these terms, efficiency is no longer seen as the achievement of a result *in a short period of time* (fostered by the "time is money" ideology), but rather as the achievement of a relevant and *qualitative* result agreeable to all the members of the group. The task-related structure of these collectives varies depending on the knowledge and skills of the members, and it is usually a combination of the horizontal and vertical staff organizations described in the *Architect's Handbook*

of Professional Practice of the American Institute of Architects.

Can these groups be expected to entirely replace the profession as it is now established? Obviously not. Without a profound change in our institutions such groups will only exist as "utopian interventions," as the piecemeal projective action of individuals and small groups, who, in setting themselves outside the present structure, attempt to create the limited conditions of a new social order. Their value can perhaps be seen in the working alternative they offer to those who endeavor to reconcile their personal and political beliefs with their professional roles and technical aptitudes.

A flexible work schedule is mandatory at the present time, if the capabilities of women are to be realized. Women find that their childrearing years overlap a critical period in their careers and are forced to make an all-or-nothing choice between having a family or continuing their professional development. Women should be entitled to work if they want to or have to, in whatever way is possible for them.

The tendency in many planning and architectural offices, however, is to separate from the "committed" professional anyone who suggests a more flexible work schedule. The latter is relegated to "low status" jobs—for example, conducting neighborhood surveys (in planning) or drafting details (in architecture). The serious full-time professional on the rise goes to client meetings and is groomed for an executive or administrative position. Lacking serious part-time work opportunities, women must often drop out during the critical years of career development and lose work continuity and the opportunity to rise in their professions. The real question is whether the capabilities of women are worth the adjustments that must be made by an office. We believe they are, not only because good professionals are always needed, but also because a person who spends a significant portion of time in activities outside the office might approach environmental design quite differently, bringing further enrichment to the professions. . . .

Alternative Arrangements

The following are some suggestions for alternatives to the standard work schedules:

1. Flexible-time contracts in which an employee agrees to work a specific amount of time per year as needed (perhaps half or two-thirds the regular total) rather than on a regular schedule. This could prove to be a definite advantage for the employer. Peaks and lows in the work load or in phases of a job could be accommodated economically without short-term hiring and firing. There might be periods of charette and periods of no work at all. The variety in itself would be stimulating, and the time spent in the office would relate to real work needs, not to an artificial schedule.

2. Task-related contracts in which an employee agrees to accomplish a specific task by a specific date with no stipulation as to where or when the work must be done. This would allow freedom to work nights or mornings or weekends, as one's best time of day or other commitments suggest. Employer and employee might agree in advance how many total hours of work the job should require. The procedure might be as simple as saying, "We need this drawing completed by Tuesday. Do you think you can do it in about 20 hours?" The employee is then free to accomplish it when and how s/he believes best, and if there are questions, can schedule him/herself to be in the office when the appropriate person is available to help. In other situations the project coordinator might estimate a schedule and amounts of time to accomplish various phases of the work and then "sub-contract" them out to various members of the team at each phase. In many cases this procedure is already being used informally, but if it is formalized, each person gains the freedom to accomplish a task in the way best suited to the person and the specific job.

3. Paired workers for one job: Two or more workers might split a job in a fashion appropriate to that specific task. Some overlap of time and a good job diary would be required to keep each worker informed of problems and decisions. This is already being done with a limited number of teaching jobs in the Brookline, Mass., public school system, and there is an employment agency in Newton, Mass., that acts as a clearing house for employees wishing to share jobs in a variety of fields. This approach requires a certain compatibility between co-workers and probably would work best if the pair is self-selected. However, the principle o

shared responsibility is already in effect in many offices where one worker covers for another on vacation or temporarily out of the office. Pairing assures a consistent backup in emergencies.

4. Expansion of the consultant approach. People with highly desired skills (spec writers, renderers, photographers, interior designers) are often able to set their own schedules, and in smaller offices where they cannot be supported full time they are welcomed in a job-by-job basis. In larger offices, several specialists could be on retainer for less than full-time work and would therefore be assured a regular income. These approaches could be extended to less specialized areas.

The work of an architect or planner is considered to be thinking work rather than mechanical, and for the committed professional the mental work often continues outside the office. Mere presence at a desk has not proved to be a guarantee of good work; there has to be trust on the part of the employer and responsibility on the part of the employee. If the employee is free to work when and how s/he believes best, dignity can be added to the roles of all personnel. This shared responsibility and respect would acknowledge the employee as a total professional rather than a tool in a hierarchy. The employer would reap the benefits of thought and effort from a whole person instead of simply buying technical ability.

(Excerpted from WALAP, "The Case for Flexible Work Schedules," *Architectural Forum,* September 1972. The following people contributed to this article: Andrea Leers Browning, Joan E. Goody, Lisa Jorgenson, Shelley Hampden-Turner, Sarah P. Harkness, Joan Forrester Sprague, Jane Weinzapfel.)

People have questioned the possibility of having a nonhierarchical structure without having a homogenous membership. Members of the Open Design Office are by no means homogenous (nor do we wish to be), varying widely in experience, capabilities, interests and life styles. We derive many benefits from this variety and have found that in a noncompetitive work environment it is possible to draw on another's fuller experience without becoming the servant of that person.

Making the distinction between learning from another person and being "bossed" by that person requires a certain vigilance on the part of all members. To a certain extent we have all been conditioned to relate to a "pecking order" based on sex, wealth, social prominence, etc.

Nonhierarchy

Working without a hierarchy, on an everyday "nitty gritty" level, means, for example, that each of us must be financially responsible. There is no "they" to see that the rent is paid, that clients pay their bills, that salaries are paid, etc. We don't have the position of the employee who is often alienated from her or his work (like the factory worker who only assembles one of thousands of parts of an automobile and has little involvement with the whole process) or who may be suddenly out of a job, nor of the employer who has to meet a fixed payroll (or fire employees) regardless of the work load.

We can accept projects to match the interests of persons who will work on the project rather than taking questionable projects to pay for heavy staff overhead. There is no "they" to decide what work we will do—what type jobs to go after, which jobs to accept and what tasks each member will perform. All of the decisions regarding rate of pay, job promotion, job acceptance, who works on what job, what tasks each member does, etc., are decided by consensus.

We will never find ourselves working on a job that conflicts with our social/political sense, nor a job we find boring. We can work in areas of our greatest experience and strength and we can also learn completely new areas of our field working with another member whose experience and strength lie in that area. We are not forced to pretend to an expertise we don't have nor do we have to minimize our knowledge in another area in order to flatter a boss.

Flexible Schedules

Critics of the concept of flexible schedules point to the difficulty of coordination and promoting job continuity. We have found little problem in these areas. Admittedly, having a nonhierarchical structure makes working on flexible schedules easier. Since we each take responsibility for the whole process of a job, there is no tendency to leave tasks undone, assuming "they" will take care of it.

There is an obligation on all of us to communicate our schedules and changes in schedule to the other members, but this is an easy matter.

Elimination of the Profit Motive

The third principle—that of not taking profits out of the firm—probably needs little explanation. By paying ourselves only for work done, we maintain a direct relationship between payment and work. This relationship has been lost in the corporate business world as a whole, and unearned profit has been one of the strongest incentives to exploit the work of others. Our profits are used to subsidize community projects, or to generate more useful work for ourselves by doing special research or promotion projects which we agree upon.

Organization Development

Building an alternative office structure is an ongoing process and the preceding description of our structure may make it sound deceptively easy. It is difficult to chronicle the false starts, misjudgments and emotional turmoil that we have experienced. Decision making in a nonhierarchical situation requires individual skills and characteristics that we may not have all developed thoroughly—self definition, a high trust level, high initiative level, impetus to ask questions instead of bluffing, and the willingness to take individual responsibility as well as responsibility to and for the other members of the office.

We have faced organizational issues involving dependency, responsibility and commitment to the office, team building, financial planning and expansion. The difficulties involved in reaching working solutions in these and other areas will decrease as we gain more experience working nonhierarchically, but the office is not rigid and the working solutions of today will be refined or perhaps entirely scrapped in the future.

The framework itself allows and encourages flexibility over time. Decisions, once made, may be changed when experience warrants it. Members of the office will come and go, depending on individual professional and personal goals. The character of the office is a factor of the individual members working at any one time and will change as the membership group changes.

As long as the basic framework that we have described remains, it will provide an effective check on any impulse to exploit co-workers. Basically, we are, as individuals and as a group, in control of our work environment, with no in-built mechanism for exploitation. Ideally, we are able to work toward individual professional goals within the framework of the group, without being obliged to sacrifice our personal lives to this end. We gain from the group to the extent that we are able to draw upon each other's strengths and fill in weakness and blind spots for one another. . . .

Drudgery vs. Creativity

As the result of our involvement with all phases of each project we have become concerned with reevaluating contract documents, bookkeeping systems, billing procedures, relationships with contractors, etc. We have found that much that has been thought of as the "drudgery" of architecture and hence has traditionally been relegated to those who have not "made it" as designers can, in fact, be creative work that affects the final result. These tasks are an important part of each architect's experience. We think they should be taught creatively in schools of architecture.

(Excerpted from "Open Design Office . . . A Working Alternative," *The Magapaper* of the Associated Student Chapters of the AIA. This article was written by Magda Brosio, Marie Kennedy, and Joan Forrester Sprague.)

An Architecture of Female Values

If the criticism leveled by both male and female critics against most contemporary architecture is that it is monumentally arrogant, impersonal, unresponsive to human needs and desires, and destructive of the environment, it may be useful to recall its origins before we conjecture what changes might be wrought by the employment of more women architects and engineers.

We know that it was out of the disastrous Chicago fire of 1871 that the new architecture was born. Huge, sprawling, crude, energetically the industrial and commercial capital of the United States, the Caliban of American· cities where, as Henry James would remark, God was Money and Money was God,

Chicago was the perfect spawning ground for a new style of building free from European influences. Five decades before the fire, Ralph Waldo Emerson lamented that the arts of America were feminine and characterless, tottering for want of the "masculine or creative" because they imitated Europe. It was another writer who supplied the necessary masculinization, the bursting out of the "feminine Victorian bonds": Walt Whitman, that paradigm of the repressed homosexual whose phallic virility and physical irrepressibility triumphed on all the muscle beaches of the mind. In offering *Leaves of Grass* to the American public, Whitman reached and transformed one of the most influential of all American architects, Louis Sullivan (1856–1924).

Lewis Mumford called Sullivan "The Whitman of American Architecture," and not by chance. For Sullivan himself could have written lines like Whitman's "I am large, I contain multitudes" or "Landscapes projected masculine, full-sized and golden." Adoring Whitman for having freed the "masculine spirit" in himself, Sullivan emulated him in his major opus on building, *Kindergarten Chats.* Here he eulogized a particular building by his Chicago colleague, Henry Hobson Richardson (1838–1886), because: ". . . here is a man for you to look at . . . an entire male . . . four-square and brown, it stands, in physical fact, a monument to trade, to the organized commercial spirit, to the power and progress of the age, to the strength and resource of individuality and force of character . . . therefore have I called it, in a world of barren pettiness, a male; for it sings the song of procreant power, as the others have squealed of miscegenation. . . ."

For what is the American male corporate obsession with "the biggest and tallest" but a reflection of the little boy's competition with Daddy. The drive is rampant and blatantly emotional. Witness this self-deluding rationalization by Sears Roebuck of its 1,450 foot, 110 story tower which will top the twin phalluses of the World Trade Center by 100 feet: "Being the largest retailer in the world, we thought we should have the largest headquarters." Not the most humane; just the largest. And the Empire State Building, once the world's biggest phallus, is now adding 11 stories.

This kind of masculine super-stereotypical competition might be amusing if it were not so devastatingly

uneconomic and ultimately destructive. What is the real rationale of the Sears tower if its electrical system itself could serve a city of 147,000 and its air-conditioning cool 6,000 homes? Can we remember Frank Lloyd Wright's fantasy, the Mile-High Building Project for Chicago's lakefront in 1956, when he proposed a needle-shaped tower to house 130,000 people? Can we look for anything rational to explain what is clearly an irrational phenomenon: the rage of bigness, for superman?

(Excerpted from Elizabeth Lindquist-Cock and Estelle Jussim, "Machismo in American Architecture," *The Feminist Art Journal,* Spring 1974.)

The inference of meaning from built form derives from our psychological associations, collective ideologies, and the cultural context of each epoch. The reading of a meaning by an observer may be different from the projected meaning intended by a designer, but this is inevitable, as it depends on each person's mental repertory of analogies and grasp of metaphor, as well as the fact that meanings change.

Analogy and metaphor lead to meaning. In analogy, the inference of meaning depends on an essential resemblance between what we look at and something we already know; in metaphor there is a transference of meaning from something where this meaning is properly applicable to something else that is different from the original reference.

It has not yet been ascertained whether analogies and metaphors exist in architecture itself or in the verbal and written language we use to talk about architecture; points of view and theories are still divided in this respect. For some theoreticians architecture is the space of representation, a language that refers to meanings outside itself (the social structure, the power of business, the idea of masculinity, the embodiment of female values, and so on). For others, architecture is a language referring to itself and its own history; it is the manipulation of pure architectural signs and of their grammar and syntax. Yet for others, it would not be proper to speak of a "language" of architecture at all, for all meanings are to be educed from the written texts about architecture. The intention of projecting a meaning, however, is inherent in both the observation and the creation of built form, regardless of whether this meaning is inside or outside of architecture itself.

Simplicity and clarity, or complexity and ambiguity, are design principles that control the range of meanings to be found in form, and design attitudes oscillate between the imposition of a formal order on the chaos of life and the formal expression of the pathos of human existence.[17]

As I become increasingly sensitive to those aspects of design which reinforce repressive attitudes and behavior, I increasingly question the desirability of simplicity and clarity. The thrust to control via design almost inevitably operates through oversimplification, enforcing a single reading or use. Control is undermined by ambiguity, choice, and multiplicity because subjective factors in the reader/user become more effective and participation is encouraged. Participation undermines control. The oversimplified, the controlled and unemotional, the unremittingly serious and emphatically rational are the consistent attitudes associated with work and adopted by our major institutions and the men and few women who inhabit them. These attitudes and the behavior that expresses them have become restricted to and associated with men and the professional environment. In the circle of cause and effect, it is these attitudes which are reinforced and reproduced as they are visually and physically extended into our environment.

One means of simplification is to assign attributes to various groups and thereby reinforce divisions, or isolating functions. The restriction of certain behavior to work and other behavior to the home creates a destructive imbalance. Design reinforces this imbalance by projecting the male tone in the public world of our large institutions (business, science, the military, and even education); valuing their anonymous, authoritarian aspects; and separating them further and further from the private world, thus continuing to isolate women, female experience and female values. . . .

When the idea and the image are simplified and complete, there is no space to bring one's own experience

and values to the forms; there is no opportunity to challenge one's habits, attitudes, and assumptions regarding men, women, work, and home. If there is no complexity or choice, there is only one possible reading; the eye is attracted once and the message understood and accepted, probably thoughtlessly. But when visual material is ambiguous or full of various aspects of the information, the different nuances often encourage alternative reactions to the same communication, and the user's participation and personal responsibility is validated. But few clients ask to be challenged. And most designers limit the problems to be solved in an effort to arrive at a potent image. The easy acceptance of gestural, single-reading, single-use designs and disregard of the symbolic content of forms result in a relationship between client and designer in which the program does not include the encouragement of a thinking audience.

The organization of material in fragments—multiple peaks rather than a singly climactic moment—has a quality and rhythm which may parallel women's ontological experience, particularly her experience of time. . . .

The linearity of time is foreign to the actual structure of a day, as well as to the rhythm of women's monthly biological time. Thought processes released from the distortions of mechanical progress are complex, repetitive, and permeated with the multiple needs of others as well as oneself. Unbounded relationships cause most women to think not only about work, but about the groceries needed for dinner, a child's dental problems, etc., in between thoughts about work. Women's tasks in the home are equally varied and open-ended—child-rearing is the classic example—while a man's work in the home has a beginning and an end; it has specific projects, such as fixing windows, appliances, or plumbing. The assemblage of fragments, the organization of forms in a complex matrix, reflects this experience of time and suggests depth and intensity as an alternative to progress. . . .

One way for the design arts to alter the public world is to develop images of the future which embody alternative values. To do this we must know what forms most communicate "female" values and which devalue femaleness and female experience and cannot incorporate such modes as emotionality, complexity, and supportive cooperation. The difficulty of infusing positive aspects of woman's role in the private

home into the public world of work is echoed in our difficulty in imagining a radically different society. The inevitability of reproducing ourselves rather than a new society could be avoided as we think of the values we wish to project into the new world.

(Excerpted from Sheila Levrant deBretteville, "A Reexamination of Some Aspects of the Design Arts from the Perspective of a Woman Designer," *Arts in Society* (Women and the Arts), Spring–Summer 1974.)

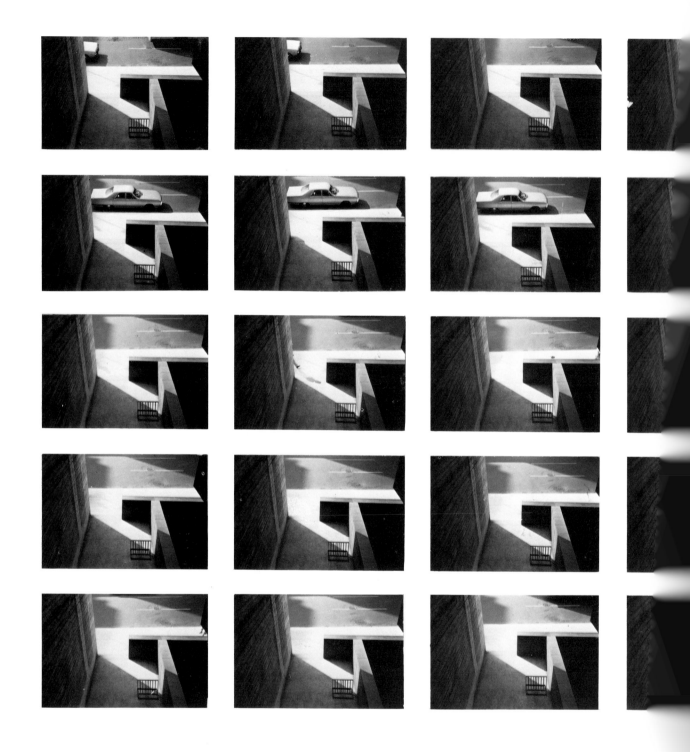

Women's Spatial Symbolism

Dorothy Alexander, White Flower, *1974.*

"Architecture remains orbicular around the static human center" —writes Sybil Moholy-Nagy in *"The Canon of Architectural History"* —*"inner and outer space are separately defined."* Although she probably did not mean to imply separate gender definitions of inner and outer space, nevertheless, cultural associations imply meanings related to attributes of maleness and femaleness. Can we then speak of an original female experience and conceptual representation of space? Is there a spatial symbolism that is uniquely woman's?

Many women artists have recently begun to consider their art as the esthetic embodiment of a new creative consciousness, based on autobiography and myth, perception of social roles, experience of time, and emotional or intellectual connections with others.

Chapter 12 discusses this creative consciousness as reflected in the art of women who use space and spatial interactions as their prime materials. These esthetic representations of space have produced an imagery of centers, *symbolically reminiscent of shelters, prisons, refuges, and sanctuaries. They have also generated an imagery of* patterns, *of social and spatial* networks, *and of* fragments *woven within matrices. Many of these works are purposely left open ended, suggesting that their form and meaning is to be completed by others.*

Chapter 13 contrasts two spatial ar-

chetypes, the Pyramid and the Labyrinth, raising some irreverent questions about the spatial materialization of male and female unconscious desires and conscious intentions. The idea of the Labyrinth, seen as the space of experience and sensuality rather than of reason, is here discussed as architecturally embodied in two extraordinary, if eccentric, buildings: Llanda Villa designed by Sarah Winchester and the Bottle Village built by Grandma Tressa Prisbey.

By Lucy R. Lippard

12. Centers and Fragments: Women's Spaces

In the arrangement of a house, and the introduction of ornamental furniture, and articles of bijouterie, there can be no doubt of the innate superiority of women.
A Lady, *The Lady's Home Companion,* Philadelphia, 1852.

. . . don't/like to travel but enjoy being in new/places. In each room I need books and yellow/roses. I try to keep my house within my head. It is enough that the heart operates/the rest of the body. I recall only/ blueprints, monuments, architectural dreams.
Rika Lesser, "The Room," *American Review,* no. 21, October 1974.

"You harmonize with your apartment, Fanny," Josée told her. "I think that's something quite unusual."
"Who decorated yours?" Fanny asked.
"Oh yes, it was Leveque and he did a very good job, didn't he?"
"I don't know. So people say. I don't think it really becomes me. I seldom feel in harmony with interior decoration of any kind. Only sometimes with people."
Francoise Sagan, *Those Without Shadows.*

No matter how sparse an interior, it is a space where things have happened, essentially an arena for anecdote and association, a sensuous stage where the handwriting is not only on the wall but nestled in every corner, on every object and surface. The outside of a building, on the contrary, is the mask of that container, which can offer a total denial of what it contains. Few people can afford to affect the exteriors of their dwellings, but an interior can be remodeled in a few hours by astute addition or subtraction and little expense.

If I stay more than a few days in a neutral space—hotel, furnished room, borrowed house—I have to change it. I can't settle down till I have shoved all the furniture around, set up a work space, stuck some personal images up on the walls. A few years ago, after living in three such places over a short time, it occurred to me how different my responses were to interior space and to exterior form. We mold interiors to the subjective shapes of our bodies and our images of ourselves. We live there. We look at exteriors with objective pleasure or indifference, in passing. The inside of a house is literary, the outside sculptural. Traditionally, inside represents female, outside male. Attention has already been drawn to the male concern with facade and monument, the female concern with function and environment; the male concern with permanence and structural imposition, the female concern with adaptability and psychological needs; the male concern with public image, the female concern with biography and autobiography.

The cliché about seeing people more clearly when you have been in their home is perfectly true. A home containing more than one person should present a complex picture—prose, perhaps, rather than poetry. At the same time, different signs are noticed, read, and connected differently by different visitors. As a mirror of the psychological needs of its inhabitants and designers, an intimate space encourages or discourages communication, comfort; manipulates or disregards certain interactions; sets up certain dramatic possibilities. The transformation of the living space usually begins with a desired transformation of the self. The changes made will reflect the changer's development. They may be a step toward increased self-confidence to venture out into broader fields; or may incorporate the expectations of interrelationships with the people and notions s/he intends to "entertain" there.

In a natural extension of this idea, several artists have made their living spaces into works of art and have even exhibited them in galleries. Tiger Morse's fantastic environment epitomized the exaggerated life-styles of the sixties. Bedroom "sculptures" are relatively common. Performance artist Colette thinks of her own apartment as "an inner sculpture" and has modeled herself on the chameleon, who becomes one with it surroundings. Her sensuous boudoir pieces frequently take transformation as their theme. In Lyn Hershman's hotel room series, wax women sleep bathe, or wait, surrounded by the careless evidence of their daily lives The viewer, or voyeur, intrudes on a intimate tableau and is invited to re the clues to the occupant's histories. The clues and clutter (or lack thereof) in an interior space is like a book open to many overlapping interpretations, a collaborative activity, the woven container of more than one past and present. Alison Knowles' *House of Dust* is both a cavelike structure and a computer printout of many combinations of inhabitants, events, and locations, making stories become the true occupants of the space.

The classic example of the "fictionalized space" was the transformation of *Womanhouse,* an old residence totally remodeled by the students and artists of the Cal Arts Feminist Art Program in 1971. It became the receptacle for the lives and fantasies of women, and it represented their final triumph over fears of house and home, confinement and release. Among its images were a mannequin emerging from the linen closet, a brutally pessimistic "bridal staircase" that began as the American dream and ended as a nightmare, a depressive sand sculpture of a figure slumped in a bathtub, a secret room within a room, a nursery with giant furniture making infants of the viewers, a menstruation bathroom, a kitchen with walls dotted by fried-egg breasts, a replica of Léa's room from Colette's novel, *Chéri,* where on exhibition days a lovely young woman made herself up, peered at herself dissatisfied, wiped off the makeup, and began again, and again, and again. Throughout the house, and the statements in the catalog, is a pervasive ambivalence about the home. An initially charming dollhouse gives way to invading monsters—ten men stare in the kitchen window, a rattlesnake curls on the living room floor, a baby is threatened by a scorpion. "Beautiful and frightening," "refuge and trap," vie with fantasies of "otherness," escape, a place to hide as *Womanhouse's* recurrent themes.

My motto, idea and hobby all rolled into one is to make home the biggest drawing card in the lives of my family.
Letter from a farm woman to *The Country Gentlewoman,* April 1945.

Above: *Alison Knowles, "House of Dust," original casting: New York, 1969; permanent installation: California, 1970. Courtesy California Institute of the Arts.*

Top: *Colette, "David's Wraith," room installation at Long Island City Center, June 1976. Photograph by Colette.*

Miriam Schapiro, "The Shrine, the Computer, the Dollhouse," made in collaboration with Sherry Brody, containing miniaturized drawings by Lee Bontecou and Sherry Brody, painting by Miriam Schapiro; from "Womanhouse," a project of the Feminist Art Program, California Institute of the Arts, 1973. Photograph by Deborah Dyer.

I always wait in suspense for a stranger to come into my room for the first time. The room has been straightened—no, set like a baited trap. The bait is not fatal either to take or to leave, but it is bait, nevertheless, bait for certain sensibilities, certain sympathies. My life alone within that room has evolved a precise shape, a formality like that of a web.

Judith Thurman, "Living Alone," *Ms.,* July 1975.

His little car started up discreetly in the deep white dust of the dry road. Then the cat appeared, like a fairy, and I went into the kitchen to light the fire . . . for I was trembling with cold and all I felt was an urgent need to soak myself in a very hot, vinegary, aromatic bath, a bath like those in which one takes refuge in Paris, on black winter mornings.

Colette, *Break of Day.*

Living space is an extension of the body, and biological as well as social experience influences a woman's preoccupations with the relationships among outside, entrance, and inside. Many women artists, whether or not they choose to acknowledge the role of interior space and the central core imagery that so often unconsciously reflects the biological and social space of a female, are consciously preoccupied with formal relationships between inside and outside. Some examples: in much of Louise Bourgeois' work, the eye and body-imagination are invited to enjoy enclosures and interior spaces, womblike labyrinths, labial "doors." Her roomlike latex tableau called *The Evening Meal* existed between an equally oppressive floor and ceiling, abstractly conveying (as the artist intended) the anxieties of the nuclear family: threatening protuberances and weights, soft things that are deceptively hard; the head of the father lies beneath the table, and the bones of a consumed fowl on its surface. Judy Rifka's series of identical wooden doors, ever diminishing in size, parallel pictorially the process of entering, entering, entering, only to reach a dead end. Athena Tacha's chalk-lined sculpture room *(Vernal Equinox Crossings of Oberlin Horizon with the Ecliptic, at 30 Hour Intervals)* makes the room

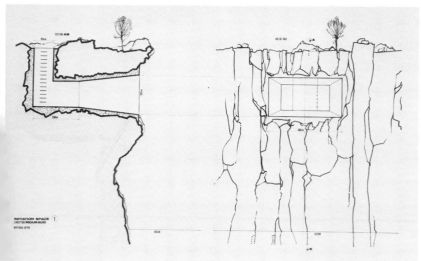

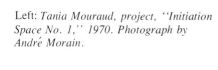

Left: *Ann Mills, "Leaf Room," from "Womanhouse," a project of the Feminist Art Program, California Institute of the Arts, 1973. Photograph by Judy Chicago.*

Above: *Louise Bourgeois, inside view, "Hanging Lair," 1963. Collection of the Museum of Modern Art. Photograph by Peter Moore, New York.*

Left: *Tania Mouraud, project, "Initiation Space No. 1," 1970. Photograph by André Morain.*

Above: *Alice Aycock, detail, earth platform with tunnel entrance, walled trench, Gibney Farm, New Kingston, Pennsylvania, 1974. Photograph by A. Aycock.*

Top: *Audrey Hemenway, "Ecological Environment," Accord, New York, 1974. Photograph by Audrey Hemenway, sculptor; Lev Zetlin, consulting engineers.*

the center of a daily circle as well as a storage place that registers nature's most grandiose movement—the turning of the earth's plane. Tania Mouraud's glowing white meditation place, her projects for sanctuaries or "initiation spaces" in the city, in the heart of a mountain, incorporate micro/macrocosmic interiors of body and mind. Ann Mills' cyclical *Leaf Room* in *Womanhouse,* with its oval ceiling, its leaves unfolding to become "large shields behind which I could hide," like Faith Wilding's *Crocheted Environment* based on "protective environments often woven out of grasses, branches or weeds" recall "primitive womb-shelters."

Alice Aycock's architectural sculptures outdoors include a mound that is almost part of the land and a bleak bunkerlike tunnel that implies defense and offense; both pieces provide an interior, a place to hide. Audrey Hemenway's fiberglass and cable tent structure is also a shelter, a functioning wildlife refuge. Jackie Winsor and Mary Miss have made monumental well-like sculptures from brick and wood, respectively, in which the exterior seems to exist mainly to tempt the viewer into the interior. In 1972, Winsor made a platform-sculpture of saplings in the Virginia woods that provides a house in nature, camouflaged by its materials. Miss, however, has also made several pieces with erect fences or barriers to unenterable spaces, and male artists Robert Morris, Lloyd Hamrol, and Charles Simonds have all made enterable, more or less protecting sculptural spaces, which, were this a longer chapter, would be interesting to contrast with those made by women.

A beautiful room with bath? A room with bath? A nice room? A room? . . . But never tell the truth about this business of rooms, because it would bust the roof off everything and undermine the whole social system. All rooms are the same. All rooms have four walls, a door, a window or two, a bed, a chair, and perhaps a bidet. A room is a place where you hide from the wolves outside and that's all any room is. Why should I worry about changing my room?
Jean Rhys, *Good Morning Midnight*

Jacqueline Winsor, ''Untitled,'' Virginia, 1972. Courtesy Paula Cooper Gallery, New York. Photograph by J. Winsor.

Mary Miss, ''Sunken Pool,'' Greenwich, Connecticut, 1974. Photograph by Mary Miss.

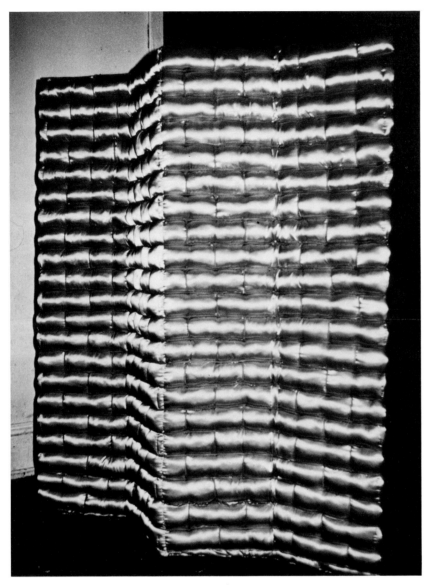

Grace Bakst Wapner, "Both Sides of the Wall," satin, polyester fill, bias tape, wood, 1972. Photograph by Grace Bakst Wapner.

Doctor Gordon's waiting room was hushed and beige. The walls were beige, and the carpets were beige, and the upholstered chairs and sofas were beige. There were no mirrors or pictures, only certificates from different medical schools. . . . At first I wondered why the room felt so safe. Then I realized it was because there were no windows.

. . . I saw the days of the year stretching ahead like a series of bright white boxes, and separating one box from another was sleep, like a black shade. Only for me, the long perspective of shades that set off one box from the next had suddenly snapped up, and I could see day after day glaring ahead of me like a broad, infinitely desolate avenue.

Sylvia Plath, *The Bell Jar*.

Interiors are seen in women's literature as prisons and sanctuaries. In the visual arts, women's images of enclosed space convey either confinement (inside looking out, as in the many paintings, sculptures, and photographs involving windows from the inside, windows as barriers) or else freedom within confinement (inside looking in, turning to the self in isolation), or combinations of the two. The Australian painter Ann Newmarch's feminist poster *Queen of the Home* ironically combines nude women caught in claustrophobic windowed interiors, a fashion magazine's advice to "take one of Vogue's colored chalks and write a hundred times a day 'I will be more beautiful,'" and a children's rhyme: "Wednesday is a day to make/ lovely buns or bake a cake/ In the kitchen you're the Queen/ And the apron keeps you clean." For the last few years Grace Bakst Wapner's work has been concerned with architectural elements (sometimes made of velvet, satin, and other incongruous materials) and ideas about communicative space—which areas of our experience allow intimacy, which are "roped off"—derived in part from Edward Hall's books.[1]

Sometimes nature is "out there," on the other side of the window, representing life and opposed to compartmentalized death. The editor of 1945 kitchen improvement contest for farm women noted, "I don't believe there was an entry that didn't menti plans for enlarging at least one window," and the first criterion for a house was one which "fits the land."[2] As the earth is identified with the female body, the garden may provide in some cases a transition to the world seen through the window. Christine Oatman's environmental sculpture, *Child's Garden of Verses,* constructed in Connecticut in 1972, is a fantasy in praise of fiction, poetry, the imagination as escape. Shoes and socks belonging to an invisible little girl are left outside the gate in the picket fence that encloses a grassy plot. Barefoot, her senses tuned, she belies her confinement by creating other worlds within, marked by piles of books and tiny constructions that seem to have emerged from their pages—a Greek temple of sugar cubes occupied by a Monarch butterfly; a glass train going through a tunnel hollowed out of a loaf of bread; a sky-painted egg. Tina Girouard's series of three house pieces in 1970–1971 included *Hung House,* a split-level mock house maintained for 6 months in her own living space; *Live House,* a performance piece with people representing different rooms in a house; and *Swept House,* a temporary floor plan outlined in dirt under the Brooklyn Bridge.

On a far more cerebral level, Jacki Apple has worked with outdoor and language conjunctions, exploring "the architecture of our psychological territories," the language of our spaces and the objects we select in various situations as a means of "breaking down the barriers, altering, extending, eliminating the boundaries between our cultural backgrounds and conditioning, our sexual and social roles/positions."[3] While many women have found an outlet for their fantasies in the home itself and in the garden, for other nonartists, a domestic audience has not always sufficed. Grandma Prisbrey—an exception to the fact that most architectural "primitives" seem to be men—has surrounded her wheel-less mobile home in a small California town by a "Bottle Village," with a wishing well of milk of magnesia bottles, "Cleopatra's Bedroom," a dollhouse, a "pencil room," and a pyramid crowned with 150 gold lipstick cases.

Above: *Tina Girouard, "Swept House,"
1971. Photograph by Carol Goodden.*

Top: *Christine Oatman, "Child's Garden
of Verses," Connecticut, 1972. Photograph by Christine Oatman.*

Above: *Patricia Johanson, "Cyrus Field," redwood, 12 in. x 2,600 ft x 2 in./30 cm x 8,000 m x 5 cm, private collection, New York, 1970. Photograph by Hans Namuth.*

Top: *Jacki Apple, "Digging," Martha Jackson West Gallery, New York, May 1975. Photograph by J. Apple.*

Since the reader ends up by making his or her characters, how they look, what the setting looks like, and so on, no matter how specific the writer is—why not a book that is openly full of holes? A follow-the-dots book, except the dots aren't numbered and the pattern is up to you, its prime virtue being that you might not have tried to draw anything at all without those few dots, a few points of departure, which are maybe the point of writing, to get people to the point of thinking for themselves, inventing. Puns are punctilio, layered, fine points of departure into the web. . . .
Latvana Greene, *I See/You Mean.*

The idea of the "crowd" is symbolically superior to that of "multiplicity" since it implies a new concept of the numerous as a totality, of Oneness as a fragmented whole.
C. Kerényi, in Jung Kerényi, *Essays on a Science of Mythology.*

Plotinus was preaching the dangers of multiplicity . . . back in the third century. Yet the problem is particularly and essentially woman's. Distraction is, always has been, and probably always will be, inherent in woman's life. For to be a woman is to have interests and duties raying out in all directions from the central mother-core, like spokes from the hub of a wheel. The pattern of our lives is essentially circular. We must be open to all points of the compass; husband, children, friends, home, community; stretched out, exposed, sensitive like the spider's web to each breeze that blows, to each call that comes.
Anne Morrow Lindbergh, *Gift from the Sea.*

The need for a "room of one's own" is the need for time, for a mental space rather than a physical one. When a woman's professional working space is open to or includes the rest of her life, it marks either an unusual integration of her roles or, more likely, an unusual determination not to let domestic duties interfere with professional ones—a kind of continuous defiance of the interruptions and demands made on her as a woman. Most women's lives are compartmented, fragmented, and necessarily far more flexible than those of men. They are conditioned by and reflected in the many rooms of the ordinary ise. A woman may be a cook in kitchen, a hostess in the living m, a mother in the children's m, a lover in the bedroom. Men's es are more concentrated on their rkplace, and they move freely ough the home like guests. Women cupy different rooms at different es of the day, and the house benes a temporal and spatial metaor for role playing.

Fragmentation need not connote plosion, disintegration. It is also a nponent of networks, stratification, interweaving of many dissimilar eads, and a deemphasis on imposed aning in favor of multiple intertations according to the wer/reader's own experience. On s level fragmentation pervades men's work in all the arts on many tle levels. It relates to the ways in ich women's conversation is struced differently from een's, to an knowledged interest in pattern over m, and more fundamentally, to men's superior ability to adapt to ried situations and to the needs of ers.

Women seem less afraid than men dilute their individual image cade) with diverse styles and ideas, ecially if better communication is the balance. It has often been noted t women "resist specialization" d preconceived notions about how ers should live their lives, that ir approach to architecture is an compassing rather than an exclusive e. For instance, architect Julia organ left so much up to her clients at the resulting variety has made re than half of her works unidentible. Eileen Gray's "layered divin of spaces encourage adaptability the use of architectural space . . . mfort, sensuality, choice and connience are provided."[4] Susana rre's *House of Meaning* facilitates rearrangement of entire living aces under different familial or sol situations. Many women sculps have also found that they prefer work with rearrangeable modules with the participation of the audice, and some have attributed this to reflection of their life-styles. By rking with image-spaces organilly generated, they build an accree structure from associated frag-

ments, which, placed together, suggest new and flexible rather than fixed meanings.

Since 1970, Patricia Johanson, painter, sculptor, landscape architect, has planned a series of works that carry these ideas into the architectural realm. After a series of large-scale, line-color sculptures in the landscape, she made *Cyrus Field,* a marble, redwood, cement and rock "path" through the woods, which structures the experience of this area and "mediates between human scale and the undifferentiated vastness of nature."[5] A cumulative piece, it is now 3 miles long. Since then, she has designed several garden, landscape, and sculpture projects among them the pavement insets for a Mitchell-Giurgola building at Yale University. Her fragmented series of glyphs, drawn from ancient languages, not only introduces almost arbitrary curves to the angular edifice, but simultaneously decentralizes (leading out to the town itself) and returns to the center (the building). Seen from the windows above, the fragments come together into a pattern readable in a number of ways, depending on the points of view and interpretation. Johanson intended this "not so much a single as a multifocus work, as *a design that will change so radically that it will literally become several different works* as the spectator changes levels, direction, context. It is really just a *series of fragments (parts) that can be put together in any number of ways* (designs within designs). . . . At the same time, I think it will be unobtrusive enough, and will involve enough *improvisation on the part of the spectator,* so that anyone who wants to ignore it can easily do so."[6]

It was in the interests of Capitalist expansion to isolate both women and the home from the spheres of public commercial life where they had become inappropriate.
Gwendolyn Wright, "On the Fringe of the Profession: Women in American Architecture," in *The Architect: Historical Essays on the Profession.*

The woman architect is interested in housing rather than houses, in community centers for the masses rather

than in neighborhood clubs for the elect; in regional planning more than in estate planning, in social aspects of her profession more than private commissions. . . . Her interest in her profession embraces its social and human implications.
Henry Atherton Frost, letter to Herbert Davis, June 20, 1941.

One can only work successfully with a community group by becoming part of it. The art is probably in the process and not in the product; the better the process is, the more involved people become with creating spaces where it feels good to be. As the architect becomes invisible, as there is no possibility for a signature or for a four-page spread in any of the professional journals, the process is probably more successful, the community is more in control, and therefore the physical form is more likely to be a true reflection of the community's own political process. This goes very much against the ideas of most designers.
Dolores Hayden, "Women and the Arts," *Arts in Society,* Spring-Summer 1974.

Women tend to sympathize with other "outsiders." The attempt to make spaces, which, in Hayden's words, "would make it easy rather than difficult for people to express in their life-style their commitment to social change,"[7] attracts artists as well as architects. Sheila Berkley's portable playgrounds or Bonnie Sherk's portable parks also extend an awareness of flexibility beyond the usual art audience. In downtown San Francisco, Sherk's temporary parks, complete with grass, a palm tree, a picnic table, and sometimes a cow, provided the model for an important landscape-art-project called *The Farm,* of which she is co-director. Begun in two old warehouses at the intersection of four low- to moderate-income and ethnically mixed neighborhoods, it will eventually be a community farm, garden, service center, and interarts workshop. In a virtually pictorial and almost surrealist manner, the farm superimposes the past (the land was once a farm) and an optimistic future on the decomposed present environment. A working situation, rather than a "model," it should have broad

Above: *Sheila Berkley, portable playground, project sponsored by New York Urban Development Corporation, New York, 1970–1971. Photograph by Harold Lehr.*

Right: *Bonnie Sherk with Harold Levine and others, "Portable Park II," San Francisco, 1970. Photograph by Bonnie Sherk.*

plications for urban design.
An example of a move in the direc-
n of a personal/communicative
de, which defies the linear projec-
n that has typified the ideologies of
 art world since the mid-fifties, is
e Morton's 1975 "flagship" at
w York's South Street Seaport.
e made some 300 small banners—
ved and painted, each dedicated to
 person important to her. These
ividual names and pictures, frag-
nts spanning a lifetime of relation-
ps, were then united by placement
 the schooner *Lettie G. Howard,*
ere during their display they pro-
ed a festive sight for the thousands
summer visitors to this popular
ce. Such work can embrace the
trograde'' impulses to pluralism,
ecticism, esthetic tolerance cur-
tly denigrated by the art world. It
mpts to reach an audience less
row and incestuous in economic
 social status than that of the art
leries and museums. Like the
men's Movement as a whole, it
estions the premise of the superior-
 of a competitive and alienated
vant-garde'' and the ''progression''
media and ideas in favor of a
wer, more content-oriented evolu-
 of motives in closer contact with
 life.
Although it cannot be said in the
e of all the women artists working
h spatial projects akin to archi-
ture that this impulse is fully de-
oped, some are tentatively emerg-
 from a strictly esthetic context
 a world where their experience as
men will, hopefully, be valued
re highly. The ideologies of the art
rld still act as repressive, neutraliz-
forces on most art by women. The
ictance to confront another audi-
e, to develop a different set
values, even to acknowledge
iinism as a political force, has
ved to maintain conflicting motiva-
ıs. Nevertheless, an increasing
nber of women artists are find-
 the strength to respond from a
sonal/communicative base rather
ın upholding the status quo that is
cifically adapted to the middle
ıss who comprise the present art
lience. In doing so, they extend a
g and generally unacknowledged
lition that is innately female.

Ree Morton, flagship, installation aboard
Lettie G. Howard, *South Street Pier, New*
York, 1975. Photograph by Ree Morton.

By Susana Torre

13. The Pyramid and the Labyrinth

"What kind of slippers are these you've got on?" he ejaculated painfully.

The master of the house looked at his embroidered slippers. Then he breathed in relief. This time he felt quite guiltless. The slippers had been made to the architect's original designs. So he answered in a superior way.

"But Mr Architect! have you already forgotten? You yourself designed them!"

"Of course," thundered the architect, "but for the bedroom! They completely disrupt the mood here with these two impossible spots of colour. Can't you see that?"

The master agreed. He took off his slippers hurriedly and was only too relieved that the architect did not object to his socks. They went into the bedroom where the rich man was allowed to put his slippers on again. "I had a birthday yesterday," he began shyly. "My dear family has showered me with presents. I wanted to consult you, dear Mr Architect, to get your advice on how best to display these items."

The face of the architect fell perceptibly. Then he let go:

"How dare you accept presents?! Haven't I designed *everything?* Haven't I taken care of *everything?* You need nothing more. You are complete."

"But," the master of the house made bold to answer, "mayn't I buy anything?"

"No, you may not! Never ever! That's all I need. Things not designed by me? Haven't I been lenient enough allowing you the Charpentier? The statue that stole all my thunder? No, you may not buy anything else!"

"But what if my grandchildren give me something they made at kindergarten?"

"Then you must not accept it."

The master of the house was devastated. But he did not give in yet. An idea, yes, an idea.

"And if I want to buy a modern painting at the Sezession?" he asked triumphantly.

"Then just try to find a spot for it. Can't you see that there's no room for anything else? Can't you see that I have designed a frame for each picture on the wall? You can't even *move* a picture. Just try finding space for a new picture."

A change took place in the rich man. He suddenly felt profoundly unhappy. He could see his future life. Nobody was allowed to give him pleasure. He had to go past the shops without desire. Nothing would be made for him any more. None of his loved ones could give him a picture. As far as he was concerned, there were no painters, no artists, no craftsmen any more. He was excluded for the future from living and striving, becoming and wishing. He felt: Now I have to learn to live with my own corpse. Yes. I am finished. *I am complete!*[1]

The gap between a space built as a ideal and the demands of human d sire is devastatingly shown in Ado Loos's savage parable. I have usec here as the opening of this brief cc to some themes of the preceding cha ter—such as women's representati of space and their concern with pa tern over form and with complexit ornament, and transformation over simplicity and immutability. The story is also interesting in that it e presses the paradox of architecture, an act forever striving towards the realization of an ideal, while as a product it is forever eroded or moc ified (depending on the view taker by new social or personal events a by the changing desires of the occu ants. It also establishes a brutal di tinction between architecture as th absolute materialization of *logos* (the Pyramid) and architecture as the evolving form of *desire* (the Labyrinth). Coincidentally, these t symbols correspond to culturally d fined ideas of masculinity and fem ninity and are associated with moc of existence and thought patterns commonly attributed to men and women.

Labyrinth. *I always found going tc her house an adventure, filled witł surprises and dangers. I would wa der about trying to find my way, n really knowing where I was, and seemingly only by chance eventuall would find myself at the steps leac down to her door.*[2]

Clichés: The Labyrinth is the space sensuality; the Pyramid, the space spirituality. The Labyrinth is the space of confusion; the Pyramid, t space of certainty.

Just how pervasive such archety can be should be measured against prevailing belief in polarities in irreconcilable rather than compleme tary opposites: order versus disord exclusiveness versus inclusiveness organization versus ad hoc; outside versus inside; public versus private reductionism versus accumulation; purism versus eclecticism. . . . Th ideas have alternately ruled the cre tion of built form, but the synthesis prescription and pleasure has been rare architectural event; and it has to become part and parcel of architectural discourse.

Being the opposite symptoms of an architectural "pathology," the Pyramid and the Labyrinth have little to do with the social and economic conditions of building; they should be seen as the expression of unconscious rather than of reason. The impulse to create either Pyramid or Labyrinth can be said to emerge, not as a "natural" force, but rather as a reflection of a culturally acquired image of the self.

A Tale of Two Labyrinths

The builders of Llanda Villa and the Bottle Village were both women. Neither of them ever gave precise reasons for their amazing creations other than their shared belief that idleness was the main cause of depression. To avoid the shallowness of a life confined to domesticity they turned instead to the monumentalization of fragments and details. The methods and resources used to achieve this couldn't have been more divergent: the construction of Llanda Villa consumed $5½ million and a profusion of precious materials, while the Bottle Village was entirely built with cast-off objects from the local garbage dump.

The history of Llanda Villa, rumored to have been inhabited by spirits, is obscured by popular myths about its creator, a 4-foot 10-inch blue-eyed dainty woman who had been educated in the best Eastern schools and had excelled as a young girl in art, mathematics, science, and music. Sarah Lockwood Pardee Winchester began her extraordinary construction in 1886 and continued to work on it until her death in 1922. Starting from an unfinished nine room ranch house that she purchased near San Jose, California, it eventually covered 6 acres on a property that grew from 40 to 160 acres over a 38-year period. The widow of William Wirt Winchester (son of the inventor and manufacturer of the legendary repeating rifle), she moved west after the death of her husband and infant daughter. With an income of $1,000 a day, she could have employed the most talented architect, but

Above: *Sarah Winchester, aerial view, Winchester House, San Jose, California, 1884–1922. Courtesy Winchester Mystery House.*

Left: *S. Winchester, dead-end stairs, Winchester House, San Jose, California, 1884–1922. Courtesy Winchester Mystery House.*

Above: *S. Winchester, ballroom, Winchester House, San Jose, California, 1884–1922. Courtesy Winchester Mystery House.*

Right: *Grandma Prisbrey, pavement mosaic patterns, Bottle Village, Santa Susana, California, 1950s to late 1960s. Photograph by Seymour Rosen.*

Opposite page: *Grandma Tressa Prisbrey, plan, Bottle Village, Santa Susana, Simi Valley, California, 1950s to late 1960s. Courtesy Walker Art Center. (1) School house, (2) Shrine, (3) Shell house, (4) Blue bottle house, (5) Pencil house, (6) Round house, (7) Wishing well, (8) Cleopatra's bedroom, (9) Mosaic card figures, (10) Doll house, (11) Rumpus room, (12) Cabana, (13) Little hut, (14) TV tube wall, (15) Leaning tower of Pisa, (16) Sanctuary wall, (17) Living trailer, (18) Bottle house, (19) Shot house, (20) Thatched house, (21) Fountain, (22) Pyramid planter, (23) Little chapel, (24) Doll's head planter.*

instead she hired a staff of 20 servants, 22 carpenters, and 18 gardeners and became her own designer and contractor.

A house of 160 rooms is all that remains of an estimated 750 chambers interconnected with deadend stairways, trick doors, and self-intersecting balconies. The wild extravagance of its Victorian splendor embraces innumerable appurtenances: turrets, towers, porches, curved walls, cornices, windows and dormers of every imaginable kind, pediments, elaborately turned posts of many sizes and styles, jigsaw ornaments, panels of exotic grainings, clusters of wooden balls, arches, trellises, cupolas, ornamental chimney stacks, and a mixture of wall materials combining horizontal wood siding with vertical paneling and shingles in a variety of shapes. Roofing, except for the flat metal decks, is extravagantly shingled, with elaborate cornice work, ridge cresting, finials, overhanging pendants, and all sorts of gables. The sunlight coming through the house's 10,000 windows and 52 skylights causes a play of shadows that enhance every facet, volume, and detail. The walls and floors of the grand ballroom, where theatrical groups and musicians were brought to perform for an audience consisting of one person, are covered with rich tapestries of materials, with rustic brick juxtaposed against some 15 different kinds of rare woods imported from many parts of the world. No plan was ever drawn of the entire house, not even after its builder's death; to record in a plan the imprint and spaces of this formidable dwelling would defy every rule of architectural representation.

There is no grand axis, no symmetry; the spaces are assembled, juxtaposed. The rooms succeed one another, communicating through passages and corridors, resembling the spatial pattern of early colonial houses, but multiplied ad infinitum. Two staircases face each other in so narrow a space that there is no recourse but to go down in order to go up again; one staircase has 7 turns and 44 risers, each 2 inches high, and ascends only 9 feet; other staircases end in the ceiling or walls.

The society that currently administers the house as a tourist attraction would have us believe that these strange architectural features were dictated to Sarah Winchester by spirits conjured up every night in the blue séance room from which she emerged in the morning carrying her blueprints for the work to be done each day. But her building patterns were affected by her physical health as much as by her desire to create a museum to display her many treasures. A room might be added just to incorporate some magnificent Tiffany glass windows, but the spiraling staircase was built when her crippling arthritis limited her movement; an odd-shaped room with four fireplaces and five hot-air registers was added when it was recommended that dry heat would ease her pain; a second floor room was transformed into a garden and magnifying glasses were incorporated into windows to observe the trees and plants in perfect detail when she could no longer tread the paths of her orchards and gardens; the deadend stairs would lead to new rooms for the nieces who never came to stay with her.

The house is awesome in its agglomeration of exquisitely crafted details, but it is no less remarkable for its minute technological innovations. There is a profusion of ingenious devices: inside cranks with burglar-proof catches on shutters over windows designed after the hammer and trigger of the Winchester rifle; fireplaces with drops for ashes; porcelain washtubs with built-in scrub boards and soap trays; curved brass plates in stair courses to foil the dust; tilting shower heads; wool insulation for temperature control; gaslights that flipped on with a switch. None of Winchester's inventions was patented or divulged, but they found their way out of the secluded mansion into the houses of neighbors all over the region.[3]

From an aerial view Llanda Villa appears to be organized around patios and courtyards as a checkered grid of built and unbuilt spaces. As it exists, it is the concrete and simultaneous record of a process spanning 38 years, where each day—filled by the demanding task of building—yielded

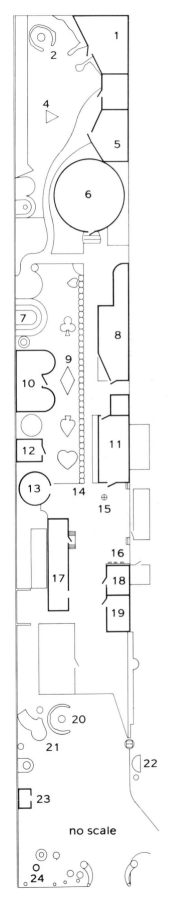

no scale

yet another figment of Sarah Winchester's insatiable energy and imagination.

South of San Jose in Simi Valley there is a curious compound of 13 buildings and 9 minor constructions fashioned out of 1 million discarded bottles and a bewildering variety of other objects. Grandma Tressa Prisbrey's Bottle Village, compressed into a narrow 40 by 300 foot lot is precariously contained by low and high boundary walls with cactus gardens and automobile headlights. It is imaginable that, had property lines not existed, Grandma Prisbrey would have continued to build, to add other constructions and engulf more space by her village. The effort she might have put into expanding was instead spent on adding layers of ornament, decorating, and accumulating and displaying her collections, which completely fill the interior of each building and shrine.

Tressa Prisbrey was born in North Dakota in 1895, the daughter of a German emigré blacksmith named Schaeffer and of Catharine Wasmuth, a second-generation German. After a lifetime of domestic responsibilities and struggle to survive on meager salaries, Tressa and her husband moved from North Dakota in the fifties to work in California war plants. Their small trailer home was settled on a ⅓-acre lot in Santa Susana. Without space to receive their sons, daughters, and grandchildren, or room to display her collection of 2,000 pencils, Grandma Prisbrey, already in her sixties, began to build, using discarded bottles that she laid on courses of concrete without frameworks. Soon the utilitarian aspect of her construction gave way to sheer pleasure and fantasy. She must have delighted in pondering the possibilities of each new object found in her daily visits to her quarry—the local garbage dump.

Grandma Prisbrey's is a world of inclusiveness and variation. It is a physical realm of glorified ad hoc, a topography of consumerism. In the concrete path leading to the ceremonial center of the village, marked by the massive Round House, are embedded the remains of things consumed and rejected: castoff car fend-ers, several thousand headlights, hub caps, old license plates, 200 spidery lead molds, frames of eyeglasses, pistols, a snorkel tube, scissors, lipstick cases, the mechanism of a pencil sharpener, jewelry, a silver dollar. The walls of "Cleopatra's Bedroom," a space glittering with golden light from translucent beer bottles, are supported by telephone poles sprayed gold and covered with bronze- and gold-painted venetian blinds. Fluorescent and television tubes, cylinders and cogs, penicillin bottles and bronze streamers are used in a fountain and in display tables. Flowers in a planter are replaced by doll heads impaled on pipes. Intravenous feeding tubes are strung together to form a screen for a fireplace. Old photographs are set among mirror splinters.[4] Grandma Prisbrey built the Bottle Village over 20 years without blueprints or master plan. Each task was undertaken as a brief endeavor, and many times constructions were entirely rebuilt or substantially transformed. She achieved a remarkable spatial continuity by creating links between spaces and fragments and through a juxtaposition of objects that evoke poetic, witty, or shocking associations.

Labyrinths cannot be synthetically described; they have to be literally "enumerated," not unlike the tasks performed by women in the home. ". . . no object is really ever completed, a sequel to the Odyssey will prove that Penelope continued her activity incessantly. . . ."[5]

Grandma Prisbrey, the Little Chapel, Bottle Village, Santa Susana, California, 1950s to late 1960s. Photograph by Seymour Rosen.

Naomi Leff

Historic Chart Relating Architectural Projects to General and Women's History in the U.S.

Throughout this book the history of women in American architecture is seen within a social context; this history can only be enriched by a detailed historical account of events arranged in order of time without interpolation. The following chart, then, is such a chronicle of events and women's history in general. The architectural images included both highlight and typify women's achievements. To maximize the amount of information, the letter **W** in bold type is used as a symbol for "woman," singular and plural. The dates in large type visually emphasize a time period of particular interest to the reader.

1630 Anne Bradstreet (1612–72), poet, settler in the Mass. Bay Colony, publishes *The Tender Muse Lately Sprin' Up in America*. **1805** Abigail Adams (1744 – 1818), letter writer, publishes *A History of the Rise, Progress & Termination of the Am. Revolution*. **1810** Elizabeth Ann Seton (1774–1821), founder of the Am. Daughters of Charity, canonized saint (1955) founds 1st free Catholic school. **1821** Emma Willard (1787 – 1870), educator, founds Troy Female Seminary, NY. (Emma Willard School), 1st academy for **W**'s studies. **1828** 1st **W**'s labor strike, Dover, Mass. **1830** Sarah Josepha Hale (1788–1879), author, editor, publishes *Godey's Lady's Book* of fashion and manners. **1832** 1st married **W**'s property law passed in Miss.; Frances Trollope (1780 – 1863), author, publishes *Domestic Manners of the Americans*. **1833** Ann

1630

Hall (1792 – 1863), miniatures painter, is 1st **W** elected to the Nat'l Academy of Design. **1836** Mary Lyon (1797 – 1849), educator, founds Mt. Holyoke Seminary (registers as College in 1893), 1st collegiate institution for **W**. **1838** Angelina Grimké (1805–79), orator, abolitionist, advocate of **W**'s rights & antislavery legislation, 1st **W** to testify before the Mass. legislature, & her sister, Sarah (1792 – 1873), both pioneers of professional public speaking for **W**, conclude a New England tour with a lecture series in Boston's Odeon Hall. **1843** Sojourner Truth (1797 – 1883), former slave, activist, leaves domestic service to preach emancipation and **W**'s rights. **1844** Dorothea Dix (1802 – 87), humanitarian, crusader for the mentally ill, founds 1st of 32 state mental hospitals. **1845** Margaret Fuller (1810 – 50), author, 1st **W**

1836

livers her 1st antislave lecture, Newford, Mass. **1855** Lucy Stone (1818 – 93), reformer, **W**'s movement leader, founder of *Woman's Journal*, marries Henry Blackwell but keeps her maiden name. **1850–60** Harriet "Moses" Tubman (1820 – 1913), abolitionist, fugitive, escaped slave, Civil War scout & nurse, guides the 1st of many to freedom on Underground Railroad. **1857** Elizabeth Blackwell (1821 – 1910), 1st **W** doctor, founds NY Infirmary for **W** & Children and adds **W**'s Medical College in 1868. **1860** **W**'s shoemakers strike in Lynn, Mass., leads to the formation of the 1st nat'l **W**'s trade union, the Daughters of St. Crispin. **1861–65 CIVIL WAR. 1861** Vassar College chartered, Poughkeepsie, NY. **1865–85 YEARS OF RECONSTRUCTION, INDUSTRIALIZATION & WESTWARD EXPANSION. 1866** **W**'s Collar Laundry Union, Troy, NY, strike & raise wages from $3 to $14/wk.; Dr. Mary Walker (1832 – 1919), Ass't Surgeon General in the Union Army, is 1st **W** to receive Congressional Medal of Honor; Louisa May Alcott (1832 – 88), novelist, nurse, publishes *Little Women*. **1868 14th AMENDMENT GUARANTEES CIVIL RIGHTS TO BLACK AMERICANS;** *The Revolution*, 1st militant feminist magazine begins.

1869 Catharine Beecher (1809–78) designs Am. **W**'s Home.

1861

1878 Margaret Hicks's (1858–83) Workman's Cottage, the earliest known published work of Am. **W** architect.

1878 Charlotte Blake Brown (1846 – 1904), physician, pioneer in sterilization & use of incubators, is 1st **W** to perform ovariotomy. **1879** Belva Lockwood (1830 – 1917), lawyer, advocate of **W**'s rights, Nat'l Equal Rights Party Nominee for US President, secures passage of a bill allowing **W** to plead before the Supreme Court. **1881** *History of Woman's Suffrage*, 1st of 3 volumes compiled by Susan B. Anthony, Elizabeth Cady Stanton, & Joslyn Gage, is published; Clara Barton (1821 – 1912), nurse, founds the Am. Red Cross; Grace Dodge (1856 – 1914), social worker, philanthropist, cofounder of Columbia Teachers Col. of Columbia U., founds 1st Working Girls Club, NY; **1883** *Ladies Home Journal* is established. **1885** **W**'s Anthropological Society founded, Wash., DC, by Matilda Stevenson.

1886 **W**'s Commonwealth Hotel, organized by a **W**'s commune.

1878

1893 Lillian Wald (1867 – 1940), social worker, pioneer in public nursing, organizes Visiting Nurse Service that later becomes the Henry Street Settlement House. **1895** Ida B. Wells (1862 – 1931), black journalist, co-founder of the NAACP, publishes 1st statistical documentation on lynching; Cecilia Beaux (1853 – 1942), portrait painter, is appointed 1st **W** instructor at the Penn. Academy of Fine Arts. **1896** Mary Baker Eddy (1821–1910), founder of the Christian Science Movement and the *Christian Science Journal* (1883), author of *Science & Health* (1875), establishes 1st Church of Christ; Rose H. Lathrop (1851–1926), nun, writer, establishes 1st free cancer home, NYC. **1897** 1st Nat'l Congress of Mothers held in Wash., DC; Phoebe Hearst (1842 – 1919), philanthropist, founder of the Nat'l Congress of Parents & Teachers, finances an international competition for the Berkeley U. Master Plan, Cal. **1898 THE SPANISH AMERICAN WAR. 1898** Gertrude Kasebier (1852 – 1934), portrait photographer, exhibits motherhood series, "The Manger," which sells for $100,000; Charlotte Perkins Gilman (1860–1935), feminist reformer, economist, advocate of child care centers, publishes *Women & Economies*. **1899** Lake Placid Conferences provide a forum fo[r] the evolving profession of hom[e] economics; Kate Chopin (1851 – 1904), author, publishes *Th[e] Awakening*. **1903** Nat'l Worke[r] Trade Union is organized; Magg[ie] Walker (1867–1934), black insu[r]ance & banking executive, b[e]comes 1st **W** bank pres. of the S[t.] Luke Penny Savings Bank. **19[..]** Ida Tarbell (1857 – 1944), jo[ur]nalist, historian, publishes *Histo[ry] of the Standard Oil Compar[y]*

1893

1900

foreign correspondent for *N.Y. Tribune*, critic, publishes the feminist manifesto *Woman in the 19th Century;* Abigail Hopper (1801 – 93), antislavery & prison reformer, Civil War nurse, welfare worker, is named head of the Female Dept. of The Prison Ass'n of NY. **1848** Maria Mitchell (1818 – 89), astronomer, 1st **W** elected to the Am. Academy of Arts & Sciences, 1st Dir. of Astronomy, Vassar College, is confirmed dis-

coverer of a comet named for her. **1848** Lucretia Mott (1793 – 1881), abolitionist, reformer, ordained Quaker minister & Elizabeth Cady Stanton (1815 - 1902), reformer, suffragist, launch the 1st **W**'s Rights Convention at Seneca Falls, NY. They adopt the "Declaration of Sentiments and Resolutions" asserting **W**'s right to vote; NY passes Married **W**'s Property Law after 8 years of petitioning led by feminist Ernestine

Rose. **1850** 1st Nat'l **W**'s Rights Convention, Worcester, NH, is chaired by Paulina Wright Davis. **1851** The Colored Girls School, Wash., DC (District of Columbia Teacher's College), is founded by Myrtilla Miner & Harriet Beecher Stowe (1811 – 96), author, donates $1,000 from royalties of *Uncle Tom's Cabin;* Gail Borden (1801 – 74), surveyor, inventor, produces 1st commercial condensed milk. **1852** Clarina How-

ard Nichols (1810 – 85), newspaper editor, temperance leader, **W**'s rights leader, petitions the Vermont legislature to grant **W**'s suffrage in school meetings. **1853** Grace Greenwood (1823 – 1904), journalist, begins publication of children's magazine, *The Little Pilgrim;* Antoinette Brown Blackwell (1825 – 1921). 1st **W** Unitarian minister, is ordained. **1854** Frances Ellen Watkins (1825 – 1911), black poet, reformer, de-

1848

1869 Harriet Irwin (1828–97) patents plan for hexagonal building.

1869 Wyoming is 1st state to grant **W** the vote; The Nat'l **W**'s Suffrage Ass'n is formed; Edmonia Lewis (1845 – 90), black sculptress, achieves distinction for "Forever Free," which depicts a black couple realizing freedom. **1871** Frances Elizabeth Caroline Willard (1839–98), **W**'s Christian Temperance Union leader, reformer, named 1st president of Evanston College for Ladies; Abigail Scott Duniway (1834 –

1915), editor, suffragist, founds the *New Northwest Journal* for **W**. **1872** Victoria Woodhull (1838 – 1927), journalist, lecturer, stockbroker, Nat'l Equal Rights Party nomination for President of the US, & her sister, Tennessee Claflin (1845 – 1923), are 1st to publish *Communist Manifesto* in English; Susan B. Anthony (1820 – 1906), reformer, suffrage leader, International **W**'s Suffrage Alliance founder, organizer of the

Working **W**'s Assn, Nat'l **W**'s Suffrage Ass'n President, is arrested & fined $100 for voting in Rochester, NY. **1876** **W**'s Pavilion, Philadelphia Centennial, is 1st public building devoted exclusively to **W**'s work; Mary Cassatt (1844 – 1926), impressionist painter, exhibits & introduces impressionism to America; Frances Flora Bond (1812 – 76), lithographer, produces 200 lithographs for Currier & Ives.

1869

1886 Emily Sartain (1841–1927), artist, becomes principal of the Phila. School of Design for **W**, 1st US school to teach industrial arts to **W**; Josephine Shaw Lowell (1843–1905), labor reformer, cofounder of the Charity Organization of NY, establishes State Training School for Girls at Hudson, NY. **1887** Sarah Winnemucca, Paiute Indian princess, lecturer, reformer, pleads Indian rights in Washington, DC. **1888**

Noted feminists attend 1st Internat'l Council of **W**, Wash., DC. **1889** Jane Addams (1860 – 1935), suffragist, Nobel Peace Prize recipient, social worker, establishes the 1st Hull Settlement House, Chicago. **1890** Mormon Church, Salt Lake City, Utah, discontinues sanction of polygamy; Am. **W** Suffrage Ass'n & Nat'l Ass'n merge into the Nat'l Am. **W** Suffrage Ass'n; Maud Nathan (1862 – 1946), social welfare

leader, suffragist, forms Consumers' League of NY to better working conditions of NY shop girls; Emily Dickinson (1830–86), poet, publishes 1st volume of poems; Carrie Nation (1846–1911), temperance advocate, begins antiliquor crusades by leading **W** in a saloon-smashing expedition through Kansas; Frances Johnson (1864–1952), architectural & news photographer, wins gold medal for essay on Wash., DC.

1893 **W**'s Building, a competition won by Sophia Hayden (1868–1953), is built for the World's Columbian Exposition, Chicago.

1886

Helen Keller (1880 – 1968), author, lecturer, blind & deaf from age 2, graduates from Radcliffe College; Anne Shaw (1847 – 1919), ordained Methodist minister, suffragist, becomes Pres. of Nat'l **W**'s Suffrage Ass'n. **1905** Mary Bethune (1875 – 1955), black educator, obtains funds to open Daytona Normal & Industrial School for Negro Girls, Daytona, Fla.; Sarah Breedlove Walker (1869 – 1919), business **W**, 1st

black **W** to become a millionaire, invents the "Walker Method" of hair straightening. **1907** Mary Adelaide Nutting (1858 – 1948), nurse, educator, founder of the *Am. Journal of Nursing,* publisher of 4-vol. *History of Nursing,* becomes 1st nurse appointed to a university chair, Columbia Teachers Coll.; Florence Lawrence (1886–1938), actress, stars in Edison's film, "Daniel Boone"; 1st Mother's Day, proposed by

Anna Jarris. **1908** Isadora Duncan (1878 – 1927), modern dancer, triumphs in NY. **1909** Campfire Girls is founded by Luther Halsey Gulick. **1910** Coll. of William & Mary (Va.) accepts **W**; general strike of NYC **W**'s Garment Workers Union results in 1st voluntary Board of Sanitary Control; the Mann Act makes it illegal for men to lure **W** across state lines. **1912** Girl Scouts is founded by Juliette Gordon Low.

1913 Cambridge School, Mass., is the first **W**'s school of architecture and landscape architecture,

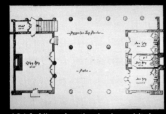

1914 Alice Austin designs kitchenless house for her feminist-socialist city plan, Llano del Rio, Cal.

1915 Julia Morgan s (1872–1957) Oakland YWCA is one of the buildings she designed for **W**.

1913 AFL votes that 1¢ per capita be spent to benefit wage earnings of **W. 1914–18 WORLD WAR I. 1914** Marietta Holley (1836–1926), author & champion of **W**'s rights, publishes *Josiah Allen on the Woman Question*, last of 20-vol. *Samantha Allen, Josiah Allen's Wife* series. **1916** Sen. Nesley Jones, Wash., DC, introduces a bill to provide a **W**'s division in the Dept. of Labor; Am. Fed. of Teachers is founded;

Dorothy Parker (1893 – 1967), writer, author of *Enough Rope* (1927), *Sunset Gun* (1928), & *Death & Taxes* (1931), becomes 1st literary critic of *Vanity Fair*; Margaret Sanger (1883 – 1966), Fania Mindell & Ethel Byrne, public health leaders, open 1st birth control clinic, NYC. **1917 W** flood into wartime industries. AFL restates support of equal pay for equal work & forms 1st corps of **W** organizers; 1,000 picket Pres.

1913

socialist lecturer, prison reformer, organizes The Children's Crusade March on Wash., DC; Emma Goldman (1869 – 1940), anarchist, feminist, lecturer, publicist, speech agitator, pioneer advocate of birth control, is named by *Nation* magazine as one of twelve greatest living Am. **W**; Rebecca Latimore Felton (1835–1930), reformer, journalist, is elected 1st **W** US senator; Willa Sibert Cather (1876–1947),

author, wins Pulitzer Prize for *One of Ours*; Emily Post (1873–1960), writer, publishes the first edition of *Etiquette*; Lillian Russell (1861–1922), actress, singer, feminist, is appointed official emissary to Europe by Pres. Harding. **1923** Alice Paul (b. 1885), suffragist, revolutionary lecturer, leader of the Independent **W**'s Party, drafts the 1st ERA; Edna St. Vincent Millay (1892 – 1950), poet, member of

Provincetown Players, author of sketches for *Vanity Fair* under the pseudonym Nancy Boyd, receives Pulitzer Prize for "The Ballad of the Harp Weaver"; Louise Bogan (1897 – 1970), poet, teacher, critic, poetry editor of *New York* magazine, publishes *Body of This Death*. **1925** Florence Sabin (1871 – 1953), anatomist, is 1st **W** elected to the Nat'l Academy of Science for her work on the lymphatic system.

1926 Virginia Woolf (1882–1941), novelist, critic, member of Hall of Fame, publishes feminist *A Room of One's Own*; Martha Graham (b. 1894), modern dancer, teacher, choreographer, makes her 1st independent debut in NYC. **1928** Margaret Mead (b. 1901), anthropologist, curator, publishes *Coming of Age in Samoa*. **1929** Museum of Modern Art is established — founders include Mrs. John D. Rockefeller,

1925

text by Elizabeth McCausland. **1939** Dorothea Lange (1895 – 1965), portrait photographer of the Southwest, publishes *An American Exodus: A Record of Human Erosion;* Anais Nin (b. 1903), author, publishes *Winter of Artifice*. **1939–45 WORLD WAR II. 1941** Karen Horney (1885 – 1952), psychiatrist, founds the Am. Institute of Psychoanalysis; Lois Marilou Jones (b. 1905), black artist, teacher, receives Corcoran

Gallery Robert Woods Landscape Prize for "Indian Shops, Gay Head." **1942** Childless **W** may join U.S. Armed Forces; Susanne Langer (b. 1895), philosopher, publishes *Philosophy in a New Key: A Study in the Symbolism of Reason, Rite & Art*; Claire McCardell (1905 – 1958), fashion designer introduces the wraparound denim "popover."

1942 Marion Mahony Griffin (1871–1961) designs the World's Fellowship Center.

1943 Ayn Rand (b. 1905), novelist, screenwriter, philosopher, publishes *The Fountainhead*; Margaret Bourke-White (1906 – 71), journalist, war correspondent, 1st staff photographer for *Fortune,* is only Western correspondent in USSR during German invasion. **1944** Rosina Lhevinne (b. 1880), pianist, Julliard teacher of Van Cliburn, Micha Dichter & John Browning, gives her 1st solo performance. **1945** Eleanor

1943

creates her role in "Member of the Wedding." **1952** Marianne Moore (1887–1972), poet, editor, author of *Nevertheless* (1944), wins Pulitzer Prize for her *Collected Poems;* Shirley Booth (b. 1909), actress wins an Academy Award for her role in "Come Back Little Sheba"; Mary Church Terell (1863 –1954), black writer, lecturer, successfully challenges restaurant segregation at age 89.

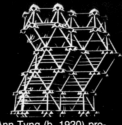

1952 Ann Tyng (b. 1920) proposes this theoretical City Tower, designed with Louis A. Kahn.

1953 Clare Booth Luce (b. 1903), playwright, Congress**W**, diplomat, named US Ambassador to Italy. **1954** Blacks of Montgomery, Ala., boycott public transportation after Rosa Parks refuses a white man her bus seat; Judy Garland (1922–69), actress, makes "A Star Is Born." **1955** Marian McPartland (b. 1918), jazz pianist, member of the Bd. of Directors of the Nat'l Endowment for the Arts, is awarded "Best Small Jazz Group" by

Metronome magazine; Helen Frankenthaler (b. 1928), abstract painter, has "Blue Territory" accepted by Whitney Museum; Beverly Sills (b. 1929), coloratura soprano, debuts at the NYC opera. **1956** Marilyn Monroe (1926 – 62) actress, appears in "Bus Stop." **1957** Marian Anderson (b. 1920) contralto, is 1st black **W** to appear at Met. Opera House, NYC **1959–73 VIETNAM WAR. 196** Joan Baez (b. 1941), folk singe

1953

Wilson's inauguration to encourage action on **W** suffrage; Jeannette Rankin (1880 – 1973), pacifist & social worker, is elected 1st **W** member of House of Rep.; **1919** 1st **W**'s Bank is established, Clarkville, Tenn.; Georgia O'Keefe (b. 1887), painter, exhibits at 291 Gallery of Alfred Steiglitz; Alice Hamilton (1869 – 1970), physician, educator, pioneer researcher of industrial diseases, becomes 1st **W** faculty

member at Harvard; Mary Pickford (b. 1893), actress, producer, cofounds the United Artists Co. with D. W. Griffith. **1920 19th AMENDMENT TO CONSTITUTION IS RATIFIED GRANTING W THE RIGHT TO VOTE. 1920** Carrie Chapman Catt (1859 – 1947), suffragist, peace leader, twice president of the Nat'l Am. **W** Suffrage Ass'n, author of *Woman Suffrage and Politics* (1923), establishes the League of **W** Voters.

1921 Chicago **W**'s Drafting Club, 1st **W**'s professional organization, publishes the *Architrave*.

1921 Alice Mary Robertson (1854 – 1931), Indian educator, Congress**W**, 1st **W** to preside over House of Rep.; Lillian Gilbreth (1878 – 1972), teacher, pioneer in kitchen design, management consultant, publishes *The Psychology of Management*; Ellen Semple (1863–1932), geographer, historian, writer, becomes 1st **W** pres. of the Ass'n of Am. Geographers. **1922** Kate Cunningham (1877 – 1948),

1921

Lillie D. Bliss, Mrs. W. Murray Crane. **1930** Jean Harlow (1911–1937), film actress, stars in "Hell's Angels"; Gertrude Vanderbilt Whitney (1885 – 1942), sponsor of the 1913 Armory Show, founds the Whitney Museum of Am. Art. **1932** Babe Didrikson Zaharias (1911 – 56), athlete, wins 2 Olympic Gold Medals; Amelia Earhart (1898 – 1937), aviator, social worker, 1st licensed **W** pilot, becomes 1st **W** to solo across the Atlantic.

ONLY 1 OUT OF 3 FAMILIES CAN AFFORD THIS MINIMUM HOUSE the cost of this house can be reduced by:

1 LARGE-SCALE PLANNING. 5%*
Reduces cost of streets, utilities, financing. Increases amount of open green space. Improves quality of architectural design by adapting lot size to house and block size to terrain.

1933 Catherine Bauer (1905–64) prepares this chart for MOMA's modern architecture exhibition.

1933 Frances Perkins (1882 – 1965), social reformer, is named 1st US Cabinet member; Ruth Bryant Owen (1885–1954), nurse, author, educator, 1st **W** foreign diplomat, is named Minister to Denmark; Gertrude Stein (1874 – 1946), author, patron of the arts, publishes *The Autobiography of Alice B. Toklas*; Katharine Hepburn (b. 1909), actress, wins Academy Award for "Morning Glory." **1934** Ruth Benedict (1887

– 1948), anthropologist, publishes *Patterns of Culture*. **1936** Dorothy Thompson (1894 – 1961), columnist, foreign correspondent, begins syndicated newspaper column, "On the Record." **1938** Pearl S. Buck (1892–1973), author of *East Wind, West Wind* (1930), *The Good Earth* (1931), is 1st **W** writer awarded Nobel Prize; Bernice Abbott (b. 1898), portrait and documentary photographer, publishes *Changing New York* with

1933

Roosevelt (1884 – 1962), humanitarian, champion of political, social & **W**'s issues, becomes US delegate to UN. **1946** Mother Frances Xavier Cabrini (1850 – 1917), nun is 1st Am. citizen canonized; Helen Hayes (b. 1900), actress, two-time Oscar winner, creator of the title role in *Victoria Regina* (1935–39), wins an Emmy for her role in "Skin of Our Teeth."

1945 Sarah Pillsbury Harkness (b. 1924) wins 2nd prize with this Smith College Competition entry.

1948 Eleanor Raymond (b. 1887) designs this solar house in Mass.

1948 Maria Mayer (1906 – 72), physicist, earns the Nobel Prize for the "Shell Theory," her discovery about the structure of the atom's nucleus. **1949** Gwendolyn Brooks (b. 1917), black poet, wins Pulitzer Prize for *Annie Allen*; Simone de Beauvoir (b. 1908), philosopher, publishes *The Second Sex*. **1950** Althea Gibson (b. 1927), tennis player, is 1st black **W** to play at Forest Hills, NY; Ethel Waters (b. 1900), black actress, singer, re-

1948

political activist, founds Institute for Study of Non-Violence, Palo Alto, Cal. Coretta King (b. 1927), civil rights leader, writer, lecturer, singer, recipient of the **W** of the Year Award, Nat'l Ass'n of Radio & T.V. Announcers (1968), is named delegate to the White House Conference on Children and Youth; **1961** Julia Child (b. 1912), chef, publishes *Mastering the Art of French Cooking*.

1959 Natalie de Blois (b. 1920) is one of the designers of the Pepsi Cola Building, NYC.

1964 Mary Otis Stevens (b. 1928) designs this living environment in Lincoln, Mass.

1963 Betty Friedan (b. 1921), feminist, founder of NOW (1966), publishes *The Feminine Mystique*; Katharine Graham (b. 1917), publisher, becomes Bd. Chairman of the *Washington Post* & of *Newsweek*; Chien-Shiung Wu (b. 1912), physicist, recipient of the **W** of the Year Award, Am. Ass'n of U.W. (1958), receives the Comstock Award, Nat'l Acad. of Sci., for her experiments on nuclear particles. **1964** Congress adds sex to

1963

Civil Rights legislation; federal equal pay legislation becomes effective; Lillian Hellman (b. 1907) dramatist of "The Children's Hour," "The Little Foxes," & "Toys in the Attic," recipient of Nat'l Inst. & Acad. of Arts & Letters Gold Medal, publishes *An Unfinished Woman: A Memoir*; Sen. Margaret Chase Smith (b. 1923) is 1st **W** to be a GOP nominee for US Pres.; Geraldine McCullough (b. 1922) black sculptor, painter, wins George D. Widener Memorial Gold Medal for sculpture; Louise Nevelson (b. 1899), sculptor, former Pres. of Nat'l Artists Equity, recipient of 1st United Society of Artists Award (1959), has 1st individual show at the Martha Jackson Gallery, NY. **1965** Mary Wells Lawrence (b. 1928), business executive, chair**W** of Wells, Rich, Greene, Inc., launches the Braniff advertising campaign. **1966** Anne Sexton (1928–74), poet, Pulitzer Prize winner, publishes *Live or Die*; Leontyne Price (b. 1927), black opera singer, opens the new Met. Opera House; Susan Sontag (b. 1933), writer, filmmaker, essayist, discoverer of the cultural phenomenon "camp," publishes *Against Interpretation*. **1967** Martina Horner (b. 1939) psychologist, educator, named Pres. of Radcliffe College following publication of her study dealing with **W**'s fear of success; **W**'s Equity Action League (WEAL) is chartered to protect educational and economic progress for **W**; 1st annual picket of Miss Am. Contest. **1969** Diane Crump (b. 1949) is 1st **W** to ride in Hialeah Parimutuel Race; Joan Ganz Cooney (b. 1929), educator, president of the Children's Television Workshop, launches "Sesame Street"; Shana Alexander (b. 1925) becomes editor-in-chief, *McCall's*, NYC; Equal Employment Opportunity

1965

Comm. rules that separate male/female help-wanted ads violate Civil Rights Act; Pres. Nixon names 20-member Advisory Council on Status of **W**. **1970** NY State legalizes abortion by a single vote; feminists demonstrate in Wash., DC, to protest male domination of birth control hearings; Boston Stock Exchange has last all-male day; Mary S. Calderone (b. 1904), physician & sex educator, director of Planned Parenthood Fed. of Am., wins Haven Emerson Award. **1971** Gloria Steinem (b. 1934), journalist, feminist, cofounder of *MS*, founds Nat'l **W**'s Political Caucus & **W**'s Action Alliance; Lucy Lippard (b. 1937), art critic & fiction writer, organizes "26 Contemporary **W** Artists Show" at the Larry Aldrich Gallery, Ridgefield, Conn.

1972–73 Professional organizations proliferate: WALAP, Cambridge; OWA, San Fran.; AWA, NYC; Archive of **W** in Architecture, NYC.

1973 The Woman's Building is created to share **W**'s culture in Los Angeles.

1970

1974–75 The years of conferences: St. Louis; Eugene, Ore.; The **W**'s Building, LA; WSPA opens in Biddeford, Me.

1973 Eleanor Holmes Norton (b. 1937), lawyer, named Chairperson of NY Commission on Human Rights; Helen Taussig (b. 1898), physician, discoverer of the cause & cure for "blue babies," is elected to the **W**'s Hall of Fame. **1974** Susan Brownmiller (b. 1936), author, feminist, publishes *Against Our Will: Men, Women & Rape*; Ella Grasso (b. 1919), economist, is 1st **W** elected Governor (Conn.) who did not follow her husband; Susie Sharp (b. 1918), lawyer, elected 1st **W** Chief Justice of a State Supreme Court (NC); Jeannette Piccard (b. 1895), aerospace scientist, 1st **W** to reach the stratosphere, becomes legal Episcopalian Deacon & illegal Episcopalian priest; Shirley Temple Black (b. 1928), child actress, politician, UN delegate, is appointed Ambassador to Ghana; Billy Jean King (b. 1943), tennis champion, feminist, begins publication *Womansport*; Addie Wyatt (b. 1925), union leader, VP of Coalition of Labor Union **W**, becomes 1st **W** pres. of Amalgamated Meat Cutters & Butcherworkmen, Chicago. **1975** International **W**'s Year; Jill Ruckelshaus (b. 1937), lawyer, heads the US Intern'l **W**'s Year Commission; US Supreme Court recognizes **W**'s right to abortion in Roe vs. Wade; Equal Rights Amendment defeated in NY; 1st **W**'s Bank of New York is estab-

1973

lished; Carla Hills (b. 1935), lawyer, teacher, named Sec. of Housing & Urban Development; Alice Rivlin (b. 1932), economist, appointed Chief of the Budget Office; Jill Conway (b. 1935), historian, feminist, educator is named 1st **W** Pres. of Smith College; Nancy Hanks (b. 1927), gov't official, becomes Chairperson of the Nat'l Endowment for the Arts; Barbara Walters (b. 1931), journalist, is designated co-host of "Today Show." **1976** Sarah Caldwell (b. 1934), conductor, artistic director of Boston Opera Co., conducts at Met. Opera; Barbara Jordan (b. 1936), lawyer, Congress**W** (Texas), 1st black member of the Texas Senate (1966), member of the House Judiciary Comm., member of the Democratic Steering Comm., *Time* nominee for **W** of the Year, is first **W** to second a presidential nomination.

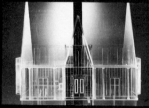

1976 The Woman's Building moves to its present location in Los Angeles.

1977 commemorates the first major exhibition (Brooklyn Museum) and book on the work of **W** in Am. architecture.

1977

Notes

Introduction:
A Parallel History

1. Linda Nochlin, "Why Have There Been No Great Women Artists?," *Art in America,* January 1971, p. 24.

2. Ibid., p. 23.

3. Vincent Scully, *The Shingle Style Today or The Historian's Revenge* (New York: George Braziller, 1974), p. 3.

4. Doris Cole, *From Tipi to Skyscraper* (Boston: i press, 1973). See Chapter 1: "Frontier Traditions: Pioneer and Indians," pp. 1–27.

5. Sherry Ortner, "Is Female to Male as Nature Is to Culture?," *Feminist Studies* 1–2, (Fall 1972), p. 10.

6. Hannah Arendt, *The Human Condition* (Chicago: The University of Chicago Press, 1958), p. 7.

7. Ibid., p. 7.

8. Kenneth Frampton, paraphrasing Hannah Arendt, in "Labor, Work and Architecture," in *Meaning in Architecture,* eds. George Baird and Charles Jencks (New York: George Braziller, 1969), p. 151.

9. Ibid., p. 151.

10. Sherry Ortner, "Is Female to Male," p. 10.

11. Ibid., p. 7.

12. Ibid., p. 7.

13. Gwendolyn Wright, "On the Fringe of the Profession: Women in American Architecture," in *The Architect: Historical Essays on the Profession,* Spiro Kostof, ed. (Fair Lawn, N.J.: Oxford, 1976).

14. For a discussion on human dwelling as process, see Martin Heidegger, "Building Dwelling Thinking," *Poetry, Language, Thought* (New York: Harper & Row, 1971), pp. 145–161.

15. Mariana Griswold van Rensselaer (Mrs. Schuyler van Rensselaer), "Client and Architect," *The North American Review,* September 1890, p. 320.

16. Lewis Mumford, "A Backward Glance," *Roots of Contemporary American Architecture,* (New York: Dover, 1972), p. 6.

17. Ayn Rand, *The Fountainhead* (Indianapolis: Bobbs-Merrill, 1943).

18. Gwendolyn Wright, "On the Fringe."

Chapter 1:
The Model Domestic Environment:
Icon or Option?

1. Helen Binkert Young, "The Modern House," in *A Manual of Home-Making,* eds. Martha Van Rensselaer, Flora Rose, and Helen Canon (New York: Macmillan, 1919), p. 1.

2. Mary Pattison, *The Principles of Domestic Engineering* (New York: The Trow Press, 1915), p. 250.

3. See Gwendolyn Wright, "On the Fringe of the Profession: Women in American Architecture," in *The Architect: Historical Essays on the Profession,* ed. Spiro Kostof (New York: Oxford, 1976); and Dolores Hayden and Gwendolyn Wright, "Review Essay: Architecture and Planning," *Signs: Journal of Women in Culture and Society* (Spring 1976) for a broader discussion of professional roles for women designers.

4. The most well-known radical was Charlotte Perkins Gilman. Her *Women and Economics* (Boston: Small, Maynard, 1898; reprinted New York: Harper & Row, 1966) and *The Home: Its Work and Influence* (Boston: McClure, Phillips & Co., 1903) were filled with insights and innovative suggestions. Among the conservative voices of the time, those who wanted settings and roles that would rekindle the home fires of the past were, for instance, H. V. von Holst, whose *Modern American Homes* (Chicago: American Technical Society, 1916) contained numerous reprints from *The Ladies' Home Journal,* and those seeking housing reform for the working class and poor, such as Winthrop Hamlin, *Low-Cost Cottage Construction in America* (Cambridge: Harvard University Press, 1917).

5. Margaret Reid carried out pioneer research in the hours devoted to housework in the 1930s while in the home economics department of Iowa State University. See *Economics of Household Production* (New York: John Wiley, 1934). A more recent study by Joann Vanek, "Time Spent in Housework," *Scientific American,* November 1974, pp. 116–120, asserts that the hours have changed very little over the past 50 years, always averaging between 52 and 60 hours per week.

6. Helen Campbell, *Household Economics* (New York: G.P. Putnam's Sons, 1897), p. 206.

7. For material on *The Ladies' Home Journal* and other popular women's magazines, see Frank L. Mott, *A History of American Magazines,* 4 vol. (Cambridge: Harvard University Press, 1957); and Edward Bok, *The Americanization of Edward Bok* (New York: Charles Scribner's Sons, 1921).

8. Christine Frederick, *Household Engineering: Scientific Management in the Home* (Chicago: The New School of Home Economics, 1915), p. 513.

9. Ibid., p. 315.

10. Ibid., p. 168.

11. Ibid., p. 316.

12. Ibid., p. 380.

13. Ibid., p. 384.

14. Greta Gray, *House and Home* (Philadelphia: J.B. Lippincott, 1923), p. 3.

15. Ibid., p. 283.

16. Two autobiographical accounts by Gilbreth's children describe what life was like when time-motion studies were applied to their own home. See Frank B. Gilbreth, Jr., and Ernestine Gilbreth Carey, *Belles on Their Toes* (New York: Crowell, 1950) and *Cheaper by the Dozen* (New York: Crowell, 1948).

17. Emily Post, *The Personality of a House* (New York: Funk & Wagnalls, 1930), p. 403.

18. Dorothy Field, *The Human House* (Boston: Houghton-Mifflin, 1939), p. 11.

19. Gwendolyn Wright, "The Woman's Commonwealth: Separatism, Self, and Sharing," *Architectural Association Quarterly* 6 (Fall-Winter 1974).

20. Catherine Bauer, *War Housing in the United States* (Washington, D.C.: National Housing Agency, 1945), p. 24.

21. Elizabeth Kemper Adams, *Women Professional Workers* (New York: Macmillan, 1921), p. 318.

Chapter 3:
Catharine Beecher and the Politics of Housework

1. Kathryn Kish Sklar, *Catharine Beecher: A Study in American Domesticity* (New Haven: Yale University Press, 1973). This biography has provided most of the background information on Beecher's life used here, and I recommend it highly. I am also indebted to Whitney Chadwick, Sheila deBretteville, Melanie Dewey, Peter Marris, and Gwen Wright for helpful discussions of Beecher's personality and to Ellen McDougall, who worked with me on a discussion of "Feminism and Domestic Architecture" in 1973 that analyzed Beecher's influence.

2. Ibid., p. 17.

3. Ibid., p. 306. Sklar states that Wadsworth executed Beecher's architectural designs. Beecher did publish a plan and view of Wadsworth's own house, but she credited this building to him. Sklar now agrees that there is no reason to attribute all Beecher's other architectural work to Wadsworth. It is also important to note that Beecher's designs for the "American woman's home" evolved in publications where she is the sole author so that these designs predate her collaboration with Harriet Beecher Stowe.

4. Ibid., p. 153.

5. Catharine E. Beecher, "How to Redeem Woman's Profession from Dishonor," *Harper's New Monthly Magazine* 31 (1865), p. 710.

6. Ibid., p. 712.

7. Ibid., p. 716.

8. Catharine E. Beecher, *A Treatise on Domestic Economy, For the Use of Young Ladies at Home and at School*, rev. ed. (New York: Harper, 1846), p. 263.

9. Ibid., p. 172, quoted in Sklar, *Catharine Beecher*, p. 307.

10. Catharine E. Beecher and Harriet Beecher Stowe, *The American Woman's Home* (New York: J. B. Ford, 1869), p. 459.

11. This is first proposed in Christopher Crowfield (pseudonym of Harriet Beecher Stowe), *House and Home Papers* (Boston: Fields, Osgood & Co., 1865), p. 223, and is repeated in Catharine Beecher and Harriet Beecher Stowe, *The American Woman's Home*.

12. This movement is discussed more fully in my article, "Collectivizing the Domestic Workplace," *Lotus* (Milan, Italy) 12 (1976), reprinted as "Redesigning the Domestic Workplace," *Chrysalis* 1 (1977).

13. Patricia Mainardi, "The Politics of Housework," in *Sisterhood Is Powerful: An Anthology of Writings from the Women's Movement*, Robin Morgan, ed. (New York: Random House, 1970).

Chapter 4:
Pioneer Women Architects

1. Correspondence with Judith Paine from Dean Kermit C. Parsons, Cornell University College of Architecture, Art & Planning, January 1974. Files of Judith Paine.

2. Phebe Hanaford, *Daughters of America; or Women of the Century* (Augusta, Maine: True & Co., 1889), p. 284; "Nolanum," *The New Century for Women*, Philadelphia (Aug. 19, 1876), p. 115; John Maass, *The Glorious Enterprise* (Watkins Glen, N.Y.: The American Life Foundation, 1973), p. 121.

3. Louise Bethune, "Women and Architecture," *The Inland Architect and News Record* 17, no. 2 (March 1891), p. 21.

4. "Architectural Education in the United States—Cornell University," *American Architect and Building News* 24 (Oct. 6, 1888), p. 157.

5. Theodor K. Rohdenburg, *A History of the School of Architecture* (New York: Columbia University Press, 1954), p. 22.

6. The most important precedent for the Woman's Building of 1893 was the Woman's Pavilion at the 1876 Philadelphia Centennial. The Pavilion, exclusively devoted to exhibits of women's work, was a novel and popular attraction. For further discussion of its background and particulars, see Judith Paine, "The Woman's Pavilion of 1876," *The Feminist Art Journal* 4, no. 4 (Winter 1976).

7. Madelaine Stern, *We the Women* (New York: Schulte Publishing Company, 1963), p. 69.

8. For a discussion of the background planning of the Women's Building as well as an analysis of the exhibits see Arlene Raven and Ruth Iskin, "The Woman's Building" (paper given at the College Art Association meeting), January 1975.

9. Maud Howe Elliott, *Art and Handicraft in the Women's Building of the World's Columbian Exposition, Chicago, 1893* (Paris & New York: 1893), pp. 9–11.

10. Unpublished report of Sophia Hayden on the Women's Building, Boston, Apr. 28, 1894; collection of the Chicago Historical Society.

11. Stern, *We the Women*, p. 75.

12. *American Architect and Building News* 28 (Nov. 26, 1892), p. 134.

13. Ibid.

14. Editorial, *The American Architect and Building News* 1 (Sept. 30, 1876), p. 313.

15. Ibid.

16. Ibid.

17. *The Inland Architect and News Record* 18, no. 4 (November 1891), p. 36.

18. Bethune, "Women and Architecture," p. 21.

19. *The Inland Architect and News Record*, November 1891.

20. Stern, *We the Women*, p. 64.

21. Bethune, "Women and Architecture," p. 2.

22. Ibid.

23. "Representative Women: Minerva Parker Nichols," *Woman's Progress* 1, no. 2 (May 1893), pp. 57–58.

24. Frances A. Willard and Mary Livermore, *A Woman of the Century* (Buffalo, N.Y.: Charles Wells Noulton, 1893), p. 596.

25. Allen Brooks, "Frank Lloyd Wright and the Wasmuth Drawings," *The Art Bulletin* 48, no. 2 (June 1966), p. 195.

26. Unpublished interview of Waldo Dean Waterman by Mary F. Ward, Jan. 11, 1971, p. 6; collection of the San Diego Historical Society.

27. Brooks Emeny, *Avon Old Farms*, privately printed, p. 45.

28. Warren Wright Parks, *The Mariemont Story* (Cincinnati, Ohio: Creative Writers and Publishers, Inc., 1967), p. 75.

29. "Workman's Cottage," *American Architect and Building News* 3 (Apr. 13, 1878), p. 129.

30. *The Technology Architectural Review* 7, p. 165.

Chapter 5:
Some Professional Roles: 1860–1910

1. Madelaine Stern, *We the Women* (New York: Schulte Publishing Company, 1963), p. 68.

2. *The Tribune* (Chicago), Mar. 28, 1891.

3. Stern, *We the Women*, p. 69.

4. *The Tribune* (Chicago), Mar. 28, 1891.

5. For example, see Frank Chouteau Brown, "Exterior Plaster Construction," *Architectural Review* 14, no. 1 (January 1907), pp. 1–8; and also by Brown, "Boston Suburban Architecture," *Architectural Record* 21, no. 4 (April 1907), pp. 245–280, which include Howe's work. For Howe's measured drawings see Lois Howe, Lois Lilley, and Constance Fuller, *Details from Old New England Houses* (New York: The Architectural Book Publishing Company, 1913).

6. It was not, however, the first partnership of women architects. Around 1912, Anna Schenck and Marcia Mead formed Schenck & Mead in New York City that continued until Schenck's death in 1915.

7. *The Tribune* (Chicago), Mar. 28, 1891.

8. Conversation with Adelaide Nichols Baker, daughter of Minerva Parker Nichols, in 1974. See also Schlesinger Library Archives, Radcliffe College, Cambridge, Mass.

9. Minerva Parker Nichols, "A Woman on the Woman's Building," *American Architect and Building News* 38, no. 885 (Dec. 10, 1892), p. 170.

10. Mahony was the second woman to receive a B.S. degree in architecture from MIT. Prior to 1894, three of the nine university architectural departments in existence granted admission and degree status to women: MIT, Cornell University, and the University of Illinois at Urbana. By 1900 another university did also: Armour Institute in Chicago, now the Illinois Institute of Technology. By 1900 there were 39 academically trained female graduates of the U.S. collegiate architectural system. This number includes the 14 women who completed the 2-year nondegree program at MIT. Statistics were compiled from the individual university archives.

11. For additional historical background see Susan Fondiler Berkon and Jane Holtz Kay, "Marion Mahony Griffin, Architect," *The Feminist Art Journal* (Spring 1975), pp. 10–14.

12. *1894 Class Book*, Massachusetts Institute of Technology, 1898.

13. Grant Carpenter Manson, *Frank Lloyd Wright to 1910: The First Golden Age* (New York: Reinhold, 1958), p. 213.

14. *1894 Class Book*.

15. Ibid.

16. Ibid.

17. Ibid. It is possible that the mountain cottage mentioned was the unexecuted house she designed for her family in Hubbard Woods, Illinois, since both were designed prior to 1899. See "The Magic of America," vol. 7, p. 75b this 8-volume unpublished manuscript written by Marion Mahony Griffin in the 1940s is in the collection of the New York Historical Society and the Burnham Library at the Art Institute of Chicago.

18. See her account in ''The Magic of America,'' vol. 7, p. 42.

19. Ibid., vol. 4, p. 159.

20. Hermann von Holst, ''A Small Stone Church of Unusual Merit,'' *Modern American Homes* (Chicago: American School of Correspondence, 1912), plate 108.

21. James Birrell, *Walter Burley Griffin* (Brisbane: University of Queensland Press, 1964), p. 13.

22. ''The Magic of America,'' vol. 7, p. 275.

23. See David T. Van Zanten, ''The Early Work of Marion Mahony Griffin,'' *The Prairie School Review* 3, no. 2 (2nd quarter, 1966), pp. 5–23; and H. Allen Brooks, *The Prairie School: Frank Lloyd Wright and His Midwest Contemporaries* (Toronto, Canada: University of Toronto Press, 1972), pp. 149–165. Brooks disputes one Van Zanten attribution—the Robert Mueller house in Decatur, Illinois, of 1909–11. While Van Zanten attributes the design-execution entirely to Mahony, Brooks views it as a joint Wright-Mahony venture. See Brooks, pp. 157–161.

24. Van Zanten, ''Early Work,'' p. 16, fn. 32. In 1916, Wright included both the Adolph and Robert Mueller houses of Decatur, Illinois, in an exhibition of his work at the Chicago Art Institute. While the latter was probably a joint venture (see note 23), the former has been solely credited to Marion Mahony. See Brooks, *Prairie School*, p. 161.

25. *The Western Architect* 19, p. 38; and Donald Kalec, ''The Prairie School Furniture,'' *The Prairie School Review* 1, no. 4 (4th quarter, 1964), p. 7.

26. *The Western Architect* 19 (October 1913), pp. 88ff.

27. *The Western Architect* 19 (May 1913), pp. 33.

28. See Van Zanten, ''Early Work,'' p. 19; and Brooks, *Prairie School*, p. 165.

29. ''The Magic of America,'' vol. 7, p. 339.

30. Ibid., vol. 7, p. 339.

31. Ibid., Birrell, *Walter Burley Griffin*, p. 30.

32. Obituary of Lola M. Lloyd, *The New York Times*, Wednesday, July 26, 1944.

33. Burnham Library at The Art Institute of Chicago.

34. Letters to Pierre Le Brun, Morgan Estate, Berkeley, Calif.

35. *Who's Who in California 1928–29;* material submitted by Morgan.

36. California Architect Certificate B-344-1903; letter from Board of Examiners, Sacramento, Calif., January 1976.

37. Walter Steilberg (engineer-architect who worked for her for many years), oral communication, October 1974.

38. Ibid.

39. Ibid.

40. In Paris Julia Morgan lived in the same house with the Maybecks, who were there to further the International Competition for the Phoebe Apperson Hearst Architectural Plan for the University of California. Letter from J. M. to Mrs. Hearst in the Bancroft Library at the University of California at Berkeley is dated February 1899, but it is possible that Hearst and Morgan met as early as 1893 in Berkeley.

41. *Y.W.C.A. News, Oakland and Alameda County Branch* 2, no. 6 (November 1975), p. 4.

42. Unpublished paper by Richard Longstreth and Robin Clements, in the records of the Archive of Women in Architecture, The Architectural League of New York.

43. Otto Haake (who helped J. M. close up in 1952), oral communication, January 1976.

44. Dorothy Wormser Coblentz, oral communication; *San Francisco Chronicle,* April 1937; article said that Boyter was the first woman to receive the certificate in Northern California since 1927 and that she trained in the offices of Julia Morgan. Boyter certificate no. C-215; letter from State Association of California Architects, Northern Section, April 1937.

45. Walter Steilberg, oral communication, October 1974.

Chapter 6:
Struggle for Place:
Women in Architecture:
1920–1960

1. *The Architrave* 11, no. 1 (July 1938); pamphlet published by Women's Architectural Club of Chicago.

2. ''Short History of the Association of Women in Architecture,'' p. 2. Archive of Women in Architecture, New York.

3. Ibid.

4. Ibid.

5. *The Architrave* 11, no. 1 (July 1938).

6. Ibid.

7. Ibid.

8. Rose Connor, AIA, Chairman of Survey, ''Women in Architecture Survey,'' Association of Women in Architecture & the Allied Arts, 1958.

9. Ibid.

10. Ibid.

11. Letter from Betty Lou Custer, historian, Feb. 19, 1958. Correspondence, Archive of Women in Architecture, New York.

12. Letter from Lucille B. Raport, AIA, May 7, 1958. Correspondence, Archive of Women in Architecture, New York.

13. ''A Thousand Women in Architecture,'' part 1, *Architectural Record*, March 1948.

14. The others were Elsa Gidoni, AIA; Ruth Reynolds Freeman; Lavone Dickensheets Scott, AIA; Barbara W. Siemens; Elizabeth Scheu Close, AIA; Larch Renshaw, AIA; Tennie Owne Wiatt, RA; Gertrude Sawyer, AIA; Marie Frommer, RA; Dr. Ing; Carina Eaglesfield Milligan, AIA; and Emily H. Butterfield, AIA.

15. ''A Thousand Women,'' part 1.

16. Ibid.

17. Ibid.

18. Doris Cole, *From Tipi to Skyscraper: A History of Women in Architecture* (Boston: i press, 1973), p. 80.

19. Ibid., p. 82.

20. Ibid.

21. Ibid., p. 94.

22. ''A Thousand Women,'' part 2, *Architectural Record*, June 1948.

23. ''Four Fine Fellows,'' *AIA Journal,* September 1969.

24. Ibid.

25. Ibid.

26. Interview with Norman Fletcher, March 1976.

27. Ibid.

28. Interview with Sarah Pillsbury Harkness, March 1976.

29. Ibid.

30. Ibid.

31. *Los Angeles Times Sunday Magazine,* Aug. 11, 1957.

32. Memo from Lucille B. Raport, AIA, Association of Women in Architecture, Apr. 5, 1958.

33. Natalie de Blois, biographical worksheet, New York, Archive of Women in Architecture.

34. ''Notes on the Design and Construction of the Dwelling Units for the Lower-Income Family,'' *The Octagon,* October 1941.

35. Ibid.

36. Ibid.

37. Ibid.

38. Ibid.

39. Ibid.

40. Ibid.

41. Ibid.

42. ''Better Housing for the Family, Prepared and Edited by Beatrice S. Friedman for the Housing Committee,'' Women's City Club of New York, Inc., 1948.

43. Jose Luis Sert was one of the international architects participating in the study, which was funded by the Iranian government. In his Lawrence B. Anderson Memorial Lecture on May 12, 1976, at the United Nations, he itemized what the housing bill of rights would contain and the social attitudes on which its implementation depends.

Chapter 7:
Some Professional Roles:
1920–1960

1. Eleanor Raymond, *Early Domestic Architecture of Pennsylvania* (Princeton: The Pyne Press, 1973); reprinted from the 1931 edition published by William Helburn, Inc.

2. ''Eleanor Raymond, '09 Builds Houses,'' *Wellesley Alumnae Magazine* (March 1953), p. 164.

3. Ibid.

4. She was, among other things, the art editor of the *Occident* magazine, a cast member of the Junior play, and an organizer of architectural exhibitions. See *The Blue and Gold Yearbook,* University of California at Berkeley, 1911, p. 88.

5. Rice apparently became acquainted with Julia Morgan during her student days at Berkeley, but there is no evidence that she actually worked in her office; based on a conversation with Rea Mowery, Rancho Santa Fe Building Commissioner, 1976.

6. Lilian Rice, ''Rancho Santa Fe—a Vision,'' *The Modern Clubwoman,* January–February 1930, p. 5.

7. Sam Hamill, correspondence with author, 1974.

8. Nathaniel Owings, *The Spaces in Between* (Boston: Houghton Mifflin Company, 1973), pp. 264–265.

9. Ibid., p. 69.

10. Henry-Russell Hitchcock, *Architecture: Nineteenth and Twentieth Centuries* (Baltimore, Md.: Penguin Books, 1971), p. 561.

Chapter 8:
New Professional Identities:
Four Women in the Sixties

1. Wolf Von Eckardt, *A Place to Live* (New York: Delacorte Press, 1967), p. 291. See also

Chapter 9 for a discussion of Catherine Bauer's efforts in housing reform.

2. Ibid., p. 338. See also Robert Goodman, *After the Planners* (New York: Simon & Schuster, 1972), p. 113. General Lucius D. Clay headed a committee composed of labor leaders and corporation presidents whose own economic interests would benefit from a vast highway building program. Secretary of Defense Charles Wilson's famous remark, "What's good for General Motors is good for the country" epitomizes the climate in which the Highway Trust Act was written.

3. For a discussion of specific examples, see Robert A. Caro, *The Power Broker* (New York: Alfred A. Knopf, Inc., 1974), pp. 962–983; as well as Chapter 9.

4. In *After the Planners* Goodman describes the milieu of the sixties that led to the questioning and protest against "a pattern of arrogant and repressive programming carried out by planners, politicians and corporate interests."

5. See Chapter 9.

6. Goodman, *After the Planners*, pp. 233–238. The advocacy team from MIT continued to work with the community redesigning and reconstructing existing structures that were turned over to neighborhood groups.

7. Chloethiel Woodard Smith, "The New Town," *Building Research* 3, no. 1 (January–February 1966), p. 11.

8. Ellen Perry Berkeley, "La Clede Town: The Most Vital Town in Town," *Architectural Forum* 129, 11:68; p. 58.

9. Ibid., p. 60.

10. Ibid., p. 61.

11. Robert Stern, *New Directions in American Architecture*, (New York: George Braziller, Inc., 1969), p. 86.

12. *Chloethiel Woodard Smith & Associated Architects/Architecture, Urban Design, Planning.* This is a brochure prepared for prospective clients by the firm.

13. Roger Montgomery, "Acorn Project," *Architectural Forum*, July–August 1969.

14. Mary S. McNulty, "The New City: Case Study of an Alternative" (unpublished). The objectives of the New City are summed up in the prospectus cited by M. S. McNulty.

15. Ibid.

16. Ibid. From this essay: "Why 100 rather than 10 or 1 thousand" is explained in a memo by Jim Morey.

17. Ibid. From this essay, citing the New City prospectus: "We are tiny in number and highly unrepresentative of the resident population we hope to attract. . . . We seek a highly diverse composition . . . of white- plus blue-collar, of black and Puerto Rican, of students and 're-tired' persons. . . . "

18. Ibid.

19. Mary Otis Stevens and Thomas McNulty, *World of Variation* (i press series on the human environment; New York: George Braziller, 1970).

20. Ibid., p. 48.

21. Ibid., pp. 49–54.

22. Ibid., p. 55.

23. Ibid., pp. 56–58.

24. Ibid., pp. 86–87.

25. Ibid., pp. 91–123.

26. Ibid., pp. 100–101.

27. See N. A. Miliutin, *Sotsgorod, The Problem of Building Socialist Cities* (Cambridge, Mass.: MIT Press, 1974).

28. See W. Boesinger and H. Girsberger, *Le Corbusier 1910–65* (New York: Praeger, 1967).

29. M. O. Stevens and T. McNulty, *World of Variation*, p. 91.

30. Related by M. O. Stevens in an interview with S. Torre. See also Mary Otis Stevens, book review on prison architecture, *Architecture Plus*, November 1973, pp. 14–16 and p. 86.

31. Related by M. O. Stevens in conversation to S. Torre. Her first thesis proposal, the design of a prison, had been rejected by her advisor.

32. "The dome is interesting not only esthetically or mathematically, but also philosophically and spiritually. . . . In its roundness it represents our modern desire for continuous mental expansion, for reaching out to the universe instead of boxing ourselves in. . . . " Swami Kriyananda, *Domebook 2: Pacific Domes* (California, 1971), p. 96. The sixties' manuals on the construction and use of domes are amazing collages where geodesic geometry and technical advice are mixed freely with funk and cosmic revelations.

33. The material on Anne Tyng in the article is from her work and writing as well as an interview of May 1976 by Jane McGroarty.

34. Anne G. Tyng, "Geometric Extensions of Consciousness," *Zodiac* 19, 1969, p. 164.

35. Ibid., p. 168.

36. Ibid., p. 166.

37. Ibid., p. 170.

38. Ibid., p. 131.

39. Ibid., p. 131.

40. Tyng quotes Plato, from the *Timaeus*: "It is impossible to combine satisfactorily two things without a third one; we must have a correlating link. Such is the nature of proportion."

41. Ibid., p. 175.

42. Anne G. Tyng, "Simultaneous Randomness and Order: The Fibonacci-Divine Proportion as a Universal Forming Principle," Doctoral Dissertation, 1975, pp. 103, 104.

43. Ibid., p. 120.

44. Ibid., p. 139.

45. For a summary discussion on metabolists and megastructures, see Charles Jencks, *Modern Movements in Architecture* (Garden City, N.Y.: Doubleday, 1973) chaps. 7 and 8.

46. Peter Wolf, *The Future of the City* (New York: Whitney Library of Design, 1974), p. 35.

47. Mary Hommann, *The Caravan Mid-town Circulation Plan*, 1965; professional monograph available from Mary Hommann Associates, 350 East 52nd Street, New York, N.Y. 10022.

48. M. O. Stevens, English translation of an article on the Lincoln House, published in *db* (Deutsche Banzeitung), November 1966.

49. Ibid.

50. Ibid. See also M. O. Stevens and T. McNulty, "Mass Movement and Hesitations," *World of Variation*, chap. 8, for an earlier discussion of concepts leading to this project.

51. A term used by Tom Wolfe to refer to custom-designed cars in his book, *The Kandy-Kolored-Tangerine-Flake-Streamline-Baby* (New York: Pocket Books, 1966).

52. See Stephen Kurtz, *Wasteland* (New York: Praeger, 1974); especially the first part, "The Road," pp. 9–19.

53. Denise Scott Brown, "Learning From Pop," *Casabella*, May–June 1971, pp. 14–40.

54. See *Signs of Life: Symbols in the American City,* catalog published by Aperture, Inc. in conjunction with the exhibition by the same name, organized and designed by Venturi & Rauch, Architects and Planners, for presentation at the Renwick Gallery, Smithsonian Institution, Washington, D.C., from February 26 through September 30, 1976.

55. Ibid.

56. D. S. Brown, "Review Article: Team 10, Perspecta 10, and the Present State of Architectural Theory," *Journal of the American Institute of Planners,* January 1967, pp. 42–50.

57. Robert Venturi, introduction to "Mass Communication on the People Freeway, or Piranesi Is Too Easy," *Perspecta 12* (The Yale Architectural Journal), 1969, p. 49.

58. Ibid.

59. D. S. Brown, "Program Extracts: Introduction and First Phase," in "Review Article," pp. 50–51.

60. Ibid., p. 50.

61. "An Interview with Denise Scott Brown," *Networks* 1, Cal Arts, 1972.

62. R. Venturi, D. S. Brown, and Stephen Izenour, *Learning from Las Vegas: A Significance for A&P Parking Lots* (Cambridge, Mass.: MIT Press, 1972).

63. Ibid., "The Philadelphia Crosstown Community," pp. 126–131.

64. Ibid., p. 129.

65. See "California City Signs," *a+u, Architecture and Urbanism,* no. 47 (November 1974), pp. 40–42; special issue devoted to the work of Venturi & Rauch 1970–1974.

66. Ibid., "International Exposition for the Bicentennial."

67. Ibid., "Benjamin Franklin Parkway Celebration for '76," pp. 62–67.

68. D. S. Brown, "On Architectural Formation and Social Concern: A Discourse for Social Planners and Radical Chic Architects," *Oppositions 5* (Journal of the Institute for Architecture and Urban Studies), 1976.

69. D. S. Brown, "Reply to Frampton," *Casabella,* May–June 1971, pp. 45–51.

70. Gwendolyn Wright, "On the Fringe of the Profession: Women in American Architecture," *The Architect: Historical Essays on the Profession,* ed. Spiro Kostof (New York: Oxford, 1976). "Essentially women used four modes of coping with . . . contradictions in their professional status. First are those who worked to become 'the exceptional woman,' just like successful men and more so: more dedicated, more determined, more prolific, giving themselves over totally to their work and their professional role. Most women, however, followed a different model: they were 'anonymous designers,' often trying to accommodate a personal family role as well as a professional one. . . . Women with an expressed social concern . . . became 'adjuncts' to the profession: planners, programmers, critics, writers, and journalists who described housing in lay terms, according to social rather than esthetic considerations. . . . Finally there have been numerous women altogether outside the profession who defined environments with architectural merit, either by advocating dramatic policy changes or by building 'alternative' institutions."

71. Chloethiel Smith chooses not to identify with women's movements, disagreeing with sexual separation in architecture. She stated in recent interview, "I never experienced discrimination, but maybe that comes from being brought up in Oregon." Anne Tyng thinks th

people are not yet ready to accept women as original thinkers and therefore disregard the possibility of a theoretical contribution to architecture by a woman. Mary Otis Stevens sees women as the "true free spirits" since life is never ready-made and therefore the choice to change life-style or career should neither be frightening nor threatening. Denise Scott Brown has pointed out the paradoxical view that many have of her role as either "the dominating wife" or the "secretary" to her architect-husband. She attributes this, among other anomalies, to the so-called "star system in architecture" (see Chapter 10).

Chapter 9:
Voices of Consequence:
Four Architectural Critics

1. "Housing's White Knight," *Architectural Forum* (March 1946), pp. 116—119ff.

2. Catherine Bauer, "Social Front of Modern Architecture in the 1930's," *Journal of the Society of Architectural Historians* (March 1965), pp. 48–52.

3. Catherine Bauer, "Exhibition of Modern Architecture at the Museum of Modern Art," *Creative Arts* (March 1932), pp. 201–206.

4. Catherine Bauer, "Dreary Deadlock of Public Housing," *Architectural Forum* (May 1957), pp. 140–142ff.

5. Catherine Bauer, "Social Front," pp. 48–52.

6. Jason Epstein, "The Last Days of New York," *New York Review of Books* (Feb. 19, 1976), p. 17.

7. Jane Jacobs, *Economy of Cities* (New York: Random House, 1969), p. 85.

8. Jane Jacobs, "Washington: Twentieth Century Capitol?," *Architectural Forum* (January 1956), pp. 92–115.

9. Jane Jacobs, "New York's Office Boom," *Architectural Forum* (March 1957), pp. 104–113.

10. Ibid.

11. Ibid.

12. Jane Jacobs, "Metropolitan Government," *Architectural Forum* (August 1957), pp. 124–127.

13. Jane Jacobs, *The Death and Life of Great American Cities* (New York: Random House, 1961), p. 373.

14. Sibyl Moholy-Nagy, "Victories and Defeats of Modern Architecture," *Progressive Architecture* (April 1953), pp. 18ff.

15. Ibid.

16. Sibyl Moholy-Nagy, "Mexican Critique," *Progressive Architecture* (November 1953), pp. 109ff.

17. Sibyl Moholy-Nagy, "Style and Materials," *Progressive Architecture* (October 1954), pp. 93–97.

18. Sibyl Moholy-Nagy, "Modular Assembly" (letter), *Progressive Architecture* (February 1958), p. 20.

19. Sibyl Moholy-Nagy, "In Defense of Architecture" (letter), *Architectural Forum* (April 1962), p. 19.

20. Sibyl Moholy-Nagy, "Of Planners and Primadonnas," *The Journal of the American Institute of Architects* (October 1961), pp. 59–63.

21. Ibid.

22. Sibyl Moholy-Nagy, "The Heritage of Cezanne," *Progressive Architecture* (August 1952), pp. 104ff.

23. Sibyl Moholy-Nagy, "Hitler's Revenge: The Grand Central Tower Project," *Art in America* (September 1968), pp. 42–43.

24. Ibid.

25. Ada Louise Huxtable, "Anyone Dig the Art of Building," *The New York Times* (Apr. 11, 1971), sect. 2, p. 26.

26. Interview with Ada Louise Huxtable, January 1974.

27. Ibid.

28. Ada Louise Huxtable, "Anti-Street, Anti-People," *The New York Times* (June 10, 1973), sect. 2, p. 24.

29. Ada Louise Huxtable, "Some Sour Notes Sound at the Kennedy Center," *The New York Times* (Sept. 19, 1971), sect. 2, p. 25.

Chapter 10:
Architecture and the
New Feminism

1. Susan Saegert and Roger Hart, "The Development of Sex Differences in the Environmental Competence of Children," *Women in Society,* ed. Pat Burnett (Chicago: Maaroufa Press, 1976).

2. Erik Erickson, "The Theory of Infantile Sexuality," *Childhood and Society* (New York: Norton, 1963), p. 103, as quoted by Saegert and Hart: "in the male the emphasis is on the external, the erectable, the intrusive, the mobile —in the female, on the internal, on the vestibular, on the static, on what is contained and endangered in the interior."

3. *The American Architect and Building News* 1, no. 1 (Sept. 30, 1876).

4. See, for example, such articles as "Female Architects," *The Builder,* Apr. 13, 1861; Lulu Stoughton Beem, *Inland Architect,* October 1884; Alberty, "Les femmes architectes," *La Construction Moderne,* Feb. 22, 1896; "The Admission of a Woman to Associateship in the R.I.B.A.," *The American Architect and Building News,* 63, no. 1204 (Jan. 21, 1899); Stan Willis, "Women Architects," *The Architect,* July 18, 1919; Pietro Belluschi, "Should You Be an Architect?," brochure of the New York Life Insurance Company.

5. "Woman as an Architect: A Profession That Calls for Recruits," *Daily Chronicle* (London), Aug. 19, 1909. Author unknown.

6. M. S. Briggs, "Notes of the Month," *The Architectural Review* 26 (Sept. 9, 1909), pp. 121–122.

7. *American Institute of Architects Journal* 15 (March 1951), pp. 111–116, 181–184, and 187–188.

8. Doris Cole, *From Tipi to Skyscraper: A History of Women in Architecture* (Boston: i press, 1973), p. 82.

9. The Cambridge School began after Harvard denied admission in architecture to several women. (It had never admitted women before.) Only after the Cambridge School was terminated by Smith College in 1942 did Harvard begin to admit women as candidates for degrees.

10. Letter from Margaret (Peg) K. Hunter to *Architecture Plus,* July 31, 1974, following publication of Doris Cole, "The Education of Women Architects," *Architecture Plus* 1, no. 11 (December 1973), pp. 30–35, 78–79. This article became the chapter on the Cambridge School in Cole's book *From Tipi to Skyscraper.*

11. These figures are from the Association of Collegiate Schools of Architecture, 1735 New York Avenue N.W., Washington, D.C. 20006. Some schools have much higher percentages of women—such as Columbia with 26.4 percent and MIT with 23.8 percent.

12. "Women in Medicine Up Sharply," *The New York Times,* July 17, 1974, p. 1.

13. This is especially true for user-needs subjects, completely neglected until now. Reena Racki's Master of Arch. thesis on housing from a mother's viewpoint, Wendy Bertrand's Master of Arch. thesis on childbirth environments, and Frances E. Kobrin's analysis on sex differences in living arrangements are a few of the many examples of women-related research. The Environmental Psychology Program of the Graduate Center of the City University of New York is now conducting a major study on sex roles in the use of space, co-authored by Val Jenson, Susan Saegert, Carol Sullivan, Gary Winkel, and Galina Zamdmer-Dubnikov. This study is sponsored by the Department of Housing and Urban Development.

14. The term "sex-typing" is ordinarily used in a social, psychological context to refer to behavior and values that are more characteristic of one sex than the other.

15. "Women and Architecture," paper prepared by Kay Stanley, Ph.D. and Bradley Soule, M.D.; Social and Behavioral Sciences Branch, National Institute of Child Health and Human Development, Bethesda, Md.

16. Ibid.

17. "The women present seem to enjoy being together but no real issues to pursue came out of the meeting," as noted in "Our Herstory: The Evolution of the West Coast Women's Design Conference," conference booklet. The conference organizers were Robbie Arnett, Georgia Bizios, Coral Cottage, Gunilla Finrow, Rosaria Hodgdon, Diane Shoemaker, Glenda Fravel Utsey, and Dorothy Victor.

18. The Women of Wurster (WOW), an organization of women staff, students, and faculty of the College of Environmental Design at the University of California at Berkeley, distributed a pamphlet in January 1976 with the following text: "What If Our Grandmothers Had Studied Architecture? Between 1906 and 1930, 79 women received architectural degrees from U.C. Berkeley. Let's find out what happened to these women." A research group coordinated by Christie Coffin resulted after the first meeting.

19. Practically in every major school or department of architecture, women realized the importance of hiring women faculty. These efforts have been particularly effective at MIT, where in 1976, Dolores Hayden prepared, in conjunction with the Affirmative Action Committee, a report documenting subtle aspects of discrimination found in the school, and at Pratt Institute, where Mimi Lobell initiated a successful lawsuit against Pratt for sex discrimination.

20. The professional conferences were places where women's organizations not only could present their views and programs, but actually help generate other groups throughout the country.

21. See section on *Exhibitions* in this chapter. The Archive of Women in Architecture, established in New York in 1973, was the basis for the organization of the first major historic and contemporary exhibit on women in American

architecture. More recently, a group called Washington Women in Architecture organized a show including 45 projects by 25 women in the area at the gallery of the InterAmerican Development Bank in August 1976. This exhibit was coordinated by Eileen Ross.

22. Although less numerous than similar courses taught by women artists in a large number of colleges and universities, women faculty have created special women-related courses. Some examples are those courses taught by Mimi Lobell at Pratt Institute in Brooklyn; Dolores Hayden at MIT; and Susana Torre at SUNY College at Old Westbury. A course on "Women in Planning and Architecture" was generated by a group of women students at Columbia University's School of Architecture and Planning. This course included topics of research such as feminist/separatist communities; the impact on women of alternate work schedule schemes; state involvement in housing and its impact on women; alternate marriage contracts; population and policy; concepts of safety and security for women; and demystification of the concept of community.

23. The Alliance of Women in Architecture in New York has been especially active in this area with the development of its own career-counseling effort, funded by NYSCA (New York State Council on the Arts) and including a videotape, a pamphlet, and a show. Other efforts have included the book, *What Can She Be? An Architect,* for readers four to ten, by Gloria and Esther Goldreich (New York: Lothrop, Lee & Shepard Co., 1974). The book features former AWA coordinating committee member Judith Edelman in the role of an active woman architect. Unfortunately, the picture of architectural practice and family life is fairly traditional in this book: readers learn that a family wanting a new house will need a weaving room for the wife, a workshop and a study for the husband.

24. As related in the *Proceedings of the West Coast Women's Design Conference,* April 18–20, 1974, University of Oregon, 20–21. The proceedings are available from the Department of Architecture and Allied Arts, University of Oregon, Eugene, Ore. 97403; $5 postpaid.

25. Unsigned review published in the Organization of Women Architects (OWA), San Francisco Newsletter, edited by Wendy Bertrand and Marian Haviland and designed by Corinne Moor Spingarn. This review also notes that the conferees were primarily young, white, and middle class. Most came from the midwest and southwest, with a few women from Boston, Toronto, San Francisco, Seattle, and New York.

26. Christie Coffin, a conference participant, said of this experience: "At 31 I found myself establishing contacts with women I had gone to school with, and was delighted to see that the students at the conference, unlike five or ten years ago were consciously organizing to support each other."

27. The keynote speaker was Gertrude Lempp Kerbis, FAIA, the well-known Chicago architect and designer of the Seven Continents Building at O'Hare International Airport and many other important buildings while working for Skidmore, Owings, & Merrill. Her speech at the St. Louis conference was on the subject "Architecture: Male, Female or Neuter?" Videotapes of Kerbis and other speakers are available from Washington University, St. Louis, Mo. 63130.

28. The organizers of "Women in Design: The Next Decade" were Rikki Binder, Sheila deBretteville, Elsa Leviseur-Fleischmann, Claire Forrest, Arlene Klasky, Jane McGroarty, Judith

Miller, Nancy Olexo, Deborah Sussman, and Bobbie Wilson, with the help of the members of the Women in Architecture and the Feminist Studio Workshop.

29. The announcement had a panel representing a blank drafting board. Participants were asked to return this panel with visual or written comments and suggestions about the questions asked in the announcement. These panels were then displayed at the entrance lobby of the Woman's Building during the conference.

30. The topics of discussion outlined in the conference brochure were: how are women designers and planners different?; the status of women working in the professions; power and achievement; conflicts between family and profession; work structure. The conference was organized by members of Women in Architecture, Landscape Architecture, and Planning (WALAP) and others.

31. The exhibit opened at the New York Chapter of the American Institute of Architects, April 30–May 28, 1974, and has traveled to a number of other locations since. It was organized by the Equal Opportunities Committee, chaired by Rosaria Piomelli, with Anna Halpin as commissioner.

32. This exhibit was the AIA Philadelphia Chapter's contribution to *Philadelphia Focuses on Women in the Visual Arts,* a festival of exhibitions, forums, and films throughout the city during April and May of 1974. Denise Scott-Brown, Elizabeth Lawson, and Robert Gutman participated in a panel discussion on the position of women in the design professions in conjunction with the exhibit.

33. "Women in Architecture," catalog of the New York AIA exhibit, 1974.

34. Cindy Cisler, "23 Are Married, 10 Have Children. So, What More Could Anyone Want to Know about Women Architects?," *Majority Report,* May 16, 1974.

35. Ada Louise Huxtable, "The Letterhead Is Solidly Male," *The New York Times,* May 19, 1974, sect. 2, col. 4, p. 26.

36. Albuquerque, New Mexico; AWA (Alliance of Women in Architecture), New York; AIA Task Force on Women in Architecture, New York; Archive of Women in Architecture, The Architectural League of New York; Bay Area Women Planners, Oakland, California; OWA/DP (Organization of Women Architects and Design Professionals), San Francisco, California; University of Michigan Women in Architecture, Ann Arbor, Michigan; WALAP (Women in Architecture, Landscape Architecture, and Planning), Boston; Women in Architecture/University of Arizona, Tucson, Arizona; Women of Wurster, University of California at Berkeley. The most recent additions to this list are Association of Women in Architecture, Clayton, Missouri; Chicago Women in Architecture, Chicago, Illinois; SHE (Sisters for a Human Environment), Seattle, Washington; Washington Women in Architecture, Washington, D.C.; Women's Design Center, Cambridge, Massachusetts.

37. Ellen Perry Berkeley, "Women in Architecture," *Architectural Forum,* September 1972.

38. This organization began as WED (Women in Environmental Design) in 1971; the name WALAP was adopted in March 1972. The following people contributed to the article: Andrea Leers Browning, Joan E. Goody, Lisa Jorgenson, Shelley Hampden-Turner, Sarah P. Harkness, Joan Forrester Sprague, Jane Weinzapfel.

39. WALAP, "The Case for Flexible Work Schedules," *Architectural Forum,* Sept. 1972.

40. Beatrice Pettit, "Women in WALAP," *Landforum,* November 1972.

41. Wall poster at the AIA New York Chapter "Women in Architecture" exhibit of 1974. This survey, however, was not done by the New York Chapter, but was possibly based on the AWA's survey.

42. "Status of Women in the Architectural Profession," report published by the American Institute of Architects, February 1975. This report was prepared by the following members of the AIA Task Force on Women in Architecture: Judith Edelman, AIA, chairwoman; Marie Laleyan, AIA; Patricia Schiffelbein, AIA; Joan Sprague, RA; and Jean Young, AIA; with Herbert Duncan, FAIA, chairman, Commission on Professional Practice; Edward G. Petrazio, AIA, administrator, Department of Professional Practice; and Alan Stover, director, Practice Programs.

43. Ellen Berkeley pointed out in a letter to Susana Torre of Sept. 1, 1976, that "these statistics are meaningless now, and were probably meaningless at the time. The total population should have been 59,484 registered architects [according to Samuel T. Balen of the NCARB], not 42,043 [as indicated by the AIA], and no one knew (or was telling) how many of these 59,484 were women."

44. "Status of Women in the Architectural Profession."

45. Ibid.

46. From the Alliance of Women in Architecture newsletter 12, August 1976.

47. Sheila deBretteville, "Eileen Gray," poster announcing an exhibition of her work. The exhibit opened at the Woman's Building on Mar. 8 and ran through Mar. 30, 1975, coinciding with the "Women in Design" Conference held at the building. The exhibit later traveled to "Princeton (School of Architecture, April 7–24); New York (Columbia University, April 28 –June 1); and Boston (City Hall, June 17–30) under the auspices of The Architectural League of New York and coordinated by Deborah Nevins. DeBretteville's poster and James Lapine's poster for The Architectural League include a short essay, illustrations of Gray's projects, and a chronology based on Joseph Rykwert's article on Eileen Gray, published in *Architectural Review,* December 1972.

48. The seven coordinators were Katrin Adam, Ellen Perry Berkeley, Noel Phyllis Birkby, Bobbie Sue Hood, Marie Kennedy, Joan Forrester Sprague, and Leslie Kanes Weisman.

49. The participants came from 21 states and Canada as well as from diverse ethnic and economic backgrounds. There were also six children. Half of the participants were in architecture and the rest in planning, interior design, landscape architecture, and other fields (a sculptor, two weavers, and a baker).

50. An underlying assumption of this course was that women, not really being integrated in the profession, are more apt to challenge the status quo.

51. Noel Phyllis Birkby and Leslie Kanes Weisman, "A Woman-Built Environment: Constructive Fantasies," *Quest: A Feminist Quarterly* 2, no. 1 (Summer 1975 Future Visions Issue).

52. WSPA is now organized as a nonprofit corporation.

53. The WSPA 1976 poster stated: "Our purpose remains two-fold: to create a personally supportive environment for the free exchange of ideas and knowledge, and to encourage both personal and professional growth through a

fuller integration of our values and identities as women with our values and identities as designers." Ellen Berkeley states in a letter to Susana Torre of Sept. 2, 1976, that "the diversity and openness of WSPA appealed to an even broader group in 1976 than it had in 1975, in terms of age, life-style and interest."

54. The complete list of course and instructor additions is "Politics and Ideology in the Urban Planning Process," taught by Harriet Cohen; "Energy-Conscious Design," taught by Polly Cooper; "Design and Construction of Architectural Tapestry," taught by Patti Glazer; "Basic Woodworking Techniques," taught by Charlotte Hitchcock; and "Architectural Design," taught by Cathy Simon.

Chapter 11:
A Current Portfolio of Projects and Ideas

1. See Reyner Banham, *Theory and Design in the First Machine Age* (New York: Praeger, 1967), pp. 71–73.

2. The Bauhaus's application of the standard was made especially on housing studies and building components. While the argument made here does not deny the technological emphasis, it suggests that there were other ideological bases for the mystique of the standard that pervades the period between the 1920s and the 1940s in modern architecture.

3. W. Boesinger and H. Girsberger, *Le Corbusier 1910–65* (New York: Praeger, 1967), p. 291. There are a large number of anthropomorphic references in Le Corbusier's writings. Some critics have gone as far as seeing "the curves of a [woman's] buttocks and shoulder arches" in his Ronchamp chapel and Carpenter Center at Harvard. See Charles Jencks, *Le Corbusier and the Tragic View of Architecture,* (Cambridge, Mass.: Harvard University Press, 1973), pp. 103–104.

4. Victor Papanek, *Design for the Real World* (New York: Pantheon, Random House, 1971), p. 92. Since 1971 there have been several studies on the handicapped, notably one by Sarah P. Harkness and James N. Groom, Jr., *Building without Barriers for the Handicapped* (New York: Whitney Library of Design, 1976).

5. Dolores Hayden, "Social Organization and Design," interview with Hayden, Sheila de Bretteville, and Clare Spark-Loeb, *Arts in Society,* Spring-Summer 1974, p. 128.

6. Janet Vrchota, "Women in Design: Developers," *Design and Environment,* Spring 1974, p. 20.

7. I have borrowed this expression from Nona Glazer-Malbin, "Woman's Place and Man's World: The Architecture of Sex Roles," professional paper presented at the annual meeting of the National Council on Family Relations, Oct. 23–26, 1974, St. Louis, Missouri. Glazer-Malbin is a professor at the Department of Sociology at Portland State University.

8. Ibid.

9. This is an S-shaped chair that allows both sitters to whisper in each other's ears as they face opposite sides. The word "confidante" is exclusively used in relation to women.

10. See Sigfried Gideon, *Mechanization Takes Command* (New York: Norton, 1969); especially pp. 396–397.

11. Phillipe Aries, *Centuries of Childhood* (New York: Vintage, 1962).

12. Nona Glazer-Malbin, "Woman's Place"; see note 7.

13. "Margaret Withers Thinks Out Loud about Women and Architecture," *The Architect,* September 1972, p. 38.

14. Henry Atherton Frost quoted by Doris Cole in *From Tipi to Skyscraper: A History of Women in Architecture* (Boston: i press, 1973), p. 98.

15. See especially Ruth Friedlander and Harriet Older, "Criteria for a Feminist Design Award," a publication available from Bay Area Women Planners, 434 66th Street, Oakland, Calif. 94609.

16. The Open Design Office is the best known of these collective offices. We have recently received news of the formation of other collectives, such as El-Ay Gray (Los Angeles), Oikos (Baltimore), and the Women's Design Collective (Cambridge).

17. Current literature on semiology and architecture is too vast to be cited here, and for the most part it is still in its inception. Interested readers should refer to the works of Umberto Eco, Michel Foucault, and Roland Barthes. In relation to this last paragraph, there is an interesting article, "De L'Eclectisme au Doute," a conversation between Eileen Gray and Jean Badovici that appeared in *L'Architecture Vivante* in 1929.

Chapter 12:
Centers and Fragments: Women's Spaces

1. Edward Hall, *The Hidden Dimension* (Garden City, N.Y.: Doubleday, 1966) and *The Silent Language* (Garden City, N.Y.: Doubleday, 1959).

2. Letter from a farm woman to *The Country Gentlewoman,* April 1945.

3. Jacki Apple, "Landscape/Mindscape," on flyer for exhibition "Survival III," New City, N.Y., Summer 1975.

4. Sheila deBretteville, poster for an exhibition of Eileen Gray's work organized by the Woman's Building, Los Angeles, 1975.

5. *Patricia Johanson: Some Approaches to Landscape, Architecture, and the City,* Montclair State College, N.J., Oct. 21–Nov. 20, 1974.

6. Ibid., italics in original.

7. Dolores Hayden, "Women and the Arts," *Arts in Society,* Spring–Summer 1974.

Chapter 13:
The Pyramid and the Labyrinth

1. Adolf Loos, "The Story of a Poor Rich Man," Apr. 26, 1900, from Ludwig Münz and Güstav Kunstler, *Adolf Loos* (New York: Praeger, 1966), pp. 223–225.

2. A description by artist Charles Simonds of one of his works, made in 1974 and entitled "Labyrinth."

3. The pamphlets and brochures on which a description of Llanda Villa appears were generously provided by Keith Kittle, General Manager of the Winchester Mystery House, 525 South Winchester Boulevard, San Jose, Calif. 95128. See also Esther Talbot, "Sarah Winchester," *Rosacrucian Digest,* July 1975, pp. 28–30, and Alan Guthertz, "The House the Spirits Built," *Occult,* July 1975.

4. For a brilliant discussion of the Bottle Village as a work of art, see Esther McCoy, "Grandma Prisbrey's Bottle Village," *Naives and Visionaries,* the catalog of an exhibition organized by the Walker Art Center, Minneapolis, Minn., and published by E.P. Dutton & Co., Inc., New York, 1974. See also "Grandma's Bottle Village," a pamphlet written and published by Grandma Prisbrey herself; it is available from The Bottle Village, 4595 Cochran Street, Santa Susana, California.

5. From "Fragments of a Conversation with Brenda Miller" in Susan Tower, "The Object Perceived/The Object Apprehended," *Artforum,* January 1974, p. 40.

By Carolyn Johnson

Selected Bibliography

The following is a basic bibliography of books and periodicals. Because of its general and incomplete nature, readers interested in more specific or recent sources should consult references mentioned in the footnotes for each chapter.

1. Books and Periodical Articles about Women in Architecture

A. Opportunities for Women in an Architecture Career

Alsopp, Bruce. *Architecture*. London: Robert Hale, Ltd., 1964. "Women in Architecture," pp. 72–73.

Belluschi, Pietro. "Should You Be an Architect?," No. 7 in a 57-booklet series issued by the New York Life Insurance Company, 1955; reprinted in *Scholastic Magazine*, April 1970.

Briggs, M. S. "Notes of the Month."

Architectural Review 26 (Sept. 9, 1909):121–122.

Cheetham, J. H. *Shall I Be an Architect?* Exeter: Wheaton Company, 1967.

Dunlop, Beth. "How One Firm Goes about 'Cutting in' Minorities and Women: Dalton, Dalton, Little, Newport." *American Institute of Architects Journal* 63, no. 2 (February 1975), pp. 41–42.

Editorial. *The American Architect and Building News* 1 (Sept. 30, 1876):1.

Epstein, Cynthia, *Woman's Place: Options and Limits in Professional Careers*. Berkeley: University of California Press, 1970, p. 153.

Frost, Henry Atherton. *Women in Architecture and Landscape Architecture*: A Study for the Institute for the Co-ordination of Women's Interests. Northampton, Mass.: Smith College, 1931.

Goldreich, Gloria, and Esther Goldreich. *What Can She Be? An Architect*. New York: Lothrop, Lee & Shepard, 1974. Photos by Robert Ipcar. (Juvenile literature.)

Greenleaf, Walter J. *Guidance Leaflets: Architecture*. U.S. Department of the Interior. Ray Lyman Wilbur, Secretary; William John Cooper, Commissioner. Washington, D.C.: U.S. Government Printing Office, 1932. U.S. Office of Education Leaflet no. 10, rev., 9 pp.

Hatcher, O. Latham. *Occupations for Women; A Study Made for the Southern Women's Educational Alliance*. Atlanta: Southern Women's Educational Alliance, 1927.

"Job Fact Sheet from *Glamour*—Architecture." New York: Condé-Nast Publications, Inc., 1961.

Kohlberg, Edith Rose. "A Battleground of the Spirit; the Pros and Cons of Architecture as a Career for Women." *Mademoiselle*, May 1966, pp. 162–163ff.

Lague, Louise. "Lady Architects Have Designs on Equality." *The Washington Star*, Aug. 2, 1976.

Morrison, Susan. "Women Architects, Planners Are Carpenters for 2 Weeks." *Biddeford-Saco Journal*, Aug. 23, 1975.

"NYC Officials Meet with Architecture Deans of Yale, Princeton, Columbia, NYU, and City University to Assure Deans There Will Be City Jobs for Qualified Women Grads; Deans Agree to Explore Recruitment of Students from Women's Colleges, Where They Had Not Previously Recruited Numbers of Students," *The New York Times*, Feb. 14, 1972, p. 26, col. 5.

Patterson, Anne. "Woman Architects, Why So Few?" *Inland Architecture*, December 1971. pp. 14–19.

Piper, Robert J. *Opportunities in an Architecture Career*. New York: Universal Publishing and Distributing Corporation, 1966.

"A Plea for Women Practising Architecture." *American Architect and Building News*, 76 (Apr. 19, 1902):20–22.

Schwartz, Felice N. *How to Go to Work When Your Husband Is Against It, Your Children Aren't Old Enough, and There's Nothing You Can Do Anyhow*. New York: Simon & Schuster, 1972, pp. 167–170.

The Status of Women in the Architectural Profession, a Task Force Report of the American Institute of Architects, February 1974. © 1975 AIA.

Turpin, Dick. "More Women Architects to Be Sought." *Los Angeles Times*, May 11, 1973, part II, p. 2, col. 1.

Verity, Terence. *Want to Be an Architect?* London: Leslie Frewin, 1966.

Winter, Elmer L. *Women at Work; Every Woman's Guide to Successful Employment*. New York: Simon & Schuster, 1967.

Woodman, Faith. "School Provides Forum for Women." *York County Coast Star*, Sept. 3, 1975.

Zapoleon, Marguerite Wykoff. "Education and Employment Opportunities for Women." *The Annals of the American Academy of Political and Social Sciences* 251 (May 1947):169–170.

B. Achievements of Women Architects

"The Admission of a Woman to Associateship in the R.I.B.A." *American Architect and Building News* 63 (Jan. 21, 1899):20–21.

Berkon, Susan Fondiler, and Jane Holtz Kay. "The First Lady: Marion Mahony (later Marion Mahony Griffin)." *Building Design* 250 (May 16, 1975):15.

Bethune, Louise. "Women and Architecture." *Inland Architect and News Record* 17 (March 1891):20–21.

Brown, Denise Scott. "Planning the Powder Room." *American Institute of Architects Journal* 47 (April 1967):81–83.

Cole, Doris. *From Tipi to Skyscraper: History of Women in Architecture*. Boston: i press (distributed by G. Braziller, New York), 1973.

"Design for a Workman's Cottage." *American Architect and Building News* 3 (Apr. 13, 1878):129.

Dott, Annabel. "The Woman Architect and Her Work." *The Architectural Review* 44 (1918):31–32.

"Female Architects." *The Builder* 19 (Apr. 13, 1861):254.

"Les Femmes Architectes." *La Construction Moderne* 11 (1896):245–256.

"The First Woman Architect?" *Country Life* 113 (Apr. 9, 1953):1077.

"Four Fine Fellows." *American Institute of Architects Journal* 52 (September 1969):86–87.

Garrett, Susanne. "Women in Architecture." *Building Design* 195 (Apr. 5, 1974):12–13.

Goldberger, Paul. "Women Architects Building Influence in a Profession That Is 98.8% Male." *The New York Times*, May 18, 1974, p. 33, col. 1ff.

"Heeded Words: Ada Louise Huxtable Has Formidable Power as Architecture Critic; Her *New York Times* Pieces Have Sway with Builders, Don't Always Win Friends." *The Wall Street Journal*, Nov. 7, 1972, p. 1, col. 1.

Huxtable, Ada Louise. "The Letterhead Is Solidly Male." *The New York Times*, May 19, 1974, sect. II, p. 26, col. 4.

Joyce, T. Athol. *Women of All Nations: A Record of Their Characteristics, Habits, Manners, Customs and Influence*. North America, vol. 3. London: Cassell & Company, Ltd., 1908, pp. 415, 445.

Joynes, Jennifer R. "Women in the Architectural Profession." *Habitat* 2, no. 4 (July–August 1959):2–6.

Karras, Maria. *The Woman's Building, Chicago 1893; The Woman's Building, Los Angeles, 1973*. Los Angeles: A Women's Community Press, 1975.

Langham-Carter, R. R. "South Africa's First Woman Architect." *Architect and Builder* 17 (March 1967):14–18.

McLendon, Winzola. "Architect Designs No Ivory Towers." *The Washington Post*, July 3 1967, sect. E, pp. 1ff.

Matthews, C. T. "Influence of Women in Architecture." *American Architect and Buildin*

News 59 (Jan. 1, 1898):3–4.

Molten, Philip L. "Asilomar: One of the Best Preserved Works of Julia Morgan, California's Pioneer Woman Architect." *Architectural Review* 157, no. 936 (February 1975):123–124.

"Outstanding Woman Architect, Leader in Professional and Civic Groups." *American Institute of Architects Journal* 56 (November 1971):62.

Paine, Judith, "The Woman's Pavilion of 1876." *The Feminist Art Journal* 4, no. 4 (Winter 1975–1976):5–13.

Pettengill, G. E. "How AIA Acquired Its First Woman Member, Mrs. Louise Bethune." *American Institute of Architects Journal* 63 (March 1975):35.

Phillips, Randal. "Women Architects, a House at Rotherfuld Greys, Near Henlay-on-Thames, Designed by Miss F. J. Gibb and Miss M. Low." *Country Life* 85 (May 27, 1939):564–565.

Poole, Daniel. "What Creates a Beautiful City?" *The Evening Star,* Washington, D.C., Mar. 12, 1965.

"Quiet Waves in the Sexual Storm." *Building Design and Construction,* September 1974, pp. 52–55.

Reif, Rita. "Fighting the System in the Male Dominated Field of Architecture." *The New York Times,* Apr. 11, 1971, p. 60, col. 1.

———. "Women Architects, Slow to Unite, Find They're Catching Up with Male Peers." *The New York Times,* Feb. 26, 1973.

Rochlin, Harriet. "Westways Women: Designed by Julia Morgan." *Westways* 68, no. 3 (March 1976):26–29.

Rykwert, Joseph. "Omaggio a Eileen Gray Pionera Del Design." *Domus* 469, December 1968.

Scherlach, Bernice. "The Legacy of Julia Morgan." *San Francisco Sunday Examiner and Chronicle,* Aug. 24, 1975, pp. 24–31.

Steilberg, Walter. "Some Examples of the Work of Julia Morgan." *Architect and Engineering of California* 55 (1918):34–101.

Stern, Madeleine B. "America's First Woman Architect?" *Society of Architectural Historians Journal* 18 (May 1959):66.

———. *We the Women: Career Firsts of Nineteenth-Century America.* New York: Schulte Publishing Company, 1963. Chapter 3, "Three American Women Firsts in Architecture," pp. 55–76.

"A Thousand Women in Architecture." *Architectural Record* 103 (March 1948):105–113, (June 1948) 108–115.

Washington Women Architects, catalog for exhibition May 1974. © Washington Women in Architecture, August 1973.

Willis, Stan. "Woman Architects." *The Architect,* July 18, 1919, pp. 44–46.

"Women Architects." *UIA: Revue de l'Union Internationale des Architectes* 35 (September 965):28–29.

Wright, Gwendolyn. "The Woman's Commonwealth." *The Architectural Association Quarterly* 6, no. 3–4(1974):36–43.

Wright, Gwendolyn, and Dolores Hayden. Review Essay: Architecture and Urban Planning." *Signs: Journal of Women in Culture and Society,* Spring 1976.

Studies and Surveys of Women in Architecture

AIA; Annual Convention; Proposed Study of Women's Status in the Field." *Architectural*

Forum 139 (July 1973):22.

American Institute of Architects. Task Force on Women in Architecture. *Women in Architecture: Task Force Report.* (Cover title: "Status of Women in the Architectural Profession.") Washington, D.C.: American Institute of Architects, 1975, pp. 38ff.

"American Women." *Time,* Mar. 20, 1972, p. 77.

Berkeley, Ellen Perry. "Women in Architecture." *Architectural Forum* 137 (September 1972):45–53.

Cisler, Cindy. "23 Are Married, 10 Have Children." *Majority Report,* May 16, 1974.

Cole, Doris. "The Education of Women Architects: A History of the Cambridge School." *Architecture Plus* 1, no. 4 (December 1973):30–35, 78–79.

Congrès International de Femmes Architects, 1st, Paris, 1963. *Rapports et Motions.* Paris, 1963, p. 311.

Conroy, Sarah Booth. "Washington Women in Architecture: Out of the Broom Closet." *The Washington Post,* Style Section, Aug. 1, 1976.

Davies, Paul. "Women in Architecture: Report of a Conference Held at North East London Polytechnic." *The Architect* (London) 4, no. 1 (February 1974):53–54.

Dean, A. O. "Board Acts on the Role of Women in Architecture." *American Institute of Architects Journal* 63 (March 1975):33–34.

DeSaules, M. "Return of Married Women to Professional Life." *Royal Institute of British Architects Journal,* Ser. 3, 71 (April 1964):136.

Dinerman, Beatrice. "Women in Architecture." *Architectural Forum* 131(December 1969):50–51.

Joynes, Jennifer R. "Women in the Architectural Profession." *Royal Architectural Institute of Canada Journal* 36 (September 1959):320–321.

Lunneborg, C. E., and P. W. Lunneborg. "Architecture School Performance Predicted from ASAT, Intellective, and Non-Intellective Measures." *Journal of Applied Psychology* 53 (June 1969):209–213.

Matthews, C. T. "Influence of Women on Architecture." *The American Architect and Building News* 3–4, January 1, 1968.

News Item. *American Institute of Architects Journal* 59 (June 1973):6.

News Reports. "Women Architects Seek Wider Role in Profession, End to Discrimination." *Architectural Record,* April 1973.

Parrish, John B. "Women in Professional Training. Report on Enrollment Trends of Women in 8 Selected Professions, 1960–1973." *Monthly Labor Review,* May 1974, pp. 41–43.

Proceedings of the West Coast Women's Design Conference, University of Oregon, April 18–20, 1974. © West Coast Women's Design Conference, 1975.

"R.I.B.A. on Equality for Women." *Royal Institute of British Architects Journal* 82, no. 4 (April 1975):6–7.

Sachs, H. "Aunty Tom Architects." *Architectural Design* 49(44), no. 2 (1974):119–120.

Standley, Kay, Bradley Soule, and Jo Standley. "Women and Architecture." *Journal of Architectural Education* 27, no. 4 (1974):78–82.

Stringer, P. "Comparison of the Self-Image of Art and Architecture Students." *Studies in Art*

Education 9 (Autumn 1967):33–49.

"Surveying the Role of Women in the Profession." *American Institute of Architects Journal* 61(June 1974):9.

van Peborgh, Sonia. "Le Premier Congrès International des Femmes Architectes. The First International Congress of Women Architects." *UIA: Revue de l'Union Internationale des Architectes* 23 (October 1963):14–15.

WALAP (Women Architects, Landscape Architects, and Planners). "The Case for Flexible Work Schedules." *Architectural Forum* 137 (September 1972):53ff.

"Woman's Work." *Newsweek,* Feb. 12, 1973.

"Women Architecture Students Meet in St. Louis." *Architectural Record* 155 (May 1974):35.

"Women in Architecture" (editorial). *Architectural and Engineering News* 1(April 1959):13.

D. Selected Articles on Women in Careers Related to Architecture

ART AND DESIGN

Birkby, Noel Phyllis, and Leslie Kanes Weisman. "A Woman Built Environment: Constructive Fantasies." *Quest* 2, no. 1 (Summer 1975):7–18.

Dreyfus, Patricia Ann. "Women's Lib and Women Designers." *Print* 24 (May 1970):29–35.

Hess, Thomas B. *Art and Sexual Politics: Women's Liberation, Women Artists, and Art History.* Edited by Thomas B. Hess and Elizabeth C. Baker. New York: Collier Books, 1973.

Lindquist-Cock, Elizabeth, and Estelle Jussim. "Machismo in American Architecture." *The Feminist Art Journal,* 9–10, Spring 1974.

Marmer, Nancy. "Womanspace, a Creative Battle for Equality in the Art World." *Art News* 72 (Summer 1973):38–39.

Nochlin, Linda. "Why Have There Been No Great Women Artists?" *Art News* 69 (January 1971):22–49ff.

"Women and the Arts." *Arts and Society* 11, no. 1 (Spring–Summer 1976).

"Women in Design." *Design and Environment* 5 (Spring 1974):1.

CONSTRUCTION

"Manpower Shortages May Push Women into Construction Work." *Engineering News Record,* May 9, 1974, pp. 24–26.

"So You Think You'll Turn the Business Over to the Boy When You Get Too Old." *House and Home* 39 (February 1971):26.

"Women Builders." *NAHB Journal-Scope,* June 3, 1974, pp. 22ff.

"Women in the Plant." *Automation in Housing,* September 1972, pp. 38–41.

LANDSCAPE ARCHITECTURE

"Gardening in New England Section." *Horticulture* 18 (December 15, 1940):1–2.

Hudnut, Joseph. "The Architectress." *American Institute of Architects Journal* 15 (March 1951):111–116; Part 2, 15 (April 1951):181–184, 187–188.

Petersen, Anne. "Women Take Lead in Landscape Art; Field Is Dominated by a Group of Brilliant Designers of Horticultural Vistas. . . ." *The New York Times,* Mar. 13, 1938, p. 1.

"Report on the Task Force on Women in Landscape Architecture," *American Society of Landscape Architects.*

PLANNING

American Society of Planning Officials, Planning Advisory Service. *Women and Blacks in Planning: 1972.* Prepared by Lisa B. Yondrof. Chicago: American Society of Planning Officials, 1972, 7 pp. (It's PAS Memo M-10.)

Criteria for a Feminist Design Award, presented at the West Coast Women's Design Conference. Available from the Bay Area Women Planners, 434 66th Street, Oakland, Calif. 94609.

Greene, Zina. "The Changing Role of Women: Implications for Planners." *HUD Challenge,* May 1974, pp. 2–4.

Hapgood, Karen, and Judith Getzels. "Planning, Women, and Change." *ASPO Planning and Advisory Service,* Report no. 301, April 1974, 78 pp.

Kaunitz, Rita D. "Planner Suggests Strategy to Give Broader Urban Role to Women." *American Institute of Planners Newsletter* 2 (November 1967):9.

E. Women as Critics (see Chapter 9)

Catherine Bauer's published articles appear in *Architectural Record, Progressive Architecture, The American Institute of Architects' Journal,* and *Architectural Forum,* as well as other publications from 1935 to 1964. Additional papers belonging to Catherine Bauer are in the Bancroft Library at the University of California at Berkeley. Information regarding personal files may be obtained by contacting her daughter, Sadie Super, through Wurster, Bernardi, Emmons in San Francisco.

Bauer, Catherine. *Citizen's Guide to Public Housing.* Poughkeepsie, N.Y.: Vassar College, 1940.

———. *Modern Architecture in England.* New York: Museum of Modern Art, 1937.

———. *Modern Housing.* Boston: Houghton Mifflin, 1934.

Ada Louise Huxtable's articles appeared frequently in art magazines (such as the now defunct *Arts Digest*) and architectural magazines during the 1950s. Many of her articles at the time appeared in *Progressive Architecture,* where she was a contributing editor and author of the series "Progressive Architecture in America." Since the early 1960s she has written mostly for *The New York Times,* although her articles have still been published in professional journals.

Huxtable, Ada Louise. *The Architecture of New York: A History and a Guide.* Garden City, N.Y.: Doubleday, 1964.

———. *Four Walking Tours of Modern Architecture in New York City.* Garden City, N.Y.: Museum of Modern Art and Municipal Art Society (distributed by Doubleday), 1961.

———. *Pier Luigi Nervi.* New York: Braziller, 1960.

———. *Will They Ever Finish Bruckner Boulevard?* New York: Macmillan, 1970.

———. *Kicked a Building Lately?* New York: Quadrangle, 1976.

Jane Jacob's articles appeared for the most part in *Architectural Forum* between 1952 and 1962, although her articles have also appeared since that time in other architectural journals.

Jacobs, Jane. *The Death and Life of Great American Cities.* New York: Random House, 1961.

———. *Economy of Cities.* New York: Random House, 1969.

Sibyl Moholy-Nagy published most extensively in *Progressive Architecture* during the 1950s and to some extent in the 1960s, although by then she was appearing frequently in *Architectural Forum.* She also wrote during those years for *The Society of Architectural Historians' Journal,* the *Journal of the American Institute of Architects,* and *Perspecta.* All her professional files and personal diaries now belong to the American Archive of Art, a branch of the Smithsonian Institution in Washington, D.C.

Moholy-Nagy, Dorothea Maria Pauline Alice Sibylle (Pietzsch). *The Architecture of Paul Rudolph,* Introduction by Sibyl Moholy-Nagy. New York: Praeger, 1970.

———. *Carlos Raul Villanueva and the Architecture of Venezuela.* Caracas, Venezuela, 1964.

———. *Children's Children.* (By S. D. Peech, pseudonym.) New York: H. Bittner and Co., 1945.

———. *Matrix of Man.* New York: Praeger, 1968.

———. *Moholy-Nagy, Experiment in Totality.* New York: Harper & Row, 1950.

———. *Native Genius in Anonymous Architecture.* New York: Horizon Press, 1957.

2. Organizations of Women in Architecture and Related Professions

AIA Chapter House
1777 Church Street, N.W.
Washington, D.C. 20036
(Washington, D.C. area)

Alliance of Women in Architecture
P.O. Box 5136
F.D.R. Station
New York, N.Y. 10022
(New York City-New England area)

American Association of University Women
2401 Virginia Ave., N.W.
Washington, D.C.
(National)

Archive of Women in Architecture
The Architectural League of New York
41 East 65th Street
New York, N.Y. 10021
(National)

Association of Women in Architecture
c/o Betsie Kniseley Marriott
2369 Kenilworth Avenue
Los Angeles, Calif. 90039
(Los Angeles area)

Bay Area Women Planners
434 66th Street
Oakland, Calif. 94609
(San Francisco Bay area)

Business and Professional Women's Foundation and Federation of Organizations of Business and Professional Women
2013 Massachusetts Ave., N.W.
Washington, D.C. 20036
(National)

Feminist Studio Workshop
Women's Building
1727 North Spring Street
Los Angeles, Calif. 90012
(Southern California area)

George Washington University
Women's Studies Program
Graduate School of Arts and Sciences
Washington, D.C.

National Association of Women in Construction
2800 W. Lancaster Ave.
Fort Worth, Tex. 76107
(National)

Organization of Women Architects
P.O. Box 26570
San Francisco, Calif. 94126
(San Francisco Bay area)

Sisters for a Human Environment
11035 14th Ave., N.E.
Seattle, Wash. 98125

Society of Women Engineers
United Engineering Center
345 E. 47th Street
New York, N.Y. 10017
(National)

l'Union Internationale des Femmes Architectes
14, Rue Dumont d'Urville
Paris XVI, France
(International)

Washington Women in Architecture
P.O. Box 32072
Washington, D.C. 20007

Women Architects, Landscape Architects, and Planners (WALAP)
c/o Boston Architectural Center
320 Newbury Street
Boston, Mass. 02215

Women in Architecture Task Force
American Institute of Architects
1735 New York Avenue, N.W.
Washington, D.C. 20006

Women in the Design of the Environment
c/o Vincent Kling
1401 Arch Street
Philadelphia, Pa. 19102

Women's Design Program
School of Design
California Institute of the Arts
Valencia, Calif. 91355

Women's School of Planning and Architecture
P.O. Box 311
Shaftsbury, Vt. 05262

3. Statistics Sources on Women in Architecture

U.S. Department of Commerce. Bureau of the Census. *1972 Census of Selected Service Industries.* Final Reports. Area Statistics.

———. *1970 Census of Population. Subject Report PC(2)-7A. Occupational Characteristics.* June 1973. xix, 805, App21pp.

———. *1970 Census of Population. Subject Report PC (2)-7F. Occupations of Persons with High Earnings.* June 1973. xiii, 119, App21pp.

———. *1970 Census of Population. Subject Report PC (2)-6B Persons Not Employed.* June 1973. xx, 242, App21pp.

U.S. Department of Health, Education, and Welfare. Office of Education. *Associate Degrees and Other Formal Awards Below the Baccalaureate, 1969–1970.* Annual, 1971. vii, 204pp., "Occupational Curriculum Awards," pp. 76–104.

———. *Earned Degrees Conferred, 1970–71.* Annual, 1973. xiii, 771pp.

———. *Fall Enrollment in Higher Education, 1971.* Annual 1973. xi, 645pp.

———. *Students Enrolled for Advanced Degrees, Fall 1970. Institutional Data.* Annual, 1971. xi, 293pp.

———. *Students Enrolled for Advanced Degrees, Fall 1970, Summary Data.* Annual, 1971. vi, 43pp. (Discontinued 1971, data in this report is currently being published in Fall Enrollment in Higher Education.)

———. *Teaching and Research Staff by Academic Field in Institutions of Higher Education, Fall 1968.* 1972. v, 37pp.

U.S. Department of Labor. Bureau of Labor Statistics. *Occupational Employment Statistics 1960–1970.* 1972. vi, 44pp. BLS Bulletin 1738.

———. *Occupational Outlook Handbook.* 1974–1975 edition. Biennial.

Biographical Notes about the Contributors

Susan Fondiler Berkon is an art-architectural historian and adjunct lecturer at the State University of New York at Old Westbury. She has published articles in *The Feminist Art Journal, Building Design* (London), and in *Victorian Boston Today*. She was born in New York City in 1948.

Sara Holmes Boutelle is an architectural historian. She received an A.B. from Mount Holyoke College and a Certificat d'Étude from the Sorbonne. Former Assistant Head of the History and History of Art Department, she is now a lecturer at the University of California at Santa Cruz Extension. She is also a Director of the Historical Preservation Association of Santa Cruz County. The subject of her essay, Julia Morgan, has been the focus of her research for the past two and a half years. In 1974 she created the Julia Morgan Association. She also assisted with the Oakland Museum's 1976 exhibition, "Julia Morgan, Architect," and mounted a Morgan exhibit at the Doe Library at Berkeley in the same year.

Doris Cole was born in 1938 in Chicago, Illinois, and grew up in Grand Rapids, Michigan. Graduating in 1959 cum laude from Radcliffe College, she received her Masters of Architecture degree from Harvard Graduate School of Design. She is a registered architect certified by the National Council of Architectural Registration Boards and is with the Architecture/ Engineering and Construction Services at the Massachusetts Institute of Technology. Cole is the author of the book, *From Tipi to Skyscraper: A History of Women in Architecture.* The biographical essay on Eleanor Raymond is composed of excerpts from her forthcoming book on Eleanor Raymond.

Sheila Levrant deBretteville, designer, was born in New York City in 1940. She was educated at Barnard College (B.A. in art history) and Yale University (M.A. in design). One of her posters was included in the Bicentennial Exhibition, "Images of an Era," at the Corcoran Gallery in 1975, and her work is represented in the Graphic Design Collection of the Museum of Modern Art. She has received awards from the American Institute of Graphic Arts, the Society of Publication Directors, and the Type Directors Club. She was a cofounder of the Woman's Building in Los Angeles where she currently teaches graphic design. Her work, which has been published here and abroad, focuses on innovative uses of new processes and materials and on the complex organization of visual images.

Dolores Hayden, social and architectural historian, is assistant professor of Architecture and History at the Massachusetts Institute of Technology. Born in New York City in 1945, educated at Mount Holyoke College, the University of Cambridge, and the Harvard Graduate School of Design, she has worked in various architectural offices and was a founder of WALAP (Women in Architecture, Landscape Architecture and Planning) in 1971. Her recent book, *Seven American Utopias: The Architecture of Communitarian Socialism 1790–1975,* published by the MIT Press, is the first major historical study of the architecture and urban planning of American utopian communities. She is currently a fellow of the Radcliffe Institute and the National Endowment for the Humanities. Work in progress includes *No Roasted Lady,* a history of the American cooperative housekeeping movement, and *Skyscraper Rape,* a collection of her essays on architecture and politics.

Carolyn R. Johnson was born in Jersey City, New Jersey, in 1947. She received her B.A. from Montclair, N.J. State College and a M.S. in library science from the University of Illinois at Urbana-Champagne. She has worked for the University of Illinois and the University of Southern California as well as MINITEX, a library network headquartered at the University of Minnesota. Her interest in architecture is avocational; she hopes to design and build her own home some day.

Naomi Leff was born in New York City in 1940. She is an environmental designer and a sociologist. She received a Masters degree in Environmental Design from Pratt Institute in Brooklyn. Her thesis was a proposal for a renovation of the U.S. Custom House in New York City. She has worked in the office of John Carl Warnecke as senior designer and project manager and is presently working on an experimental approach to space and construction techniques as applied to store design. Leff is a cofounder of the Archive of Women in Architecture.

Lucy R. Lippard is an internationally known feminist art critic. She has published hundreds of articles, is a contributing editor to magazines such as *Heresies, Chrysalis,* and *Art in America,* and has organized a large number of exhibitions. Her ten books, some of which have been translated into several languages, include: *Changing: Essays in Art Criticism, Eva Hesse, Six Years: The Dematerialization of the Art Object,* and *From the Center: Feminist Essays on Women's Art.* She has lectured extensively here and abroad and over the last six years has concentrated on the work and special concerns of women artists. Lippard was born in New York City in 1937.

Jane C. McGroarty is an architect. Born in Callicoon, New York, in 1943, and graduated from Barnard College in 1965, she obtained her Master of Architecture degree from the University of California at Los Angeles in 1975. She has been a guest lecturer at the State University of New York at Old Westbury and is now adjunct professor at the New York Institute of Technology. She has also developed new techniques for architectural representation, such as the model illustrated on the cover of this book.

Judith Paine was born in Minneapolis, Minnesota, in 1946, attended Smith College, and graduated from Sarah Lawrence College in 1972. She received a Masters degree in architectural history from Columbia University in 1975 after spending a year working on the collection of American decorative arts at Yale University Art Gallery. Her present position is as the historical preservation specialist in architectural history with the Connecticut Historical Commission.

Suzanne Stephens was born in Washington, D.C., in 1942, graduated from Cornell University in 1964, and since then has been on the editorial staff of *Progressive Architecture* three times, where she is currently a senior editor. She was also an associate editor of *Architectural Forum,* an editorial researcher at the Museum of Modern Art, and has published articles in *Artforum, The New York Times, Print,* and *Design and Environment.*

Mary Otis Stevens was born in New York City in 1928 and educated at Smith College (B.A. in philosophy in 1949) and MIT (M.A. in architecture in 1956). After working a short while with The Architects Collaborative, she joined the office of Thomas McNulty, whom she married in 1958. Since then Stevens and McNulty have collaborated on private projects as well as inner-city and prison studies and proposals and a book, *World of Variation,* published in 1969. That same year, Stevens founded i press and published a series on the human environment. In 1974, she founded the Design Guild, an office of architects/builders working in South and East Boston. Her most recent project, sponsored by the National Endowment for the Arts, is a major historical survey of the process of American settlement and the vernacular tradition in planning.

Susana Torre was born in Bahia Blanca, Argentina, in 1944. She obtained her professional architectural degree from the University of Buenos Aires in 1967 and continued her graduate studies in the United States. She has taught at Pratt Institute and at the State University of New York at Old Westbury, where she established the guidelines for an architectural design curriculum. As an architect and author, her work has been published in international architectural magazines and exhibited at the Museum of Modern Art and the Institute for Architecture and Urban Studies in New York. She is cofounder and coordinator of the Archive of Women in Architecture.

Gwendolyn Wright was born in 1946 in Chicago. An architect and a former journalist, she is completing her Ph.D. in architectural history at the University of California at Berkeley. She has written and lectured extensively on the evolution of American housing and on the role of women in the architectural sphere.

Index